Current Topics in
Clinical and Community Psychology
VOLUME 2

Contributors

DOUGLAS N. JACKSON
JAMES G. KELLY
JOHN E. KOOIKER
EUGENE E. LEVITT
EDWIN I. MEGARGEE
JAMES A. NORTON
OSCAR A. PARSONS

Current Topics in Clinical and Community Psychology VOLUME 2

EDITED BY

CHARLES D. SPIELBERGER
Department of Psychology
Florida State University
Tallahassee, Florida

ACADEMIC PRESS   New York and London   1970

ACADEMIC PRESS, INC.
111 Fifth Avenue, New York, New York 10003

United Kingdom Edition published by
ACADEMIC PRESS, INC. (LONDON) LTD.
Berkeley Square House, London W1X 6BA

LIBRARY OF CONGRESS CATALOG CARD NUMBER: 72-84224

PRINTED IN THE UNITED STATES OF AMERICA

Contents

CLINICAL NEUROPSYCHOLOGY

OSCAR A. PARSONS

A SEQUENTIAL SYSTEM FOR PERSONALITY SCALE DEVELOPMENT

DOUGLAS N. JACKSON

THE PREDICTION OF VIOLENCE WITH PSYCHOLOGICAL TESTS

EDWIN I. MEGARGEE

DEPRESSION AND ORAL CONTRACEPTION

EUGENE E. LEVITT, JOHN E. KOOIKER, AND JAMES A. NORTON

THE QUEST FOR VALID PREVENTIVE INTERVENTIONS

JAMES G. KELLY

List of Contributors

Numbers in parentheses indicate the pages on which the author's contributions begin.

DOUGLAS N. JACKSON (61), Professor of Psychology, Department of Psychology, University of Western Ontario, London, Canada

JAMES G. KELLY (183), Professor of Psychology, Department of Psychology, and Research Associate, Institute for Social Research, University of Michigan, Ann Arbor, Michigan

JOHN E. KOOIKER (157), Professor of Psychiatry, Indiana University School of Medicine, Indianapolis, Indiana

EUGENE E. LEVITT (157), Director, Psychology Section, and Professor of Clinical Psychology, Indiana University School of Medicine, Indianapolis, Indiana

EDWIN I. MEGARGEE (97), Professor of Psychology, Department of Psychology, Florida State University, Tallahassee, Florida

JAMES A. NORTON (157), Professor of Biostatistics, Indiana University School of Medicine, Indianapolis, Indiana

OSCAR A. PARSONS (1), Professor of Medical Psychology, Department of Psychiatry and Behavioral Sciences, University of Oklahoma Medical Center, Oklahoma City, Oklahoma

Preface

In the year that has passed since the publication of the initial volume in this series, we have witnessed an increased incidence of drug abuse and alcoholism, and an escalation in militant activism and violence. The Vietnam War continues and fighting has been extended into Cambodia and Laos. The aggressive postures of the new Left, the Black Power advocates, and the proponents of the Women's Liberation Movement are now recognized as significant forces to which the society must accommodate. Hijacking airplanes, destruction of buildings on college campuses, and physical assaults upon policemen occur with such frequency that they have come to be regarded as symbols of the prevailing *Zeitgeist*.

The technological achievements of our modern industrial society have produced a higher standard of living and given greater social mobility and more leisure time to more people than any other culture has ever known. Paradoxically, however, economic gain and increased personal freedom have been accompanied by a profound sense of alienation of the individual. The resulting feelings of frustration and discontent have stimulated demands for greater personal relevance in the present while spawning a pervasive pessimism about the future. In the slums of our cities and on the college campus, the establishment is under continuous attack and there is mounting impatience for changes deemed necessary to improve the quality of American life.

The contributions to Volume 2 of *Current Topics in Clinical and Community Psychology* reflect the increasing relevance of scientific work in these fields to the problems of modern society. In the first chapter of this volume, Oscar A. Parsons defines in broad outline a new area of specialization—clinical neuropsychology. Through the accumulation of neuroanatomical and electrophysiological evidence of brain–behavior relationships, investigators in this emerging field seek to identify and measure the behavior deficits that result from brain damage in humans that may result from agents such as mind-altering drugs, alcohol, tranquilizers, and inadequate diet. Parsons also provides a comprehensive review of current work on lateralization and localization of neuropsychological processes, and highlights significant theoretical and methodological issues in brain–behavior research.

Douglas N. Jackson and Edwin I. Megargee, in Chapters 2 and 3, introduce insightful new approaches to the measurement of personality. In this traditional area of concern to clinical psychologists, Jackson emphasizes the importance of translating progress in personality research into valid psychometric assessment procedures. As an exercise of his faith in the proposition that personality can be measured objectively, Jackson describes in detail a program of research in which recent developments in personality assessment, psychometric theory, and computer technology were applied to the development of a new test, the *Personality Research Form*.

Megargee's chapter provides a timely analysis of theoretical and methodological issues associated with research on the nature and prediction of violence. He also reviews the considerable research evidence that has accumulated on the assessment of violence with structured personality inventories and projective techniques. In his attempt to synthesize these two areas, Megargee shows that accurate prediction of violence with psychological tests will depend upon progress in personality research that clarifies the complex interaction between personality traits and the situational variables that serve to instigate violent behavior.

In Chapter 4, a clinical psychologist, a psychiatrist, and a biostatistician combine their talents to investigate the relationship between depressive mood changes in women and the use of oral contraceptives. Levitt, Kooiker, and Norton studied over two hundred women who were taking "the Pill" for periods of up to 4 months, and compared their mood changes with various control groups. Their study failed to substantiate the hypothesis that the Pill produces depression as a side-effect, but the results clearly indicate the importance of carefully controlled research as a check on the validity of hypotheses derived from clinical practice. They also call attention to some of the complex methodological problems that must be solved in studying the effects of drugs on emotional states.

The chapters by Megargee and Levitt *et al.* are concerned with important contemporary social issues as well as clinical phenomena, and are thus relevant to both clinical and community psychology. In the final chapter of this volume, James G. Kelly addresses a major area of concern in community psychology, namely, the effectiveness of individuals in organizations and in communities. Noting that different communities may require different models for preventive intervention, Kelly describes three approaches, each with different aims and contrasting premises about the community change process. Kelly also gives examples of each approach and suggests appropriate evaluative criteria and research paradigms for assessing the effectiveness of these interventions in producing community change.

For technical and clerical assistance in processing the manuscripts for this volume, I am deeply indebted to Mrs. Ellen Amatea, Mrs. Helen Thomas, and Mrs. Margaret Skelly.

Contents of Volume 1

Clinical Neuropsychology[1]

Oscar A. Parsons
Department of Psychiatry and Behavioral Sciences
University of Oklahoma Medical Center
Oklahoma City, Oklahoma

The field of neuropsychology is concerned with the relationships between brain and behavior. As a behavioral science, neuropsychology seeks to establish the empirical bases of these relationships, to develop explanatory concepts for them, and to order the phenomena from theoretical points of view.

The data of neuropsychology have derived from investigations of both animals and men. Those experimental approaches which attempt

[1] Preparation of this chapter was facilitated by earlier versions of various relevant topics, prepared while the author was Fulbright Lecturer in Clinical Psychology at Copenhagen University, Copenhagen, Denmark. Research cited from our laboratories was supported in part by NINDS grants NB 05359, NB 2507, and NB 05797. I am indebted to former and current colleagues and students who have shared in the research and contributed to formulations ensuing from it. These co-workers are named specifically where appropriate. I am particularly grateful to my colleagues, Drs. Ronald Krug, Kathryn West, and Arthur Vega, for their critical reading of the pre-publication manuscript.

1

to alter structure and function directly (ablation studies or direct electrical and chemical stimulation) have been restricted, with certain notable exceptions, to subhuman animals. Other experimental approaches have generated data from both animals and humans by inducing temporary or transient changes in states of consciousness through drugs, sleep, lowered oxygen levels, etc. Historically, however, the greatest contributions to the understanding of the neuropsychology of "higher mental functions" have come from clinical-experimental studies of brain-damaged or brain-dysfuctional humans.

I. Clinical Neuropsychology: A New Discipline

In this chapter we shall be concerned with the emerging discipline of clinical neuropsychology. As Pribram (1962) has pointed out, there are several disciplines directly interested in neuropsychology, i.e., neurology, neurosurgery, and psychology, representatives from any of which might qualify as neuropsychologists. In this discussion, however, we shall consider neuropsychology as an aspect of psychology. The prefix "neuro" designates the focus of the area much as the terms "social," "developmental," and "personality" distinguish special domains of investigation and knowledge.

Clinical neuropsychology may be defined more specifically as that branch of psychology which applies knowledge derived from relevant experimental and clinical investigations to specific brain-behavior problems in humans. The clinical neuropsychologist is concerned primarily with identifying, measuring, and describing changes in behavior that relate to brain dysfunction. Thus his activities contribute to a variety of important clinical problems: differential diagnosis; lateralization and localization of lesions; establishing baselines of sensory-motor, perceptual-cognitive, and intellectual functioning from which subsequent improvement or decline can be determined; identifying specific deficits resulting from noxious agents such as drugs; developing methods for remediation of deficits; helping to determine competency in the aged; and developing better diagnostic and remedial methods for the minimally brain-damaged child.

Does a neuropsychologist function in ways significantly different from a clinical psychologist so as to warrant his separate, "specialized" identification? We feel that he does in terms of the needs and developments of the field. Just as clinical child psychology has emerged as a specialized area in Division 12 (Clinical Psychology) of the American Psychological Association (or as Clinical Psychology itself achieved recognition as a special area of applied psychology), so there are signs that clinical neuro-psychology is becoming identified as a specialty in its own right.

First, there are indications of special recognition within the profession itself. The term "neuropsychology" has received increasing use in the literature (Benton, 1969; Butter, 1968; Luria, 1966). The selected papers of one of the most influential psychologists of our century, Karl Lashley, were edited almost a decade ago under the title of "The Neuropsychology of Lashley" (Beach, Hebb, Morgan, & Nissen, 1960). New journals such as *Neuropsychologia* and *Cortex* are devoted to studies explicitly neuro-psychological in nature. During the mid-sixties the International Neuro-psychology Society was formed, primarily composed of psychologists of whom many identified themselves as specialists in neuropsychology. Professorships in neuropsychology have been created at several universi-ties and at least one university Ph. D program offers an area of specializa-tion in neuropsychology. Summer workshops in clinical neuropsychology have attracted the attendance of professionals working in this area. Re-cently four postdoctoral clinical training programs in neuropsychology have been established.

Underlying these changes and basic to them is the recognition that sophisticated and skilled work in this area requires specialized knowl-edge and experience. Technical advances during the last decade have led to "breakthroughs" and to the accumulation of data far beyond the wild-est expectations or fervent hopes of the neuroscientists or psychologists of twenty years ago. It is no longer enough for the professional to have a general textbok familiarity with the central nervous system, as do most clinical psychologists. Rather, the clinical neuropsychologist must have appropriate education and training in modern biological aspects of behavior before he can utilize neuropsychological data in a meaningful clinical or experimental fashion.

Finally, one cannot ignore the social matrix. We live in a society whose youth experiments with multifarious mind (brain) altering drugs, whose over-thirty population is ridden with alcohol and tranquilizers, whose underprivileged frequently suffer from inadequate diets which directly (in the neonate) or indirectly (in the pregnant mother) affect the growing brain (Eichenwald & Fry, 1969), and whose automobile drivers provide a toll of head injuries from accidents that outstrips that of wartime casualties. Such a society requires the services of individuals trained to appreciate both the biological and the psychological aspects of central nervous system functioning.

Clinical neuropsychology indeed has emerged as a distinct discipline among several that are concerned with brain-behavior relationships, and all indications point to its continued growth and emphasis. What, then, is the current status of the field? What issues and problems, be they substantive, theoretical or professional, confront this developing discipline?

Some questions it seeks to answer are as old as psychology itself: What are the effects of brain lesions upon behavior? To what extent is there localization and lateralization of functions in the brain? Other questions are relatively new: Is there sufficient evidence to warrant continuing efforts to develop and extend psychodiagnostic methods? Should effort rather be devoted to the identification and measurement of deficit behavior without reference to psychodiagnosis? To what extent does brain injury result in a disturbed psychophysiology?

Still other problems are those that confront any scientific activity: the identification and description of those relevant variables that directly or indirectly affect the measurement and interpretation of empirical relationships in one's area of inquiry. Some relevant variables already are identified: the nature of the stimuli, instructions, experimenter attitudes, and subject components such as age and the nature, extent, and location of the lesion.

Of a different level, one asks about the status of theory development in clinical neuropsychology and whether or not there are promising new conceptual orientations. Furthermore, what does the future hold? What techniques will be developed, what areas investigated, and what educational needs must be anticipated for the clinical neuropsychologist of tomorrow?

Throughout this chapter many of the problems and issues mentioned above will be discussed but selectively so. Since space does not permit thorough coverage of all aspects of the field, our focus will be upon the postadolescent and presenescent adult human. Detailed consideration is not given to the relationship between intrahemispheric localization and the age at which brain damage occurs, nor to the studies of subhuman species from which have come important contributions to neuropsychology. Work emanating from our laboratories is referred to extensively, but key references to other studies, both specific and general in nature, are provided.

The development of clinical neuropsychology received its greatest impetus from the psychodiagnostic activities and concerns of psychologists. Thus, psychodiagnosis is an appropriate topic with which to begin our detailed discussion.

II. Psychodiagnosis in Clinical Neuropsychology

The traditional psychodiagnostic contributions of clinical psychologists to problems of brain-damaged patients form the basis for much of the present-day clinical neuropsychologist's activities. However, just as clinical psychology proper recently has questioned its diagnostic role (see past and current issues of *The Clinical Psychologist,* Newsletter, Division 12), so neuropsychologists have raised questions concerning these activities (Meyer, 1957; Spreen & Benton, 1965; Talland, 1963). The basic issue is whether or not it is legitimate for neuropsychologists to continue their efforts to determine the presence or absence of brain damage or to differentiate brain damage from alternatives such as neurosis, psychosis, and psychophysiological reaction. The fruitfulness of a diagnostic orientation is at the core of the debate.

Evidence for continuation of diagnostic efforts comes from several sources. At the clinical level, the psychodiagnostic approach has proven itself many times over. Clinical psychologists functioning in medical settings are familiar with the experience of examining a patient in whom brain damage was not suspected and finding positive behavioral indications of such a condition with subsequent confirmation by other methods. More importantly, diagnostic accuracy is improving with increased sophistication in measurement and models. We have moved a great distance along the road first mapped by Kurt Goldstein (1942) in his classic monograph "Aftereffects of Brain Injuries in War." However helpful and heuristic Goldstein's formulations and methods have been (and we shall demonstrate their usefulness later), his description of abstract and concrete behaviors was vague and ill-defined. The specification of any given behavior on these dimensions was frequently done after the fact and his clinical methods were impressionistic and generally inadequate for the more detailed and penetrating questions gradually emerging.

Quantification of behavior through the application of multiple measures and multivariate models (Haynes & Sells, 1963; Satz, 1966) has led to decided advances. An example of a quantitatively measured perceptual-motor test which has promise has been provided by Canter (1968). Reproduction of the Bender-Gestalt figures on an interfering background resulted in greater decrements for brain-damaged patients than other patients and a particularly good diagnostic hit rate of 92%. Whether other laboratories will provide cross-validation remains to be seen but certainly such attempts are indicated.

Spreen and Benton (1965) have provided a most interesting analysis of the hit rates, i.e., correct predictions of brain damage or no brain damage based on a survey of published experiments. The average of correct predictions made with a single test for the detection of brain damage in general was 71%. If the cumulative predictive value of several measures were pooled, an average of 80% correct prediction was obtained, with a reported maximum of 94%. When scores were weighted by special predictive formulas and discriminant function analyses were used, an average of 83% correct predictions with a reported maximum of 91% was achieved. Spreen and Benton point out such figures correspond favorably with the hit rates reported for diagnostic techniques such as the electroencephalogram, brain scan, pneumoencephalography, angiograms.

Another aspect of progress in diagnosis has been the demonstration by Ralph Reitan and his associates that a multivariate quantification of tests for brain damage can lead to specific statements as well as general diagnostic categorization (Reitan, 1962, 1967; Wheeler, Burke, & Reitan, 1963; Wheeler & Reitan, 1963). Using the Halstead Battery of Neuropsychological Tests (Halstead, 1947; Reitan, 1962), Reitan has developed a large pool of data based on the examination of several thousand brain-damaged patients. His laboratory has reported well over a hundred studies comparing the responses of heterogeneous brain-damaged patients, specific groups of lateralized cases, and normal controls to the same test battery. Reitan has concerned himself not only with the question of presence or absence of brain damage (Reitan, 1955a), but also with the lateralization, localization, nature, and type of lesion (Reitan, 1964).

Not only has greater specificity been introduced but also more sophisticated and searching analyses of comparative contributions of various techniques have been made. Satz, Fennell, and Reilly (1970) compared the EEG, brain scan, pneumoencephalogram, skull films, arteriograms, and Block Rotation Test (BRT) as to hit rates, strength of predictive association, and conditional probabilities as a function of base rate and the cost efficiency of each test. The results, based on a large sample of brain-injured, showed that no single method of criterion was both necessary and sufficient. Questions which must be asked by diagnosticians include the differential signs provided by the test, the base rate of the population involved, and the risks associated with types of misclassification error. Satz *et al.* (1970) conclude that psychologists should not be discouraged in that the relatively low discriminative power of psychological tests are shared by many techniques used by neurology. Indeed, psychologists should be encouraged in that all the tests examined provide useful information in the diagnosis of brain damage. The psychological test (BRT) under certain conditions would be one of the preferred tests.

As impressive as these arguments and examples may be in support of a diagnostic orientation, there are many counter arguments. The opposing position states that there is sufficient evidence questioning the ultimate worth of pursuing the psychodiagnostic approach to suggest that other strategies or activities be emphasized by the neuropsychologist (Heilbrun, 1962; Meyer, 1957; Reitan, 1966; Smith, 1962; Spreen &

Benton, 1965; Talland, 1963). The arguments here are fourfold. First, the criterion measures for validating psychodiagnostic tests are not very exact when the full range of brain-damaged cases is considered. In many cases, e.g., mild diffuse damage, there is not a satisfactory independent way of proving or disproving the presence, extent of severity, and location of the damage.

Second, validating populations that have been clearly defined are composed of cases so obviously brain-damaged that one need only look at them or talk with them briefly in order to ascertain their affliction. Of what meaning, then, are the psychodiagnostic measures which are developed in reference to such populations? If there is a diagnostic need, it is for measures which will aid in the identification of the questionable and borderline cases.

Third, the nosological category of brain damage is so heterogeneous and includes such a diversity of neurological conditions that valid generalizations from any one population to another are next to impossible. When a subpopulation can be clearly defined, it is composed either of patients with gross pathology (as described above) or patients with lesions so specialized and restricted (e.g., temporal lobectomies) that inferences are limited. To generalize about *the* brain-damaged person is to commit the error of generalizing about *the* schizophrenic. It is when the population of schizophrenics has been subdivided into groups such as "process *vs.* reactive" (Kantor & Herron, 1966) or "good *vs.* poor premorbid" Garmezy, 1965) that fruitful results have been obtained.

Finally, the development of new biomedical techniques of diagnosis lessens the need for psychodiagnosis. The brain scan, for example, has proved singularly successful with a large variety of brain lesions (Spreen & Benton, 1965), averaging some 90% accuracy, and the risk compared with older neurosurgical procedures such as the pneumoencephalograph and angiogram is extremely small. This advance coupled with refinements in EEG techniques make possible by new data reduction methods (Livanov, 1969), new developments in measurement of cerebral blood flow (Obrist, Ingvar, Chivian, & Cronqvist, 1968), and biochemical assays in tumor cases (Paoletti, Vandenheuvel, Fumagalli, & Paoletti, 1969) all suggest that psychodiagnosis will not be as pressing a need as it once seemed to be.

These are indeed compelling arguments and if the activities of the clinical neuropsychologist were limited to the restrictive question "brain damage or alternative," justification of his role would be difficult. Spreen and Benton (1965), at the conclusion of their review, state ". . . it is felt that the search for screening devices has reached its culmination point, has served its purpose and should not be indefinitely continued.

Further progress is seen in the prediction of a specific locus of lesion by use of special methods according to neuropsychological hypotheses [pp. 332–333]." Thus, if the question posed to the neuropsychologist is that of identification and measurement of the various behavioral deficits associated with brain damage (Talland, 1963), there is ample rationale for his role and function. In this context he could describe the nature of the deficits, e.g., sensory-motor, perceptual language, cognitive, intellective, temporal acuity, and their corresponding implications for efficiency in behavior as well as localization and lateralization. The effective level of functioning of the individual at the time of examination with implications for rehabilitation could be noted. An evaluation of the contribution of personality reactions to the specific and general deficits of the patient could be provided.

There is little doubt that this alternative formulation of the desirable activities for the clinical neuropsychologists is the preferred one at this point in time. But it should be immediately apparent that implicit in the focus upon specification of deficit is the development of knowledge which will ultimately provide more reliable and valid information for answering psychodiagnostic questions. Despite the advances in other diagnostic techniques, as Satz, Fennell, and Reilly (1970) noted, there will always be some error in diagnosis, some cases missed, and some cases where risky medical techniques should be avoided. Finally, from a humanistic point of view, if only one brain-damaged patient per clinical neuropsychologist were positively identified by psychodiagnostic methods, and that identification resulted in treatment which otherwise might never be applied, the diagnostic approach, as one of several orientations for the practicing neuropsychologist, is justifiable.

In summary then, there are many reasons why clinical neuropsychologists have shifted from a simplistic preoccupation with psychodiagnosis to an emphasis upon description and measurement of behavior deficits in brain damage. The shift in emphasis does not exclude diagnostic inferences but rather seeks to place such inferences on a firmer footing of empirical knowledge. Progress in this direction is considered in the next section.

III. Lateralization and Localization of Neuropsychological Processes

At the outset it should be noted that there are at least two classes of "psychological processes" which are of great interest to those of us working in the neuropsychological area: (*a*) traditional conceptual classes of higher mental functions (Luria, 1966) such as attention, perception, memory, language functions, problem-solving, concept formation, judgment; (*b*) motivational, emotional, psychodynamic, and personality processes that, together with the conceptual entities of the first category, comprise the more important aspects of our intrapersonal and interpersonal behavior. Obviously, the behavior of the human organism in any given situation is a product of all factors and variables noted in both classes, but the functions noted in the first category are more clearly identified and easily measured than the molar variables of the second category and have received greater attention in investigations of neuropsychological localization.

It is not surprising to learn that many of the old arguments are still with us as regards localization and nonlocalization of higher mental functions (Krech, 1962; Yacorznski, 1965). It is safe to say, however, that the evidence is rather consistent for two classes of effects, two types of impairment of psychological functions in response to brain damage: *specific* and *general* effects. The general effects are probably heavily dependent upon the mass of cortical tissue destroyed or malfunctioning. Chapman and Wolff (1959), in a classic study, demonstrated a positive relationship between amount of destruction of brain tissue and impairment of all psychological functions including the reaction to failure and the frustration and adaptability of the patient to the problems of everyday living. These general effects will be discussed later but are mentioned here as background considerations which must be kept in mind as we deal with more specific effects.

Most of the controversy noted above consists of disagreement about the role of particular portions of the brain in the higher mental functions. None would deny that specific deficits in sensory and motor functions can be attributed to lesions of the post- and pre-Rolandic areas, or the fact that the left or "dominant" hemisphere is implicated more commonly in aphasic reactions than the right hemisphere. Further, the role of the right or "nondominant" hemisphere in certain aspects of perception has received increasing recognition. But beyond these general statements there lie multitudinous problems of specification and explanation. To illustrate some of the problems, it is appropriate to examine research on the differential psychological functions of the two hemispheres as measured by the most commonly employed and best standardized intelligence tests, the Wechsler Scales (Wechsler, 1944, 1958). Obviously, if these scales could provide us with relevant information, a huge pool of data from both clinical examinations as well as specific research studies would be available.

A. LATERALIZATION AND THE WECHSLER SCALES

There is, in fact, good reason to expect that the Wechsler Scales would contribute to knowledge concerning the differential pschological functions associated with the two hemispheres. Repeated factor-analytic studies (Guertin, Ladd, Frank, Rabin, & Hiester, 1966) have reported two major factors on both Wechsler-Bellevue I (W-B) and the Wechsler Adult Intelligence Scale (WAIS) which correspond to the Verbal Scale and Performance Scale. The role of language in the Verbal Scale is obvious and the perceptual and perceptual-motor abilities involved in the Performance Scale have been recognized since Wechsler devised the tests (Wechsler, 1944). In view of the clinical and experimental evidence for control of verbal and language functions by the left hemisphere and similar evidence for the salience of the right hemisphere in perceptual and visuo-constructive behavior (Millikan & Darley, 1967), the straightforward predictions can be made: left hemisphere lesion cases should have lower Verbal IQs (VIQs) than Performance IQs (PIQs) and the converse for right hemisphere lesion cases. What has been found?

Almost all studies have reported that groups of patients with left hemisphere lesions have significantly lower VIQs than right hemisphere damaged patients (Vega & Parsons, 1969). Some investigators have also found PIQs significantly lower in right compared with left lesion cases (Balthazar & Morrison, 1961; Dennerll, 1964; Reitan, 1955a). But other experimenters have failed to confirm the differential PIQ impairment in right compared to left hemisphere cases (Heilbrun, 1956; Satz, Richard, & Daniels, 1967; Smith, 1966). A similar lack of PIQ differences has been found in our laboratories (Vega & Parsons, 1969). There are a number of reasons why discrepant results might be obtained in testing hypotheses involving the PIQ. One problem is the nature of the subtests comprising the Performance Scale, a problem extensively discussed by Parsons, Vega, and Burn (1969) and noted by Benton (1962) and Heilbrun (1956). In sum, compared to the Verbal Scale, the Performance Scale is not as good a criterion measure for testing hypotheses about neuropsychological localization.

However, such a conclusion does not preclude utilization of a subtest from the Performance Scale which might best represent the perceptual and visuo-constructive abilities in question. The results of several factor-analytic studies (Berger, Bernstein, Klein, Cohen, & Lucas, 1964) indicate that Block Design consistently has the highest loading on what Guertin *et al.* (1966) called the "perceptual organization" factor. Vocabulary occupies a comparable role on the Verbal factor. Would use of these two "best measures" give rise to evidence of differential lateralization of function?

This question was examined by Parsons, Vega, and Burn (1969).
The first hypothesis, derived on the basis of the above reasoning, was that
patients with left hemisphere damage would perform more poorly on the
Vocabulary than on the Block Design subtests and right hemisphere cases
would manifest the opposite pattern. The second and more important
hypothesis was that patients with left hemisphere damage would perform
more poorly on the Vocabulary than the right hemisphere lesion group,
while the opposite relationship would hold for the Block Design. The
WAIS was administered in two separate experiments to populations of
middle-aged male veterans. In Experiment 1, there were three groups
of brain-damaged subjects (Ss): 20 Ss with predominantly left hemisphere damage (LHD), 16 Ss with predominantly right hemisphere
damage (RHD), and 8 Ss with bilateral or diffuse damage (BHD). The
control group consisted of 45 non-brain-damaged Ss from the general
medical and surgical wards. In Experiment 2, similar groups were
examined: LHD ($N = 24$), RHD ($N = 25$), BHD ($N = 49$), and controls ($N = 50$). Details on these groups are given in Parsons *et al.*
(1969). Age-corrected scaled scores were used to test the hypothesis.

The results are presented in Figure 1. The expected differences were
found with remarkable consistency in both experiments. LHD had significantly lower Vocabulary than Block Design scores and were significantly
lower than the RHD on Vocabulary. The RHD group were significantly
lower on Block Design than Vocabulary scores and significantly lower

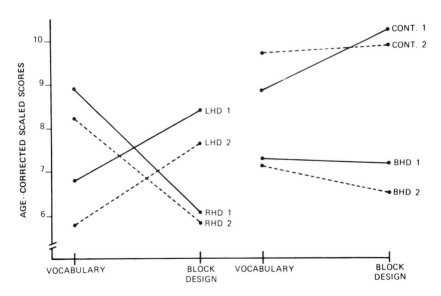

Fɪɢ. 1. Mean Vocabulary and Block Design age-corrected scaled scores for all
groups in both experiments (Parsons, Vega, & Burn, 1969).

than the LHD on Block Design. With one exception, the within-group comparisons in the controls and the BHD were not significant.

Another approach to the hypothesized difference in hemispheric functions could be taken. If the hypotheses above are valid, the implied "dissociation" in functions should lead to lower correlations between Vocabulary and Block Design in the unilateral lesion groups than in the BHD and control groups. In Table 1, Pearson rs are given for the combined groups. In the RHD group the correlation is lower than in any of the other groups and is nonsignificant. As judged by these results, the dissociation between verbal and visuo-constructive abilities is more clear-cut in the case of the RHD than the LHD. Recalling the point made earlier about the possible role of language mediation in performance subtests, the significant correlation obtained in the LHD is not surprising. Considering all of the results, there is strong support for the concept of lateralization of neuropsychological processes, and two of the most reliable subtests from the WAIS may be used to measure these lateralized functions.

TABLE 1

CORRELATIONS BETWEEN VOCABULARY AND BLOCK DESIGN AGE-CORRECTED SCALED SCORES[a]

Group	N	p
LHD	44	.369*
RHD	41	.235
BHD	57	.549**
Controls	95	.442**

[a] From Parsons, Vega, & Burn (1969).
* $p < .05$.
** $p < .01$.

Returning to the initial problem posed, i.e., the lack of consistent differences between LHD and RHD on Performance IQ, there is another point which must be considered. Left hemisphere damage could result in impaired sensory-motor functioning in the preferred hand (almost all Ss used in the experiments above were right handed). Since the Performance tests are timed and typically call for manual manipulation of test materials, the possible role of sensory-motor dysfunction was investigated.

To examine this issue, the performance of the LHD, RHD and control groups of Experiment 2 on four sensory-motor tests was compared with their Verbal and Performance IQs (Vega & Parsons, 1969). It was expected that LHD patients who had comparatively little contralateral sensory-motor impairment would perform better on the Performance Scale of the WAIS than LHD patients with greater contralateral involvement. Since this could be due to either or both of the two factors mentioned earlier (the effect of impaired language functioning and the sensory-motor impairment), correlating both VIQ and sensory-motor impairment with PIQ should give some indication of their relative saliency. In contrast, it was thought that within the RHD group, contralateral sensory-motor impairment would not have as great an effect on PIQ, since neither the preferred hand nor language functions would be affected.

Sensory-motor tests were administered to the Ss. ("Sensory-motor" in this context is used for tasks that involve sensory and perceptual factors and require motor functions such as strength, rapidity of movement and coordination.) The Ss were examined on the Purdue Pegboard Test and three tests from the Halstead Battery (Halstead, 1947): the Finger Tapping Test, the Dynamometer Test, and the Tactual Performance Test. Ss performed the tests with both right and left hands. All scores were converted to normalized T scores derived from the controls (Vega & Parsons, 1967), and averaged across tests for each S.

In Figure 2, the results typical of so many experiments in this area are found: significant differences in all comparisons except that of the PIQ scores for LHD and RHD. In Table 2, the sensory-motor scores for the two groups are given. In considering these data, it should be kept in mind that the corresponding T scores for controls are 50 for each hand. Two important conclusions can be reached. First, the contralateral

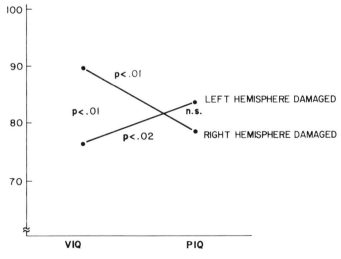

Fig. 2. WAIS IQs of left and right damaged Ss (Vega & Parsons, 1969).

14   *Oscar A. Parsons*

TABLE 2
RIGHT-HAND AND LEFT-HAND SENSORY-MOTOR PERFORMANCE IN RHD AND LHD GROUPS[a]

Group	Left-hand T Score	Right-hand T Score
RHD	38.1	45.9
LHD	44.5	35.1
t	3.18*	5.22*

[a] Vega & Parsons (1969).
* $p < .01$.

impairment in each group is substantial; in fact use of two of the tests (Purdue Pegboard and Finger Tapping) provides discrimination between brain-damaged and control groups at a level greater than that of the complete Halstead Battery (Vega, 1969). Second, both groups were impaired to about the same degree in their contralateral and ipsilateral hands. This suggests that both LHD and RHD were neurologically impaired to the same degree. Table 3 presents the correlations among the variables. The LHD correlations among the VIQ, PIQ, and contralateral sensory-motor impairment score (right hand) are all significant and similar in magnitude to that of the controls, whereas none of the correlations among VIQ, PIQ, and contralateral hand (left hand) are significant in the RHD.

Partial correlations were calculated in which the relationship between

TABLE 3
CORRELATIONS BETWEEN SENSORY-MOTOR PERFORMANCE WAIS SCORES[a,b]

Group		PIQ	R Hand	L Hand
LHD				
	VIQ	.66**	.60**	.17
	PIQ	—	.41**	.41*
RHD				
	VIQ	.32	−.03	−.03
	PIQ	—	.43*	.09
Control				
	VIQ	.68**	.33*	.28*
	PIQ	—	.44*	.46**

Scores

[a] After Vega & Parsons (1969).
[b] Italicized scores refer to the comparisons cited in the text.
* $p < .05$.
** $p < .01$.

contralateral sensory-motor deficit and PIQ was examined, partialling out the VIQ. In LHD the previously significant correlation of $+.41$ becomes essentially zero (.02); in the RHD the nonsignificant correlation of $+.09$ remains a nonsignificant $-.08$. These findings suggest that impaired sensory-motor performance in the preferred hand of the LHD group (all Ss except one in each group were right handed) does not contribute significantly to the performance on the subtests comprising the PIQ. It seems likely that the high correlation between VIQ and contra-lateral sensory-motor impairment in the LHD is due to the proximity of the brain areas classically associated with aphasic difficulties (Penfield & Roberts, 1959) and sensory-motor areas. These findings are similar to those of Semmes, Weinstein, Ghent, and Teuber (1960) who reported that impaired sensory-motor functions and language deficits were likely to coexist in LHD groups.

Another way of viewing the data is seen in Figure 3. Here the LHD and RHD have been subdivided into groups with maximal and minimal contralateral deficits (above and below the median for their group). The two upper graphs of the figure show that significant differences in level on VIQ and PIQ are obtained in the LHD but not in the RHD. In fact, the maximal sensory-motor subgroup of the RHD shows a higher level of performance, but after these data were adjusted for educational levels, the performance of the two subgroups was almost identical. Neither age nor education could account for the differences found in this figure.

The most important aspect of the findings is illustrated in the lower graphs of Figure 3. When minimal contralateral deficit groups are com-pared, significant differences appear only on the PIQ; when maximal contralateral deficit groups are compared, significant differences are present only on the VIQs. It is the LHD subgroups that account for the difference, which points to the crucial importance of the LHD group in this type of research. Is sensory-motor deficit the critical variable? After an analysis of partial correlations, we concluded that it probably was not sensory-motor deficit but rather impaired language functioning. To provide a direct test of this, the LHD were divided into maximally dysphasic and minimally dysphasic groups. When the dysphasic Ss were excluded, the lower left graph of Figure 3 was virtually reproduced. When the dysphasic Ss were compared to the RHD, the lower right graph was reproduced.

While these findings and explanations may not account for all factors resulting in discrepant results in this problem area, they certainly could explain many of them. To the extent that LHD patients with contra-lateral sensory-motor deficits (and thereby language difficulties) are included, the difference between the LHD and RHD groups will decrease

Oscar A. Parsons

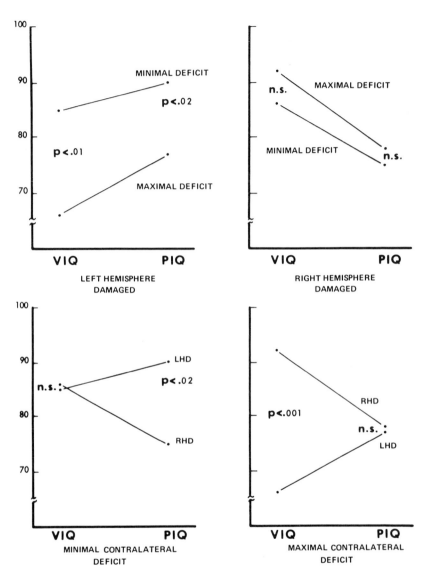

Fɪɢ. 3. Relation of sensory-motor deficits to WAIS scores (Vega & Parsons, 1969).

on PIQ and increase on VIQ, moving through the relationships depicted in the lower left graph of Figure 3 to those in the lower right. Indeed most of the patterns which have been reported in the literature could be reproduced by an appropriate seasoning of LHD patients with dysphasic patients.

A final study illustrating the potential usefulness of the WAIS in clinical neuropsychology may be mentioned. Pattern analysis of the Wechsler Scales has been the subject of many studies (Guertin *et al.*, 1966; Wechsler, 1958), most of which have been devoted to the question of differentiating brain-damaged patients from other psychopathological groups. Few studies have been reported to our knowledge which attempt to use a quantified pattern analysis to distinguish left and right hemisphere cases (Balthazar & Morrison, 1961; Dennerll, 1964). Simpson and Vega (1969) used a method described by Sullivan and Welsh (1952) for analyzing coded MMPI profiles. This method, as applied to our data, involved comparing the rank orders of all possible pairs of age-corrected subtest scores in a LHD ($N = 21$) group with those of a control group ($N = 50$) and selecting as LHD "signs" pairs of relationships which differed beyond the $p < .05$ level. The RHD ($N = 23$) were treated similarly. Note that the hemispheric signs were developed with reference to the control group and not on the basis of comparing the LHD and RHD directly. On this basis, the following signs were found (Table 4).

TABLE 4
LEFT HEMISPHERE AND RIGHT HEMISPHERE WAIS SIGNS

Left Hemisphere Signs	Right Hemisphere Signs
Vocabulary > Comprehension	Information > Picture Arrangement
Vocabulary > Arithmetic	Information > Object Assembly
Vocabulary > Similarities	Digit Span > Digit Symbol
Picture Completion > Arithmetic	Digit Span > Picture Arrangement
Picture Completion > Similarities	Picture Completion > Object Assembly
Picture Arrangement > Arithmetic	

The number of signs for each S in each group was tabulated and appropriate cutoff scores assigned. On this basis, a patient was classified as LHD if he had four or more left hemisphere signs and RHD if he had four or more right hemisphere signs (Table 5). The results indicated significant separation of the groups; LHD and RHD differed on left

TABLE 5
DISCRIMINATION AMONG GROUPS BY HEMISPHERE SIGNS

Groups	LHD Signs		RHD Signs	
	<4	≥4	<4	≥4
LHD	10	11	19	2
RHD	19	4	6	17
BHD	37	7	28	16
Controls	42	8	40	10

hemisphere signs ($\chi^2 = 6.0$, $p < .02$) and right hemisphere signs ($\chi^2 = 18.5$, $p < .001$). Interestingly, the LHD signs do not discriminate the groups as well as do the RHD signs. Considering all groups including controls and bilateral-diffuse damaged patients (BHD), presence or absence of RHD signs is associated with a high probability of correct classification into RHD or non-RHD categories (75%). Presence of LHD signs is associated with correct classification, but absence of LHD signs does not contribute as much (i.e., there are many false negatives). It was also found that only one control, two LHD, two RHD and two BHD patients had both LHD and RHD signs and that correlations between LHD and RHD signs were essentially zero in control and BHD groups whereas they were negative in the lateralized groups. For the combined lateralized groups, the correlation between the hemispheric signs was $-.46$ ($df = 42$, $p < .01$).

These results must be considered tentative and subject to cross-validation with age-corrected scores for other groups of brain damaged Ss. However, application of the lateralization signs to the *mean* scores (non-age-corrected) for LHD and RHD cases in a number of published studies with various Wechsler Scales gave rise to the data in Table 6, in which the results are encouraging and informative. For example, it is

TABLE 6
HEMISPHERE SIGNS APPLIED TO GROUP MEANS OF PUBLISHED DATA

Study and Wechsler Scale	Group	LHD signs	RHD signs
Balthazar & Morrison	LHD	4*	1
(1961) WB & WISC	RHD	0	4*
Dennerll	LHD	4*	2
(1964) WAIS, WB & WISC	RHD	0	5*
Fitzhugh & Fitzhugh	LHD	4*	3
(1964) WB-I	RHD	2	5*
Reitan	LHD	5*	2
(1955b) WB-I	RHD	3	4*
Wheeler & Reitan	Early LHD	5*	2
(1963) WB-I	Early RHD	3	5*
	Late LHD	5*	1
	Late RHD	1	5*
	Early BHD	2	3
	Late BHD	4*	5*
	Early controls	2	3
	Late controls	2	3

* Discriminating signs above cut-off point.

apparent that the signs discriminate the group means equally well in the WB-I Ss as in the WAIS studies. Furthermore (from data not presented here), it became apparent that one of the LHD signs (Vocabulary > Comprehension) did not hold up. This is in accord with clinical practice, i.e., Comprehension is frequently the highest Verbal Scale score in brain-damaged patients, so it is likely that when the signs are applied to individual Ss (in other studies currently underway) this one will not be retained. It should be noted that Arithmetic and Similarities appear to be the subtests most affected by LHD since five of the signs involve them. On the other hand, in the RHD signs, Picture Arrangement and Object Assembly form the basis for four of the comparisons. Finally, while the Verbal minus Performance IQ discrepancies are significantly related to hemisphere signs, the correlations are such that the signs could be used as an independent measure. Perhaps a combination of both discrepancies and signs will be useful. Whether this new sign approach will prove helpful in lateralization remains to be seen. However, the results strongly point to different lateralized functions in the two hemispheres and suggest lines of future investigation.

Three studies involving the WAIS have been presented in some detail. In the first study, the differential psychological functions subserved by the left and right hemispheres were demonstrated by use of two subtests, Vocabulary and Block Design. In the second study, an explanation for the equivocal evidence concerning differences between LHD and RHD groups on PIQ was developed in terms of the important role of language dysfunction in the LHD group. Finally, a new method of pattern analysis was described which seems to have promise for discriminating right and left hemisphere damage. Considered as a whole, the studies provide ample evidence for continuing interest on the part of the clinical neuropsychologist in one of the most commonly used, best standardized and multipurposed psychological tests currently available.

B. Lateralization of Functions: Commisurotomy Cases; Neuroanatomical and Electrophysiological Differences

While the discussion of laterality in the previous section was restricted to the evidence from the Wechsler Scales, there is an extensive body of literature which points rather conclusively to neuropsychological lateralization. One of the more dramatic sources of new evidence has come from the work of Sperry (1968), Gazzaniga (1965), and Bogen (Gazzaniga, Bogen, & Sperry, 1967). They have investigated intensively a small number of patients in whom the cerebral hemispheres have been surgically divided for treatment of seizures (severing the corpus callosum, anterior and posterior commissures). Essentially, then, there are two brains unconnected except at the subcortical level. Each hemisphere can be examined for differential function by presenting material differing in stimulus characteristics and response requirements to it. Presentation of visual language stimuli to the left brain (in the right visual field) resulted in comprehension, expression, and communication at a level which was similar to the normal intact brain. But visual stimuli, e.g., drawings of figures, when presented to the left hemisphere resulted in an impaired copying performance. Another variation in their procedure involved the patient doing the Block Design test with the right hand and the left hand. The performance of the right hand, under the control of the left hemisphere, was more impaired than that obtained with the same patient's left hand, under control of the right hemisphere.

When language stimuli were presented to the right hemisphere, i.e., in the left visual field, the patient was unable to initiate speech or writing. However, if tasks were used which required only the choice of a correct response from among several alternatives, the right hemisphere could "perceive, think, emote, learn and remember at a level characteristically human" (Gazzaniga, 1965, p. 372) but the comprehension proceeded outside of the awareness of the left hemisphere. These investigators conclude (Sperry, 1968) that the primary difference in the hemispheres does not lie in differential memory, i.e., traces or engrams are bilaterally deposited. Rather, differences lie in the specialized executive functions of the two hemispheres, especially the left hemisphere.

In the field of neuroanatomy, asymmetries in the temporal region have been convincingly demonstrated in a quantitative fashion for the first time (Geschwind & Levitsky, 1968). Using 100 human adult brains at postmortem, these investigators found that 65% of the brains had a larger left than right planum temporale, an area which makes up part of the temporal speech cortex (immediately posterior to Heschl's gyrus). In only 11% of the brains was it larger on the right. The length of the planum was about one third longer on the left than right ($p < .001$). The differences in neuroanatomical structure of a region known to be involved in language function, by both cortical stimulation and lesion effects, has given renewed emphasis to structural approaches to brain function.

Differences in hemispheric electrophysiological functioning in response to verbal and nonverbal stimuli have been demonstrated in recent studies (Giannitrapani, 1967). To give an example of these findings, Buschbaum and Fedio (1969) studied the average evoked response (AER) to word patterns, design patterns, and random patterns of dots visually presented. AER wave forms for verbal and nonverbal stimuli differed to a significantly greater extent in the left hemisphere than the right hemisphere. Verbal stimuli had shorter AER latencies. The discrimination of word *vs.* random dot patterns was found to be superior in the left hemisphere at certain presentation levels (64–192 msec) while the word *vs.* design patterns were better discriminated at the same millisecond interval by the right hemisphere.

Thus, neuroanatomical and electrophysiological evidence is beginning to accumulate in support of the behavioral differences obtained for left *vs.* right hemisphere.

C. Left Hemisphere, Language Disturbance and Cognitive Behavior

Given the evidence cited so far for control of language functions by the left hemisphere and the importance of the latter in awareness, what remains to be explicated? Many problems and issues remain. Since the time of Broca, explanations for aphasia or disturbance in language function have been the source of continual debate. The current situation is no exception. There are exponents of specific language deficits associated with specific neuroanatomical lesions (Geschwind, 1965; Goodglass, Quadfasel, & Timberlake, 1964) and champions of the general language deficit irrespective of lesion location (Goldstein, 1959; Schuell, Jenkins, & Jimenez-Pabon, 1965). Interested readers may consult the above and following sources for extended discussions of issues dealing specifically in aphasia (Brain, 1961; Millikan & Darley, 1967; Penfield & Roberts, 1959).

Brief mention should be made, however, of studies with aphasics which hold promise for future work on relatively specific problems in left hemisphere functioning. Butters and Brody (1968) investigated cross-modal matchings (visual-tactual, etc.) in patients with dominant parietal lobe damage in the region of the angular gyrus *vs.* patients with fronto-temporal damage. The parietal lobe patients were impaired on cross-modal matching but fronto-temporal patients were unimpaired. Efron (1963) has presented data on impaired auditory sequencing in aphasics. In his studies, two tones of quite different frequencies were presented briefly and the subject had to distinguish which came first. Comparison with visual stimuli similarly presented indicated that aphasics did poorly on the auditory but not on the visual sequencing task. However, despite these replicated differences between aphasic and nonaphasic brain-damaged groups, no correlation has been found between degree of aphasic impairment and auditory sequencing deficit *within* aphasic groups (Millikan & Darley, 1967, p. 31). Both of these studies should provide the basis for more extensive investigations in the future.

Dominance and language function is a related problem which again has been treated extensively in other sources (Mountcastle, 1962; Piercy, 1964). One important finding which has received increasing support is that even in left-handed subjects, the executive functions for speech and language are predominantly in the left hemisphere (Piercy, 1964). Piercy's critical review will repay the concerned reader. We shall return to the problem of dominance later.

Despite the long history of controversy and proliferation of confusing terminologies, language behavior remains a fascinating area for neuropsychologists. Language and communication are so intimately involved in the human condition that they cannot be ignored. But even more cogently, language appears to be unique to man. If this is so, then it can only be studied in man. Consequently, the study of humans with brain lesions will continue to illuminate the problem area. An example of this is the current concern over the old problem of the relation of language to thought. Does impairment in language behavior mean impaired thought or can aphasia be present while other cognitive activities are relatively unimpaired?

Interesting and provocative background contributions to this topic have come from two recent sources. Furth (1966) has investigated language and nonlanguage cognitive performance in the congenitally deaf. He found that deaf children exhibit impairment on cognitive tests that involve language but not on measures of cognitive activity and problem solving which do not. Furth concluded that "logical intelligent thinking does not need the support of a symbolic system, as it exists in the living language of society . . . the internal organization of intelligence is not dependent on the language system; on the contrary, comprehension and the use of the ready-made language is dependent on the structure of intelligence [Furth, 1966, p. 228]." Lenneberg (1967, 1969) has adopted the position that language is one form of cognitive activities which are rooted in the biology of man. He comments that man's brain is not simply that of a chimpanzee with greatly enlarged association possibilities but has undergone restructuring and reintegration as in other biological evolutionary structures. Similarly, as regards language, "man's cognition is not essentially that of every other primate with merely the addition of language; instead, I propose that his entire cognitive function of which his capacity for language is a specific part, is species-specific [Lenneberg, 1969, p. 642]." Language, then, from this point of view, is an intimate part of cognition and thus neither a cause nor an effect or product. From Furth's statement one might expect that impaired language functioning could exist in the absence of other cognitive impairment. Lenneberg's approach on the other hand seems to imply a close relationship between language and other basic cognitive activities, i.e., deficit in language would mean deficit in other cognitive operations.

What are the findings? Weinstein (1964) reported that of a group of diverse head-injured Ss only those with left parieto-temporal lesions showed a significant decline on a retest of general intelligence (AGCT). Evidence for impaired abstracting behavior associated with aphasia using the Weigl Sorting Test has been equivocal. In one of the better controlled studies (De Renzi, Faglioni, Savoiardo, & Vignolo, 1966), it was found that right and left nonaphasic brain-damaged patients performed at almost the same level as control patients, but an aphasic left hemisphere group was grossly impaired in performance on a refined version of Weigl's test. These results held even when correction was made for the effects of general intelligence by a nonverbal test, Raven's Progressive Matrices. Perhaps one of the important variables is indicated by their finding that the aphasics' Weigl score was correlated highly with an auditory verbal comprehension score but not with visual naming or an ideomotor apraxia score. Ruling out the possible contribution of ideomotor apraxia was of particular importance. On tests involving nonverbal sorting behavior, if the S were to have difficulty in implementing his response motorically, he, of course, would manifest a deficit.

Russo and Vignolo (1967) replicated the results of Teuber and Weinstein (1956) on the Gottschaldt Hidden Figure Test; aphasics were found to perform more poorly than either nonaphasic left hemisphere cases or right hemisphere patients. On the other hand, right hemisphere cases performed significantly more poorly than nonaphasic left hemisphere cases. The authors conclude that poor visual figure-ground discrimination in the aphasics "is the consequence, not so much of the language disorder *per se*, but of a specialized intellectual defect . . . aphasics do poorly on the Gottschaldt Test because of the same kind of defect which causes them to fail on Weigl's test [Russo & Vignolo, 1967, pp. 123–124]."

Archibald, Wepman, and Jones (1967), impressed with the conflicting evidence concerning the role of aphasia in nonverbal cognitive tasks, examined the performance of appropriate groups on four such tests: Raven's Colored Matrices, Shure-Wepman's Concept Shift, Grassi Block Substitution Test, and the Elithorn Mazes. They found that the more severe aphasic patients were impaired in their cognitive performance. However, their general conclusion was that "aphasia, itself, is specifically a defect of language and memory for language which may or may not be accompanied by impaired cognitive functioning [p. 293]." The most significant finding in their study was the extremely low performance of the RHD on the Elithorn Mazes, a fact to which we shall return later.

Another group of studies provides relevant evidence. The Halstead Category Test, one of the most discriminating of the neuropsychological tests of the Halstead Battery (Reitan, 1955a; Vega & Parsons, 1967), has been used to investigate possible differential effects of left and right lesions on abstracting behavior. The Category Test is essentially a non-verbal concept identification task in which a series of slides, each with geometric figures which differ on a number of dimensions, are presented visually. The task for the subject is to select (by pressing a button) one of the stimulus figures on each slide which best represents the concept or principle in that series. There are seven subtests each of which involves different categorizing principles.

Shure and Halstead (1958) found that LHD patients performed more poorly on the Category Test than RHD patients. They attributed this to the language and symbolic manipulation involved in abstracting behavior. But Chapman and Wolff (1959) found a trend in their study for RHD to do more poorly than LHD groups. Reitan (1960) reported that dysphasic and nondysphasic brain-damaged groups attained similar levels of impaired scores on the Category Test despite markedly poorer perform-ance by the dysphasics on the Wechsler Verbal Scale. Doehring and Reitan (1962) found no significant differences between LHD and RHD in level of impairment or in pattern of performance on the Category Test.

One study in our laboratories gave rise to results similar to those reported by Chapman and Wolff (1959). Groups of patients given the Category Test were ordered in terms of errors, as follows: RHD, LHD, BHD, and controls. Each group was significantly different from the other groups. Neither Vocabulary nor the Halstead-Wepman Test for Aphasia (Reitan, 1962), both of which were significantly impaired in the LHD compared to the RHD groups, correlated significantly with performance in any of the brain-damaged groups; thus, lowered performance by LHD on a test of abstracting ability could not be attributed to language dysfunction. A second study which employed a visual concept identifica-tion task of a more stringently controlled nature (Burn, 1967) gave rise to results similar to Doehring and Reitan (1962). LHD and RHD groups did not differ from each other in performance although both groups were significantly poorer than controls and the LHD group had significantly lower Vocabulary scores than the RHD.

To return to the question of the relation of language to thought, support for both Furth and Lenneberg's positions has been found. Studies which have compared aphasic and nonaphasic LHD cases appear to find some evidence for greater deficits in performance on certain tasks such as the Gottschaldt Hidden Figures and, in some instances, the Weigl Sorting Test. But on the Category test, one which demands much more "reasoning" and conceptual behavior than the other two tests, aphasia or LHD in general does not seem to play a significant role. How can these discrepant results be explained? What is this "specialized defect" postulated by Russo and Vignolo (1967) which could account for deficits on the two tests but not be found on the Category test?

The answer lies in future experimentation in which there is a better delineation of the psychological functions which are measured or are salient in these specific tasks. One avenue which certainly should be explored is the possible contribution of defects in the visual scanning process. Tyler (1969) has recently presented evidence that visual scanning patterns for aphasics differ from normals and other brain-damaged. Restricted visual scanning, unusually long fixations, ineffective search patterns are found to some extent in the motor (expressive) aphasic but are most pronounced in the sensory (receptive) aphasic. The Weigl Test as used by De Renzi *et al.* (1966) involves presentation of stimulus materials scattered over a table; the Hidden Figures Test requires sustained visual search. It seems plausible that abnormalities of visual scanning might affect performance on both tests. The Halstead Category Test, on the other hand, with its restricted field of presentation and simple geometric figures and relative emphasis on conceptual activity, might not place as great a demand on the scanning process.

A second avenue of exploration certainly will be devoted to explication of the possible role of impaired auditory verbal comprehension and ideational apraxia in cognitive task performance by aphasic patients. Recall that De Renzi *et al.* (1966) found that Weigl performance and auditory verbal comprehension were highly correlated in aphasics and that Efron (1963) demonstrated marked impairment in auditory sequencing in aphasics. Consider also the findings of another study (De Renzi, Pieczuro, & Vignolo, 1968) in which ideational apraxia (inability to demonstrate the use of actual objects) was found in 34% of aphasics, 6% of nonaphasics (LHD) and 0% of RHD, and in which ideational apraxia and auditory verbal comprehension were significantly correlated (+.58). De Renzi *et al.* (1968) further point out that in their laboratories, aphasics have been found to be inferior to other brain-damaged patients in matching drawings of objects with their corresponding sounds and colors. Considering these attributes of the LHD aphasics it is unlikely that deficits in their performance could be attributed to one specialized defect. Depending on the stimuli, instructions, and response required, aphasic subjects would perform poorly on one task because of impaired verbal comprehension, on another because of ideational apraxia, another because of defective visual scanning, and still another, as suggested by De Renzi *et al.* (1968), because of inability to associate different aspects of the same concept. Yet, despite these factors, aphasics can perform as well as other brain-damaged groups on certain tasks, such as Raven's

Progressive Matrices and the Halstead Category Test, when severity of defect is taken into consideration. Obviously there is work here aplenty for the future!

D. RIGHT HEMISPHERE AND PERCEPTUAL BEHAVIOR

As noted earlier, the commisurotomy cases have provided particularly valuable information concerning the right hemisphere (Sperry, 1968). The striking inability of the right hemispheres of these patients to respond with either speech or writing when stimuli are presented solely to that hemisphere certainly raises questions about its role in awareness and functioning. The ingenious tests described by Sperry (1968) reveal that the right hemisphere can perform intermodal or cross-modal transfer of perceptual information; make simple generalizations; calculate simple arithmetic problems; comprehend both written and spoken words to some extent (although of course, this comprehension could not be expressed verbally); sort objects; respond with appropriate emotion, although the left hemisphere cannot verbalize why; and perform tasks that involve drawing spatial relationships and constructing block designs better than the left hemisphere. Sperry concludes, "Observations like the foregoing lead us to favor the view that in the minor hemisphere we deal with a second conscious entity that is characteristically human and runs along in parallel with the more dominant stream of consciousness in the major hemisphere [p. 732]."

But commisurotomies exist only in a few people. What evidence is there of specialized right hemisphere functioning from other sources? The concept that the right (nondominant hemisphere) is salient in certain aspects of perception is nearly a century old. As pointed out by Smith (1969), Hughlings Jackson described the function of the right posterior lobe as "leading" in visuo-ideational processes, contrasted with the left hemisphere's "leading" in language. However, much of the evidence which points to the specific disabilities associated with RHD has been gained in the last two decades.

Neglect or imperception of the contralateral side of the body and extrapersonal space has long been described in clinical literature (Piercy, 1964) as more characteristic of RHD than LHD. Construction dyspraxias, i.e., the imperfect execution of construction tasks in which visual control is important, have also been noted (Arrigoni & De Renzi, 1964). An example of a typical experiment has been provided earlier in this chapter were defective performance on the Block Design Test was found to be greater in RHD than LHD. Impaired performance by RHD on visually guided motor behavior such as maze performance has also been cited earlier (Archibald, Wepman, & Jones, 1967) and repeatedly confirmed. Numerous other experiments have been reviewed by Piercy (1964) which clearly point to impaired perceptual functioning in RHD.

The problem for the neuropsychologist has been to specify these defects more clearly. Does deficit result from defective information processing at the sensory-perceptual level or is it in the perceptual-motor feedback system? Is there evidence for intrahemisphere localization, i.e., are certain regions of the right hemisphere more intimately involved in the deficit behavior in a fashion analogous to the specific regions in the left hemisphere which have greater saliency in aphasia? Are there perceptual deficits in other modalities? What is the role of visual field defects in the impaired performance? What is the role of recency *vs.* chronicity of damage in performance? Warrington and James (1967) compared unilateral RHD and LHD on three tests of visual recognition (using incomplete figures) and one of immediate visual retention. RHD were significantly poorer on all three perceptual recognition tests, but were not significantly different on visual retention. An analysis of subgroups of patients by lesions indicated that the temporal lobe patients did not differ significantly but the parietal lobe patients did; RHD parietal cases had greater impairment than LHD groups on all tests including visual retention. The LHD group did not differ from the control group on any of the visual tests. The pattern of correlations obtained among the visual tests suggested that the tests of visual retention and visual recognition involve different functions or patterns of functions which are then differentially affected by lesions in the right parietal lobe. Finally, performance on the Block Design Test was highly related to visual retention scoring in RHD but not in LHD. Thus, immediate memory for a visual spatial arrangement was associated with failure on a task of a visual-spatial constructive nature.

In an important contribution, marred only by confusion in the labeling of data in their tables, Newcombe and Russell (1969) studied men who suffered missile wounds in the head 20 years previously. RHD patients performed significantly poorer than LHD on a test of visual closure and visual maze learning. The LHD performed as well as controls on these tasks. Evidence was also found for a differential impairment within the right hemisphere; there was no overlap of those who were severely impaired on the closure test with those severely impaired on the maze test. Visual field deficits could not account for the poor performance.

Deficits in learning of geometric forms (but intact verbal paired-associate learning) following right hemisphere unilateral electroconvulsive shock treatment have been found (Cohen, Noblin, & Silverman,

1968). Left hemisphere shocked patients, in contrast, had deficits in verbal paired-associate learning but minimal difficulty with learning of forms. Milner (1968) summarized a number of studies on visual memory tests after right temporal lobectomy and reported deficits in that group for any *method* of testing but not for *type* of stimulus. No memory loss was seen on any task which had a visual presentation of verbal material but definite impairment occurred on tasks using nonverbal stimuli, including nonsense figures and snapshots of human faces. Benton and Van Allen (1968) examined RHD and LHD for recognition of faces by matching one of six choices, concurrently presented, to a stimulus figure. The task was varied in difficulty by matching full-faced pictures with three-quarter views and different lighting. RHD had significantly more errors than the LHD who performed at the level of the controls. Visual field deficits could not account for these differences. The investigators conclude that the RHD disability involves faulty integration and discrimination of sensory data rather than simple sensory deficit.

De Renzi (1968) reviewed several experiments involving visual field defects and performance on visual tasks. RHD patients remembered significantly fewer recurrent nonsense designs that LHD patients but the greatest impairment was in the RHD subgroup with visual field defects. In a subsequent experiment, RHD patients performed more poorly than LHD patients over a series of trials on a tactual formboard test administered while the subject was blindfolded. Again, the subgroup of patients with visual field defects performed worse than the rest. This finding suggests that the poor performance of the RHD visual field defect group in the nonsense figure experiment is probably not attributable to the visual defect *per se* but that the areas of the brain which were damaged subserve both the visual field and visual memory. Thus, a lesion in the parietal lobe could interrupt the optic radiations, leading to a visual field defect, but at the same time impinge on areas where sensory-spatial information is integrated and stored.

Results cited in these experiments suggest that answers to the questions posed earlier are beginning to be found. Deficits in RHD functioning exist at the level of integration of sensory information, especially with visual stimuli of a spatial nature, in visual memory, in visually guided maze performance and visuo-constructive tasks. Further, there are suggestions that different regions of the right hemisphere are of varying importance in the brain processes underlying the psychological functions noted above. The greatest deficits appear to occur with damage to post-Rolandic areas, the parietal and temporal lobes. Deficits have been found in RHD patients examined 20 years subsequent to injury, suggesting that permanent alteration of function has occurred. Visual field defects appear to be concurrent effects, a point which emphasizes the importance of temporal and parietal lobe functioning in diverse aspects of the perceptual process.

The last question, i.e., "Are there perceptual deficits manifested in other modalities?" is answered in the affirmative. Following up the work reported by De Renzi (1968) from the very active neuropsychology laboratories in Milan, De Renzi and Scotti (1969) found decided deficits in RHD patients on a tactual test of shape discrimination. Their RHD and LHD patients had no difficulty in recognizing shapes visually, when allowed to palpate by hand comparable forms hidden from view. But when allowed only to run the forefinger around the lateral edge of the shapes, again hidden from sight, the RHD group was markedly impaired in visual choice of the corresponding forms. LHD patients were slightly impaired but quite significantly better than the RHD group. The investigators conclude that the posterior portion of the right hemisphere is heavily involved with the integration of spatial information regardless of sensory modality. Carmon and Benton (1969) have demonstrated that RHD patients, compared to LHD, have deficits in detecting spatial direction of tactual stimuli although perception of number of stimuli is intact. The deficits were particularly apparent in the ipsilateral hand comparisons. In a study of tactile maze learning in unilateral lesion cases, Corkin (1965) found that RHD patients were much more impaired than LHD cases. Evidence for other types of differential impairment in somato-sensory functioning of RHD and LHD are reported in Semmes, Weinstein, Ghent, and Teuber (1960).

Asymmetries in auditory functioning for the two hemispheres have been reported. Milner (1962) found that right temporal lobectomy cases performed more poorly than left temporal cases on several of the Seashore Tests of musical aptitude, particularly on timbre, time, loudness and tonal memory. The area of dichotic stimulation (simultaneous presentation of stimuli to both ears) is currently yielding a rich harvest of studies. Kimura (1967), one of the pioneers with the technique, has reported that right temporal patients performed significantly poorer on a test of recognition of melodies compared with left temporal cases. These results were confirmed by another laboratory (Millikan & Darley, 1967, p. 135). Of even greater interest is that normal subjects can recognize melodies better with the right hemisphere (left ear), and distinguish dichotically presented digits or words better with the left hemisphere (right ear). The development of a technique, dichotic stimulation, which enables differential hemispheric functioning to be studied in normal individuals has spurred neuropsychologists on to an intensive exploration with the technique, as a glance at current journals will show.

The evidence reviewed here indicates substantial differences in certain aspects of right hemispheric functioning. These differences suggest a relative saliency of the right hemisphere in perceptual functions in at least three modalities: vision, audition, and tactile. The intact right hemisphere seems to be the "leading" hemisphere for integration and retention of sensory-perceptual information of a spatial and perhaps temporally patterned nonverbal nature. Is this what we would call dominance? This brings up one of the most interesting theories of neuropsychlogical functioning to appear in recent years.

E. HEMISPHERIC SPECIALIZATION

A provocative paper by Semmes (1968) has presented a model for differential organization of the two hemispheres. In brief, Semmes proposes that sensory and motor abilities are represented focally in the left hemisphere and diffusely in the right hemisphere. Schematically this could be depicted as overlapping circles in the right hemisphere, indicating diffuseness of functional representation, and nonoverlapping circles of focal representation in the left hemisphere. Such an organization, she points out (Semmes, 1968, pp. 19–21), may lead to a different understanding of "dominance." A small lesion in the RHD patients might not have much effect, since that hemisphere's functions are diffusely organized. But a small lesion in the LHD patient could cause a severe deficit because of the focal nature of the left hemisphere organization. Thus, the left hemisphere would appear to be dominant for that function. If more complex tasks were presented, tasks which involve several abilities, a lesion in the right hemisphere might give rise to greater impairment in performance than in the case of a left hemisphere lesion similarly placed, because of the diffuse representation of the functions underlying the abilities. The result would be an apparent "dominance" for that task. Such a condition she terms "pseudodominance."

Semmes bases her model on results gained largely from the extensive study of somatosensory disorders previously mentioned (Semmes et al., 1960). There are two types of findings which are important: first, the evidence for a greater incidence of ipsilateral sensorimotor deficits in LHD and second, lack of relationship between localization of lesion and deficit in sensorimotor performance in RHD compared to LHD. To exemplify the first finding, the LHD group had a significantly greater percentage of patients who manifested deficits in touch-pressure, two-point discrimination, point localization or sense of passive movement of the left hand than the RHD cases had for the right hand. The second finding is illustrated by the difference found on sensorimotor tests within the LHD group; the nearer the lesion to sensorimotor cortex, the greater the performance deficit. In the RHD, the deficits obtained did not differ as a function of location. Other findings, both clinical (Critchley, 1953) and experimental (De Renzi & Faglioni, 1967; Vaughan & Costa, 1962; Wyke, 1968), support Semmes' position.

Some evidence for Semmes' notion of ipsilateral control of sensory processes has been found in several studies in our laboratories. Parsons, Majumder, and Chandler (1967) plotted the visual fields of unilateral lesion groups by means of thresholds for flicker detection. If Semmes' hypothesis were valid, a greater deficit in the left visual (ipsilateral) field for LHD patients would be found than in the right visual (ispsilateral) field of the RHD. The contralateral field threshold for both groups was decidedly impaired and at the same level but, in accord with Semmes' notion, the ipsilateral field for the LHD was significantly more depressed than that of the RHD. Analysis of data from a previously published study with other groups of patients but using the same technique gave rise to the same results (Vega, Parsons, & Chandler, 1966).

As regards Semmes' second finding, i.e., that sensorimotor (and more complex) functions are more diffusely represented in the right hemisphere, additional support has been gained from De Renzi and Faglioni (1967). But there is reason to question the generality of Semmes' model in light of the results cited earlier. Both Warrington and James (1967) and Newcombe and Russell (1969) have presented evidence for a relative dissociation of function within the right hemisphere. In both experiments, different visual processes in RHD were either unrelated or not highly correlated despite being significantly impaired. Unpublished research in our laboratory also raises questions. Correlations among performances on two sensorimotor tests comparable to those Semmes reported (dynamometer and finger tapping) did not differ for the ipsilateral hand of RHD (+.71) and LHD (+.59) although they were in the expected direction. Further, the differences between the right and left hands within the two groups did not differ as would be expected if greater ipsilateral damage were to be found in the LHD group. On the other hand, a significant correlation was found between performance on the Halstead Category Test involving visualspatial geometric figures and the Block Design Test (+.35, $p < .05$) in the RHD but not in the LHD (+.18), a finding which would be in accord with the "diffuse representation" of functions as well as the salience of the right hemisphere in visual-spatial functions.

It is obvious that much work lies ahead to delineate the experimental conditions and lesion characteristics of subjects under which the Semmes' model generates valid predictions. However, it is equally clear that through the introduction of such a model, and as the result of the successors that it will provoke, clarification of the nature of hemispheric organization and function ultimately will emerge. But any model for brain function will also have to include consideration of the general effects of brain damage for reasons which will become apparent in the next section.

IV. General Effects

A number of investigators have emphasized that in addition to specific effects, general impairment of behavior may be found subsequent to brain injury (Chapman & Wolff, 1959; De Renzi & Faglioni, 1965; Goldstein, 1959; Huse & Parsons, 1965; Luria, 1966; Parsons, 1968; Satz, 1966; Teuber & Weinstein, 1955). These general or nonlateralizable, nonlocalizable effects have been described in behaviors ranging from one of the simplest yet most basic aspects of behavior, vigilance, to the broadest aspects of behavior involving adaptation to changing life situation requirements.

Before detailed analysis is attempted, it is instructive to consider the study reported by Chapman and Wolff (1959). Their presentation, one of the most extensive studies of brain-damaged patients ever undertaken, is particularly rewarding despite the formidable number of unhappily placed tables and figures in the article. After studying subjects, in whom known amounts of brain tissue had been removed, on laboratory tests of psychological functioning, and conducting extensive interviews with wives, friends and employers, Chapman and Wolff concluded that the degree of impairment of the "highest integrative functions" was directly related to the mass of cerebral tissue lost from the isocortex. Their second conclusion was that this relationship was independent of site and lateralization. While the generality of the latter conclusion is questionable in view of their subject selection (excluding patients with "significant" impairment of speech or language) and the findings of other recent studies, the evidence for the first conclusion is impressive.

Of particular interest for our present purposes is the description of the patients' life behavior gained from the interviews described earlier. The following is an adapted summary of what they term the "early stage of waning cerebral hemisphere function" in patients with developing brain disease, or in patients with 30 to 60 grams of brain tissue removed. The patients were seen as having less energy, drive, and initiative. Learning new material was fatiguing; they did not catch on to points being made in conversation or work as readily as before. They could not shift as rapidly from one role or problem and thus tried to do one thing at a time. There was increasing difficulty in eliminating or extinguishing responses to irrelevant stimuli and thus in concentrating on the pertinent aspects of problems with which they were confronted. At the personal level, they withdrew, manifesting less overt demonstration of affection or warmth and less concern over the well-being of others. They were less active physically, interpersonally, and socially. They tended to avoid new and different siuations and when unavoidable were greatly fatigued by them. Interests were more circumscribed and creative activity dropped off. The prevailing premorbid defenses were much more conspicuous; frustration tolerance was low. Goals and purposive activity were maintained but less effectively and at greater personal cost. As the number of grams of brain tissue removed increased (above the 30 to 60 range), the characteristics described above were intensified.

It is obvious that loss of brain tissue of as little as 30 grams (out of an average brain weight of about 1300 grams) results in changes throughout the full spectrum of the human organism's behavior. Depending on the approach to and methods used with the brain-damaged patients, investigators will focus on different aspects of the disturbances and develop different explanatory concepts. In the summary provided above, there is ample reason to investigate the question of reduced vigilance (Head, 1963), memory, and arousal as fundamental to the impaired behavior. On the other hand, much of what was stated could be formulated in terms of what Goldstein (1942, 1959) has described as the outstanding characteristic of brain damage, an impairment of the abstract attitude. Research and concepts of both approaches will be looked at next.

A. Vigilance, Memory, and Arousal

1. *Vigilance*

The concept of vigilance dates back to Henry Head's (1963) intriguing discussion in 1926 of what he considered to be an extremely important aspect of brain-injury, i.e., a lowered level of physiological efficiency. This state of "lowered vitality" he pointed out was not to be confused with heightened or lowered excitability, rather a condition in which the organism responded with less high-grade adapted behavior to stimuli. In an eloquent passage he stated:

What wonder that the complex powers demanded by speech, reading and writing can be affected by a lesion which diminishes neural vitality. Vigilance is lowered and the specific mental aptitudes die out as an electric lamp is extinguished, when the voltage falls below the necessary level, the centres involved in these automatic processes, which form an essential part of the conscious act, may continue to live on a lower vital level, as when under the influence of chloroform; they do not cease to function, but the vigilance necessary for the performance of their high-grade activities has been abolished by the fall of neural potency [Head, 1963, p. 487].

Evidence for a nonlocalized impairment of central nervous system (CNS) functioning on tests of vigilance and reaction time (RT) has been provided in a number of studies reviewed by De Renzi and Faglioni (1965). These investigators point out that simple RT is a technique of choice as an estimate of overall severity of impairment of CNS function-ing because it is independent of laterality of lesion (providing the hand or foot ipsilateral to the lesion is used); it is not affected by presence of aphasia; it is not related to educational level and it is as good a predic-tion of brain damage as other more complex tests. In unpublished studies in our laboratories, we also have found significant decrements in RT in heterogenous brain-damaged patients with no differences due to laterality of lesion. Still other evidence comes from Sperry (1968). Commisurectomized patients and controls were presented with two separate visual discrimination tasks, one to each hemisphere simultan-eously. Reaction time to these presentations did not produce an incre-ment in RT (over single presentation to one hemisphere) in the patients. For the controls there was a marked slowing of RTs for the simultaneous presentation. However, the RTs for the commisurectomized patients were markedly higher under both types of presentations than were those of the controls.

These data suggest a basic interference with the temporal aspects of information processing in the brain-injured person, regardless of site of damage. If so, it should be apparent in other types of sensory and per-ceptual tests involving temporal dimensions. Experiments in flicker detection provide such evidence. Shure and Halstead (1958) have re-ported significant inverse relationships between flicker thresholds and size of lesion, i.e., the larger the lesion the poorer the flicker detection. Again, these results were independent of lateralization. Chapman and Wolff (1959) found a similar relationship for flicker thresholds and mass of brain tissue removed. Parsons, Majumder, and Chandler (1967) found that flicker detection thresholds in unilateral lesion patients were significantly lower for the half-fields subserved by the uninjured as well as the injured cortex. Battersby (1951) has reported similar results. As an example of another experimental situation involving temporal resolu-tion, it long has been recognized that brain-damaged patients mani-fest deficits in perception when presented with visual stimuli tachistoscopically (Goldstein, 1942). Apparently CNS dysfunction of almost any type results in a deficit in temporal acuity (i.e., the ability to detect temporal intervals between stimuli), deficits in the rapidity with which responses can be given to stimuli, and deficits in the perception of material briefly presented. Is there evidence for general deficits when time is not the paramount factor?

2. Memory

While specific deficits in memory have been stressed in the earlier sections, there is little doubt that general effects are more the rule than the exception (Talland, 1963). Chapman and Wolff (1959) have stated that "impairments of memory result from damage in any region of the cerebral hemisphere, the degree of impairment being closely related to the mass of brain that is damaged [p. 75]." In a study in our laboratories, Burn (1967) found that brain-damaged patients manifested impairment of some 15 points on the Wechsler Memory Scale compared with controls, a highly significant difference ($t = 4.40$, $p < .001$). There were no differential effects on the subtests attributable to the LHD and RHD except on the learning of paired verbal associates. Here the left hemisphere cases scored significantly lower than the right hemisphere cases but the later scored quite significantly lower than the controls. This study merely exemplifies one of the most widely recognized criteria of both acute and chronic brain damage: loss of memory (Maher, 1966; Redlich & Freedman, 1966).

As in the case of the specific effects, we must ask the question, what is the nature of this "memory loss"? Are the traces destroyed or are the organizational and functional patterns disrupted in a way which effectively precludes rapid and satisfactory retrieval? There is much evidence to support the latter notion. Talland (1965) studied patients with Korsakoff's syndrome, a syndrome in which the primary psychological symptom is "loss of memory." After an experimental analysis, Talland came to the conclusion that the so-called memory deficit of these patients was probably due to defective activation and persistence. "The dysfunction characteristic of the amnesic syndrome seems to arise from the most general activating operation that determined the rate, range and persistence of scanning [Talland, 1965, p. 313]." Others, Talland pointed out, have arrived at similar conclusions for other types of brain conditions. He cites Lashley who stated that amnesias resulting from brain injury were not caused by the destruction of specific memory traces, "but represented a lowered level of vigilance, a greater difficulty in activating the organized patterns of traces, or a disturbance of some broader system of organized functions [p. 319]." Russell (1959) seemed to be hinting at the same thing when he described, in patients who have had concussions, the recovery of memory occurring when they seemed to be making an effort to piece the memories together. Shure and Halstead (1958) suggested that lesions almost anywhere in the cerebral cortex interrupt reticular activating system (RAS) projection and corticofugal fibers. This could, they point out, "reduce the total cortical afferent influence and cortifugal feedback which normally maintains synchronous, brain rhythms and a high level of conscious awareness [p. 23]." Chapman and Wolff (1959) concluded that removal of even small amounts of brain tissue from the cortex reduced the capacity for most complex human activity including the capacity to initiate and maintain appropriate adaptive reactions.

It appears obvious that such statements have wide implications for understanding general deficits in the higher intellectual functions. Could such deficits result from interrupted cortical-subcortical circuits which are fundamental to mechanisms sustaining general alertness, vigilance, and the ability to maintain the scanning operations which lead to (a) the matching of previous experience with incoming sensory stimulation and (b) the sequential undertaking of cycles of search, match, and confirmation, all of which have implication for the future direction of the organism (Talland, 1965)? Does this approach mean that patients with brain dysfunction are less "activated" or "aroused"? Certainly, the well-established disturbances of the electroencephalogram demonstrate that normal brain rhythms are affected adversely by brain injury. But what about other measures of arousal which have been associated with RAS activity, such as the autonomic variables of skin conductance level (SCL), skin conductance response (SCR), heart rate? To explore this question, a series of studies (described below) was undertaken in our laboratories.

3. Arousal

The first experiment (Parsons & Chandler, 1969) dealt with three straightforward questions: (a) Does the level of arousal, as measured by SCL and SCR, differ in brain-damaged (BD) and non-brain-damaged (NBD) patients? (b) Is there a differential arousal in the groups as a function of the task? (c) Is level of arousal related to performance on the task? Continual electrodermal polygraph recordings were made on all Ss under the following conditions: basal rest, startle stimulus, passive stimulation (listening to a periodically sounded buzzer), a choice reaction time, and a paired-associate learning task with easy and difficult items. All conditions were interspersed with rest periods. Two groups of middle-aged male veterans were studied: a heterogeneous

but clearly diagnosed group of BD and a NBD group of general medical
and surgical patients. The groups were equated on relevant variables
including extent of emotional disorder. In answer to the first question
regarding level of arousal, BD differed from NBD in that they had
higher SCLs on the average, significantly so under rest conditions. In
answer to the second question regarding differential arousal, the two
groups did *not* change in their relative mean difference in levels over
the conditions. (SCR data were very similar and thus will not be reported
here.) Since this was the first experiment in an essentially unchartered
field, we decided to replicate it with a new group of patients and controls (Parsons & Chandler, 1969).

The abscissa of Figure 4 presents conditions and the ordinate the
level of SCLs. A group of schizophrenics were included for comparisons.
The results were more clear-cut than in the first experiment. BD differed
from NBD on almost every condition. Schizophrenics were significantly
different from the BD in the beginning of the experiment but under
paired associates conditions they were significantly different from NBD.
Again, however, the BD and NBD groups did not have a differential
level of arousal as a function of the nature of the task; their curves were
essentially parallel. BD patients on both experiments were also signifi-

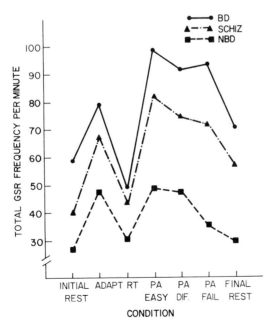

Fig. 4. Mean log conductance over conditions for brain damaged, schizophrenics,
and controls (Parsons & Chandler, 1969).

cantly poorer on reaction time and paired-associate learning than the NBD. This brings us to our third question, is the level of arousal related to the impaired performance? One way of examining this question was to correlate performance and electrodermal measures. Correlations were generally low and nonsignificant. However, both the SCL and SCRs correlated positively with performance in the BD and negatively in the NBD and schizophrenics. For example, the SCL *vs.* Paired-Associate learning score was +.35 in Experiment I and +.25 in Experiment II for the BD, while the corresponding correlations were —.38 and —.11 for the NBD. (The correlation for the schizophrenics was —.31.) The positive correlations in the BD mean that the greater the arousal, the better the performance, but since they had significantly higher levels of arousal than the NBD and also significantly lower levels of performance, it does not seem likely the arousal levels as measured by electrodermal measures are a significant factor in the performance levels of BD.

There are reasons, however, for believing that electrodermal measures are not the psychophysiological measure of choice in trying to unravel the performance deficit problem. In the next experiment (Holloway & Parsons, 1969), 19 NBD and 23 BD patients were utilized. The BD groups was subdivided into three subgroups: eight patients with only (or primarily) left hemisphere involvement (LHD), eight patients with right hemisphere involvement (RHD), and seven patients with diffuse or bilateral involvement (BHD). Patients were approximately of the same education and age levels as those in the previous experiment. The RHD and LHD groups were similar with respect to the extent and nature of the brain lesion. Again the groups were subjected to different tasks while psychophysiological responses were being recorded on an 8-channel Beckman Dynograph (R). There were five experimental conditions: a five-minute rest period, a series of 10 habituation trials (no response required) with a 2″ buzzer, the same procedure with a 10″ buzzer, 10 trials of a motor reaction time test (using the right foot), and 10 trials of a simple perceptual-memory test. The following measures were recorded: SCLs and SCRs from palmar and dorsal surfaces of the *right and left* hands, and heart rate.

In Figure 5, left minus right SCL difference scores were computed for both palmar and dorsal recordings. (A negative sign means that the SCL of the right hand is greater than the SCL for the left hand; a positive sign means the opposite.) Looking at the palmar portion of the curve, it is quite apparent that the LHD has higher SCLs on the right hand than on the left (negative scores) while the RHD group has the opposite (positive scores). Thus, the relationships reported for the first two experiments for brain-damaged as a whole were also found for a com-

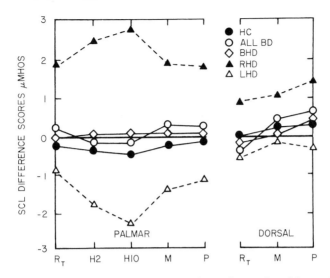

Fig. 5. SCL palmar and dorsal differences in brain-damaged and hospital control groups (Holloway & Parsons, 1969).

parison within the BD of more-injured *vs.* less-injured patients. But these data suggest that brain injury results in a cortical "release" phenomenon, i.e., that the electrodermal measures are directly affected by brain injury and thus cannot give a very clear picture of the "involvement" or "arousal" of the S.

We next investigated the heart rate component of the orienting response. This response and its adaptive significance has been discussed in depth in Stern and Plapp's (1969) chapter in Volume 1 of this serial publication. Suffice it to say that any new stimulus or change in stimulus pattern evokes a "what is it?" or orienting response (OR) (Sokolov, 1963). This response is characterized, among other measures, by brief cardiac deceleration. As the same stimulus recurs the response diminishes and habituation is said to have occurred. Lacey (1967) has reported that the cardiac deceleration component of the OR is associated with active preparation for stimuli in normal subjects. What happens in brain damage?

Using the data recorded in the experiment previously cited (Holloway & Parsons, 1969), we found the following: (*a*) BD had higher heart rates than NBD during habituation (passive stimulation) but not in rest or in the other situations; (*b*) BD had greater heart rate change "OR" scores to the offset of the stimulus; and (*c*) BD "ORs" did not habituate to the stimulus, while the NBD showed the usual habituation effect (Figure 6), a finding similar to that of Davidoff and McDonald (1964).

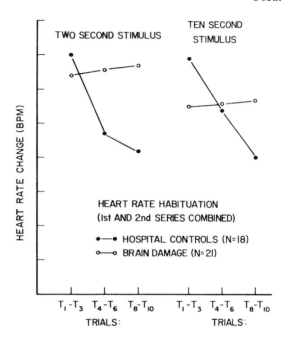

FIG. 6. Habituation of heart rate for 2-second and 10-second stimulation.

It would appear that the BD are susceptible to stimulation by nonmeaningful stimuli, and that once they are tracking a stimulus its cessation produces a greater reaction than in NBD. Finally, the OR cardiac component in BD does not habituate over trials as it does in NBD.

To return to performance, according to previous experimenters (Lacey, 1967), cardiac deceleration (OR) is associated with the active preparation for reception of stimuli. In the motor reaction-time test of our experiment we have partial measurement of this psychological state in that the more alert the subject is after receiving the warning signal, the more rapidly he would react. Thus, a correlation between OR and RT would be expected. The correlation of the cardiac component of the OR (heart rate change score) with RT in the NBD was $-.456$ ($p < .05$). The greater the OR, the faster the reaction time in accord with expectation. In the BD, however, this correlation was $-.03$; speed of RT was unrelated to the OR cardiac component response to the warning signal.

Thus, there are indications that electrodermal measures are affected by brain damage, giving rise to a "cortical release." These measures, however, do not seem to be related significantly to performance. A similar phenomenon is found with the heart rate response component of the orienting response, which may have implications for performance in that BD are susceptible to "nonmeaningful" stimulation, i.e., they do not appear to habituate. This suggests a loss of inhibitory controls which are thought to be important in habituation. Further, BD have significantly greater ORs to offset than to onset of stimulus. This result is similar to Stern's (1968) finding that GSR offset responses in children are inversely related to age, i.e., the younger the child, the greater the offset response.

It may be, then, that part of the performance deficit in the BD may be accounted for by interference with inhibitory controls that lead to the integrated, effective performance of any type of task. These inhibitory processes enter into the multiply determined aspect of performance at all levels: at the level of immediate central response to stimuli (as shown in our experiment); at the central integrative level; and, finally, at the initiation of effector activity. Given the feedback control of afferent-efferent and central processes, as emphasized by Luria (1966), it seems likely that defects in inhibitory controls at any level of this process may ultimately affect the level of performance. Perhaps at a different level of discourse, these disturbances in inhibitory regulatory processes are what Talland (1965) has described in more psychological terms as deficits in activation and persistence patterns or, at the more molar level of Goldstein (1959), deficits in "sets" and higher levels of abstracting behavior. It is to the latter area that we now turn.

B. Abstracting Behavior, Sets, and Interpersonal Behavior

1. *Abstract-Concrete Behavior*

The terms "abstract" and "concrete attitudes," as applied to brain-damaged patients, are indubitably linked with Kurt Goldstein (1942, 1959). As noted earlier in this chapter, many criticisms can be leveled at his formulations and methods of testing, but the fact remains that his "organismic" approach stresses molar behaviors and is thereby a healthy antidote for too heavy a dose of localization. Goldstein did not deny localization of neuropsychological processes. In fact, as Geschwind (1964) has pointed out, he often became very specific in his localization statements. Rather, Goldstein was concerned to a greater degree with certain types of disturbed behaviors in his patients that were similar to those described by the relatives and friends of the patients of Chapman and Wolff (1959). These disturbances had the greatest implications for the patients of a rehabilitation neurologist after World War I, the role in which Goldstein developed his concepts.

To encompass the diversity of symptoms with which he was confronted, Goldstein (1959) formulated the presence of a basic defect accompanying brain damage: an impairment of the abstract attitude. He advanced the notion that human beings possess two kinds of attitudes toward the world: the abstract and the concrete. In the concrete attitude, the individual's response is to the immediate experience of situations and things. In the abstract attitude, the individual "transcends" the immediately given aspect of sense impressions and considers the situation from a conceptual point of view. The normal person can use both attitudes appropriately, shifting his levels of functioning. The brain-damaged person cannot shift as easily; he is impaired in his abstract attitude and this impairment springs from a disturbance in figure-ground relationships of neural activity. Goldstein (1959) gave a list of some 10 characteristics of the abstract attitude centering on being able to initiate a set, to shift set, to abstract common properties, to grasp the essence of a given whole, and to assume the "as if" attitude.

The overall implication of deficits in abstract attitude is that the brain-damaged patient has impaired performance in many areas. Furthermore, he manifests a reduced capacity to evaluate, or place in perspective, his altered performance capabilities. He thus becomes more dependent upon external or environmental cues to evaluate his behavior.

Goldstein's orienting statements have served as guides for understanding and explaining impaired behavior in brain damage for many years. Rather than reviewing the many studies in this area, we have selected some of the work from our laboratories to exemplify how Goldstein's concepts and orientation have been used.

It is important to note, however, the similarity between what Goldstein has described as "impairment in the abstract attitude" and what Talland (1965) has called "deficits in the sequential undertaking of cycles of search, match, confirmation and the implication of these for the future direction of the organism." Inability to initiate a set, to shift set, to adopt the "as if" stance, etc., could easily be seen in terms of impaired information processing, lack of sustained search for matching and confirming patterns of incoming stimuli with stored information, and lack of consideration of the implications or outcome of the search and comparison for the future of the organism. It should not surprise us to find that the explanatory concepts arising from two different conceptual approaches can be translated. Both conceptual orientations were developed to account for the same facts, the behavioral deficits of brain-injured patients.

In the studies reported below, the behavior of brain-damaged patients was investigated as a function of the following: the degree of ambiguity in the stimuli presented, the type of instructions given, the use of "anchors" in tasks requiring psychophysical judgment, and the experimenter's attitude and helping behavior.

2. Stimuli, Sets, and Instructions

Our first experiment in this area was conducted over a decade ago (Gottlieb & Parsons, 1960). Twenty definitely brain-damaged patients and 20 suspected (but eventually shown not to be brain-damaged) patients were given the Rorschach Ink-Blot Test. The study was directed toward several aims which need not concern us at the moment, but one of the major findings was that the definitely brain-damaged patients had significantly more poor form (F—) whole responses than did the comparison group. As Goldstein would predict, in the face of ambiguous stimuli the brain-damaged patients had difficulty initiating an appropriate set. In Talland's terms, the scanning and match operations were faulty and the patients settled for a lower level of congruence and appropriateness. Parenthetically, a recent experiment by Hall, Hall, and Lavoie (1968) demonstrate clear-cut laterally differences between left and right hemisphere lesion cases on selected variables from the Rorschach Test. One of the more discriminating indices was form level in which poor form was associated with right hemisphere lesions.

In the next study, an unpublished doctoral dissertation (Sternlof, 1964), we were interested in a totally different problem: the differential perception of males and females (both actual pictures of persons and symbolic representations of them) by paranoid, depressed, and brain-damaged patients. Combined male and female pairs of pictures were presented as stereograms using the telebinocular. Male adult patients were given 2 or 3 seconds to view each pair and were asked to tell what they saw. Under such conditions, subjects usually report either male or female and are not aware that photographs of both sexes have been presented. The results were very clear. As predicted, paranoid patients reported significantly more males, depressed patients tended to report more females, and the control groups (hospital aides and a group of heterogeneous brain-damaged patients) reported both sexes about equally. Most important for our purpose, the brain-damaged group had the greatest difficulty when *symbols* of male and female were presented. They have significantly greater "don't know" responses to the symbols than each of the other groups. Again, under conditions where the task calls for rapid organization of perception with stimuli of symbolic nature, brain-damaged patients manifest maximal deficit. When more extended periods of time were given for viewing the symbolic stimuli, the brain-damaged performed as well as the other groups.

The above experiments deal with the characteristics of the stimuli (ambiguous or representational) and the temporal aspect of stimulus presentation (limited or non-limited). An equally important dimension is

that of the instructions given by the experimenter and the possible interaction of the instruction-induced sets of the patient with performance
on different types of tasks. Lodge, in her doctoral dissertation (Lodge,
1966), examined performances of brain-damaged and control patients
on three perceptual tasks: a flicker detection test (where the stimulus
actually was changing), the Archimedes Spiral aftereffect (where the
stimulus had changed but no longer was changing at the time of the
response measure), and the Necker Cube (reversible figures which never
change in physical stimulus characteristics). Three sets of instructions
were given: "facilitating" instructions which described the phenomena
and thus tuned the subject appropriately to the task, "neutral" instructions which asked the subject to describe what he saw when it was
different, and "inhibiting" instructions which gave the subject the set
that nothing was going to change.

As expected, the brain-damaged patients performed significantly more
poorly on all three tasks. The greatest differences in their performance
were obtained under the "neutral" instruction condition, as exemplified
in Figure 7, which presents the results for the spiral aftereffect. The
differential effects of facilitating and inhibiting instructions depended
somewhat on the type of task, but as a whole, they suggest strongly
that instructions defining the task for the subject are of crucial importance
in studies of brain damage. To the extent that the situation is un-

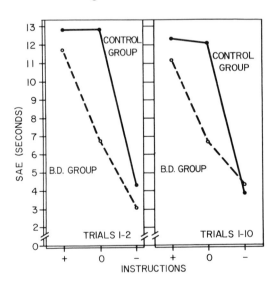

FIG. 7. Mean duration of spiral aftereffect (after Lodge, 1966).

structured and the brain-injured patient must impose a set in the situation, he is much more likely to manifest deficit performance.

Several other aspects of the role of stimulus variables and instructions were examined in the next experiment. In this study, an unpublished doctoral dissertation, Majumder (1966) was interested in the effects of "anchor" stimuli on the psychophysical judgment of brain-damaged and control patients. "Anchor" stimuli in this instance were stimuli differing markedly in intensity from other stimuli in the series and were introduced without informing the patient. Reasoning from Goldstein's (1959) and Helson's (1964) positions. Majumder predicted that brain-damaged patients would have greater anchor effects in judgment of stimuli and that they would be less able than control patients to ignore the anchor stimulus when instructed to do so. The subjects were given five stimulus intensities to judge on a 9-point scale in three modalities (vision, audition and tactual) under three conditions: "no anchor" introduced in the range of stimuli presented; an "anchor" introduced without informing the subject; and, finally, an "ignore anchor" condition where the subject was told before each presentation of the anchor stimulus that he should ignore it. A common logarithmic scale in decibel units was utilized (Stevens, 1966) to describe all three stimulus qualities, thus rendering a common metric. Sixteen brain-damaged patients and a group of control patients equated or relevant variables were studied.

The results indicated that in the "no anchor" condition the psychometric curves for the category judgments were not significantly different for the groups (Figure 8). For analysis of the "anchor" condition, Helson's (1964) approach was utilized rather than a simple substractive procedure of "no anchor" minus "anchor." The adaptation level procedures provide a more sensitive test of the impact of focal (series stimuli) and background (anchor stimuli) factors. The analyses indicated that controls were four times as influenced in their judgments by the series stimuli as by the anchor stimulus; for the brain damaged the ratio was two to one. These were highly significant differences, and in each modality. In the "ignore anchor" condition, the ratio for the brain damaged was about the same but increased to about six to one in the controls. The result is also evident in Figure 8. It can be seen that the controls in the "ignore anchor" condition shifted their judgments back toward the "no anchor" condition and they did so significantly. The brain damaged did not shift. In fact, in the modality of vision they moved significantly further away from the control condition.

Majumder (1966) interpreted the results of the study as reflecting the brain-damaged patient's difficulty in distinguishing figure and ground

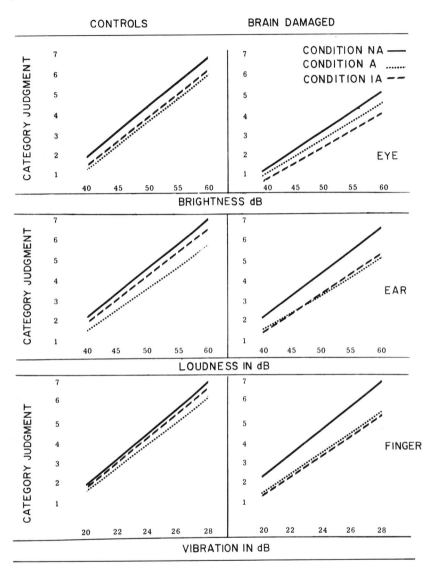

CONTROLS   BRAIN DAMAGED

CONDITION NA ——
CONDITION A ·········
CONDITION IA — —

Fɪɢ. 8. Psychometric curves (fitted) under various experimental conditions. Each point based on 160 judgments (Majumder, 1966).

in accord with Goldstein's position. Even more striking was the inability of these patients to adopt the "as if" attitude, to ignore the anchor stimulus. In Goldstein's terms the patients were tied rather concretely to the immediacy of their sensory experience. Just as we found with respect to arousal and the orienting response in brain-damaged patients, these patients are vulnerable to irrelevant (in this case, background) stimuli and cannot habituate. The "concrete" behavior of the brain-damaged might very well be due to interference with inhibitory controls which permit selective filtering, processing, and responding to stimuli.

3. *Experimenter's Attitudes and Helping Behavior*

Another significant aspect of the stimulus situation under which experiments with brain-damaged subjects are conducted is the experimenter. Recalling Goldstein's (1959) conclusions concerning the reliance of brain-damaged patients upon external structure, Parsons and Stewart (1966) hypothesized that the performance of brain-damaged patients would be affected to a greater extent by the "supportive" or "disinterested" attitude of the experimenter than would neurotic control patients. Two experiments were conducted, both employing essentially the same method but differing in experimenters. In the first Dr. Stewart conducted the interviews; in the second, a female graduate assistant conducted them in a very different hospital and setting. Since the findings of the two experiments were comparable, we shall present the second only. The subjects were administered a short psychomotor task, the Stein Symbol-Gestalt Test (Stein, 1961). The experimenter then gave either a warm, supportive interview, a cold, disinterested interview or a "neutral treatment" during which the subject read magazines. The "treatments" lasted 7 to 12 minutes. The Stein was administered a second time and was followed by a 3- to 5-minute repetition of the same type of treatment. Finally, there was a third administration of the Stein Test. Groups of brain-damaged and neurotic subjects who were equated on relevant variables were assigned to the three treatment conditions.

The results are presented in Figure 9. Replicating the first experiment, the brain-damaged patients performed significantly more poorly than the controls and showed a significant treatment $\times$ trials effect that was not found in the controls. As can be seen on the graph, the "disinterested" treatment gave rise to the greatest difference in both groups, but the effect was more pronounced for the brain damaged. Analyses of components of the total score indicated that the differences between the groups as a function of treatments were due primarily to the speed factor rather than errors. Apparently, the "disinterested, cold" experimenter affected the motivations of the brain-damaged patient to a greater extent than it did the other patients.

Interestingly, in the above experiment, the effects of "warm, supportive" and "neutral" interviews were not different. Apparently, "love is not enough" for the brain-damaged patients. Perhaps more specific

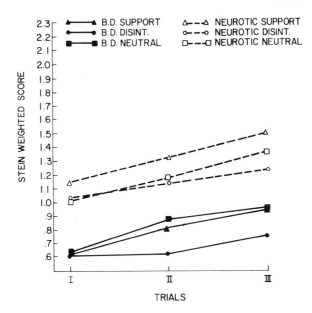

Fig. 9. Stein weighted scores over trials (Parsons & Stewart, 1966).

forms of interest and help could give rise to greater facilitating effects in brain-damaged than other patients. In an unpublished experiment by Monk (1965), some data bearing on this notion were obtained. Previous to her study (Parsons & Klein, 1969), we had demonstrated that brain-damaged patients and process schizophrenics performed similarly on a test of abstracting ability comprised of alternating easy and difficult sub-tests, the Herron Category Test (Herron, 1962). In Monk's study we were interested in whether direct help provided in the form of cues would lead to improvement in performance in brain-damaged and schizophrenic patients.

If brain-damaged patients rely more on external structure and feedback than do other groups, they might well benefit to a greater extent from the help (cues) provided by the experimenter than would the interpersonally handicapped process schizophrenics. On the other hand, if the cognitive deficit in the brain-damaged were the major factor, it might be expected that the process schizophrenics would improve more. Carefully diagnosed male adult process schizophrenics, brain-damaged, and control patients, equated on relevant variables, were given the Herron Category Test twice. On the first administration (Trial 1) cues were provided at certain points during performance on the eight subtests. The patients were then readministered the test immediately (Trial 2) but with no further clues given. On Trial 1, both the process schizophrenics and the brain-damaged had significantly more errors and needed significantly more cues than the controls. The two pathological groups did not differ on these variables. When improvement from Trial 1 to Trial 2 on easy and difficult subtests was considered, the improvement patterns were similar for brain damaged and controls (Table 7). In these groups there was greater improvement on Difficult *vs.* Easy scores, while in the process schizophrenics this pattern was reversed, giving rise to a significant interaction. The interaction, however, comes from the greater improvement of the control group on the difficult items and of the process schizophrenics on the easy items. The brain-damaged patients manifest little change from easy to difficult.

TABLE 7
IMPROVEMENT: TRIAL 1 MINUS TRIAL 2 ERRORS

	Easy	Difficult	Total
Control	2.4	9.6	12.0
Brain-damaged	1.1	3.8	4.9
Process schizophrenics	6.1	2.1	8.2

In answer to the questions raised earlier, it would appear that brain-damaged patients did not respond differentially to clues provided by the examiner. Their improvement scores were quite low, lower, in fact, than process schizophrenics. Apparently, on tests of abstracting ability, the cognitive deficit in brain injury is such that the patient connot utilize direct help from the examiner in the form of relevant cues. This raises the interesting question as to whether cognitive retraining procedures can be used with brain-damaged patients. According to Goldstein (1959), improvement in abstracting behavior cannot be expected until the brain condition improves. However, other evidence suggests that brain-damaged groups can significantly benefit from the experience of merely taking the same abstracting test twice, without having the "help" of the experimenter (Parsons & Klein, 1969). It is possible that the cues provided in Monk's experiment (for example, "In this subtest shape is not included in or important to the principle you are trying to find.") actually served to confuse the brain-damaged patient by calling attention to an irrelevant detail which he could not (as suggested by Majumder's experiment) then ignore? The question lends itself to a straightforward experiment, the outcome of which could have much relevance for rehabilitative efforts.

In this section on "general" effects, it has been pointed out that brain-damaged patients manifest deficits at almost any level of behavior. Deficits in vigilance, memory, perception, and cognitive functions appear to be directly proportional to the amount of tissue destroyed or dysfunctional. Evidence from several sources suggests that cortical brain damage results in disruptions of the inhibitory and regulatory controls of lower brain centers. It seems likely that these disruptions contribute to lessened effectiveness in performance. Faced with impaired effectiveness in meeting experimental and life situational demands, the brain-damaged patient places greater reliance on environmental structure, including the experimenter or examiner, than do other patients. Instructions, "sets," nature of task, and attitude of the experimenter interact in a complex way, thus posing challenges for the clinical neuropsychologist interested in the experimental psychopathology of brain damage.

V. Prospects

Given the foregoing review of progress, what are the prospects for the future? The next decade promises to be even more exciting than the past. As noted at the outset of this chapter, there is every indication that clinical neuropsychology is a vital and expanding field. The human mind remains one of the most fascinating of all scientific puzzles, and problems of brain-behavior relationships will be of increasing importance as time goes on. It seems quite probable that four experimental strategies or lines of investigation will be emphasized in the immediate future.

First, it is likely that international cooperative studies will be stressed. One of the rewards for the clinical neurophsychologist interested in the lawfulness and generality of behavior is the fact that certain brain-behavior relationships can be demonstrated across the cultures. Differential left and right hemisphere functioning has been reported in various countries, regardless of social-cultural-linguistic differences. Theories of neuropsychology might well apply across cultures to a greater degree than do our current theories of psychopathology. One of the first steps in this direction is the development of common metrics. Benton (1969) has reported on the development of a "Multilingual Aphasia Battery." The construction and standardization of a test battery in four languages (English, French, German, and Italian) should provide a firm ground for better communication and interpretation of research findings.

Second, the current rapid progress in electrophysiological methods and technology and their increasing use in brain-behavior research suggests that the study of intrabrain processes under certain stimulus and response conditions will be the center of much activity. Computer-averaged evoked responses have already been shown to be effective in distinguishing left and right hemisphere functioning (Buschbaum & Fedio, 1969). Electroencephalographic responses during the course of recognizing visual stimuli, as reported by Beyn, Zhirmusnskaya, and Volkov (1967), have led to detailed inferences concerning processes such as "sets," decision making and feedback evaluation. Psychophysiological responses which define such important events as the "orienting response" (Parsons, 1968), examined in a variety of stimulus situations, are likely to lead to further understanding of the role of cortical release in inhibitory processes in brain damage. Depth electrode stimulation and recording by means of FM radio waves in completely mobile patients has been reported (Delgado, Mark, Sweet, Ervin, Weiss, Bach-Y-Rita, & Hagiwara, 1968). Abnormalities in behavior and subjective reports by the patients were correlated with abnormalities on the electroencephalogram recordings. The promise inherent in the above methods undoubtedly will be realized in the future.

The third strategy is a reemphasis of an old approach: the intensive experimental analysis of a single subject. Luria (1966) and Luria, Sokolov, and Klemkowski (1967) have provided a model of this type of approach. In the latter study, in order to explain disturbances in acoustic-verbal memory, two patients with left temporo-parietal lesions were thoroughly investigated using memory tests for various stimuli given under different "trace holding" conditions. While both patients showed memory disturbance, the "neurodynamic processes" involved for each patient were decidedly different. In a similar vein, Geschwind and Kaplan's (Geschwind, 1965) analysis of a single case provided compelling evidence for Geschwind's "disconnection" model. Given quantitative techniques and meaningful methods of study, the single case should reappear in our literature.

The fourth strategy is also a familiar one. Essentially, it is the continual application of knowledge and theories from the basic advances in psychology proper to problems of neuropsychology. The studies in dichotic stimulation cited earlier (Kimura, 1967) are a good example of the application of a technique worked out in the context of information-processing models. Another example is the experiment of Burn (1967) in which he applied concept identification techniques to the investigation of brain damage effects on cognitive processes. Still another experiment is that of Huse and Parsons (1965) which illustrates the value of using a technique (pursuit-rotor) in which the parameters have been thoroughly investigated. Finally, use of Helson's adaptation level theory has provided a rather striking demonstration of the effect of background stimuli in the functioning of patients with brain damage (Majumder, 1966).

What do these trends imply for the education of the clinical neuro-psychologist? First, he must have a thorough grounding in his basic area of psychology at the substantive, theoretical and experimental levels. As new developments occur in his area, he must be prepared to apply them to problems in neuropsychology and, in turn, feed back into those basic developments new knowledge from his investigations. Second, he must have a thorough grounding also in modern concepts of structure and function of the central nervous system and more than passing familiarity with techniques of electrophysiological measurement. Finally, as a clinical neuropsychologist, and in the best tradition of the sciences of man, he should be prepared to learn from his patients. A background in personality, psychodynamics, and psychopathology is necessary for understanding his patient as a person as well as for advancing the state of knowledge in neuropsychology. Impossible? No. It can be done, but perhaps not in the time usually allotted for a doctoral program. At present, the optimal educational program would be one in which sound training in clinical and experimental psychology were followed by postdoctoral training in neuropsychology. The next decade will see many more such programs established.

VI. Summary

Clinical neuropsychology is an emergent discipline which applies the knowledge gained from clinical and experimental investigations to specific brain-behavior problems in humans. All indications point to a rapid growth and emphasis of this new discipline. The historically important psychodiagnostic role of the clinical neuropsychologist is currently questioned. There is a growing consensus that the greatest contribution from the clinical neuropsychologist will derive from his identification measurement, and explanation of deficit behaviors. Such in-depth analysis on his part will not only provide the background for answering pressing diagnostic questions but will also advance the state of knowledge concerning determinants of human behavior.

There is substantial agreement that brain damage results in both general and specific deficits. Any comprehensive neuropsychological theory will have to include an accounting for both effects. Progress in understanding specific deficits, especially the lateralization of neuropsychological processes, has been rather dramatic. The role of the left hemisphere in executive functions involving language and verbal manipulations and the role of the right hemisphere in perceptual and visuo-spatial behavior has been well established. The Wechsler Scales may be used meaningfully to explore lateralization in the psychological functioning of the hemispheres. Recent experiments with commisurotomy cases have confirmed differential psychological functioning in the two hemispheres, and neuroanatomical and electrophysiological evidence gives additional support.

Left hemisphere dysfunctions in the form of aphasic disturbances have continued to engage investigators. Defects in auditory sequencing and comprehensive appear to be important variables for further investigation. The role of language in thinking has received renewed attention. Disturbance in language functioning may or may not be associated with visual tests of conceptual functioning (depending on task conditions), and perhaps defective visual scanning is important here. The right hemisphere has been shown to play a leading role in the integration of visual stimuli, in visual memory, and in visually guided behavior. Similar effects have been found for tactual and auditory modalities. The dichotic stimulation technique has been very useful in demonstrating differential functions in normal subjects as well as in brain damaged patients.

A model of hemispheric specialization by Semmes has proved to be of heuristic value. The model depicts the functions within the left hemisphere as organized "focally" while right hemisphere functions are organized diffusely. Evidence supporting her model and evidence raising questions as to its generality were presented.

In considering general effects, the many changes in the molar behavior of the patient in his life situation were described. Two major aspects were selected for special review: behaviors which might be attributed to deficits in vigilance, memory, and arousal, and deficits which were due to impairment of the abstract attitude or "sets." There is little doubt that vigilance is lowered in brain damage and that reaction time provides a reasonably good measure of the severity of impairment. Memory deficit also is related to the severity of the disorder. However, the question has been raised as to whether the memory "loss" in so classic an example as Korsakoff's disease is not so much "loss" as defective activation and persistence in the pattern of search, match, and confirmation. Questions also have been raised as to whether cortical lesions achieve their general effect by interrupting cortical-subcortical feedback circuits which sustain the higher mental processes.

Studies of arousal in brain-damaged patients were considered. Brain-damaged patients have higher levels of skin conductance and heart rate under certain conditions (passive stimulation) than do non-brain-damaged patients. But laterality effects were found which suggest that the control of skin conductance is directly affected by lesions of the contralateral hemisphere, and therefore skin conductance is not the most appropriate measure for investigating some questions. Heart rate change components of the orienting response suggest that brain-damaged patients do not habituate to repetitive stimuli and thus suffer from defective inhibitory control of autonomic functions with attendant implications for defective inhibition at various stages of information processing.

Attention was given to Goldstein's postulation of impairment of the abstract attitude in brain-damaged patients. The critcisms directed toward Goldstein's formulation were recognized, but Goldstein's interest in the broader aspects of the patients' behavior was acknowledged as having provided a framework from which useful experimentation has ensued. Examples of such research were given.

Experimental evidence was offered for the importance of the degree of ambiguity of the stimulus, the crucial role of instructions, and the effect of anchor stimuli on psychophysical judgments. Brain-damaged patients not only have difficulty in initiating and shifting sets but also are markedly affected by background stimuli, a condition which probably has its roots in disturbed inhibitory control patterns of neural processes. Finally, brain-damaged patients were shown to be more deleteriously affected in performance on a psychomotor test by the experimenter's attitude of disinterest than were neurotic patients, and they did not benefit as much as schizophrenic patients from the experimenter's helping behavior (cues) in performing an abstracting task.

All of these observations have direct implication for the neuropsychologist's current clinical and experimental investigations. The future prospects are even more exciting. International cooperative studies, expanding utilization of electrophysiological and psychophysiological techniques, intensive examination of single cases and continued application of developments in basic psychological knowledge to brain-behavior problems will contribute substantially to the neuropsychology of the next decade.

Implications for education and training programs for the clinical neuropsychologist are obvious; emphasis on modern biological and technological advances in the neurosciences must be added to the basic doctoral training in clinical and experimental psychology. It is likely that this will best be accomplished in postdoctoral training programs specifically oriented toward clinical neuropsychology.

REFERENCES

Archibald, Y. M., Wepman, J. M., & Jones, L. V. Nonverbal cognitive performance in aphasic and nonaphasic brain-damaged patients. *Cortex*, 1967, 3, 275–294.
Arrigoni, G., & De Renzi, E. Constructional apraxia and hemispheric locus of lesion. *Cortex*, 1964, 1, 170–197.

Balthazar, E. E., & Morrison, D. H. The use of Wechsler Intelligence Scales as diagnostic indicators of predominant left-right and indeterminate unilateral brain-damage. *Journal of Clinical Psychology*, 1961, **17**, 161–165.

Battersby, W. S. The regional gradient of critical flicker frequency after frontal or occipital lobe injury. *Journal of Experimental Psychology*, 1951, **42**, 59–68.

Beach, F. A., Hebb, D. O., Morgan, C. T., & Nissen, H. W. *The neuropsychology of Lashley*. New York: McGraw-Hill, 1960.

Benton, A. Clinical symptomatology in right and left hemisphere lesions. In V. B. Mountcastle (Ed.), *Interhemispheric relations and cerebral dominance*. Baltimore: Johns Hopkins Press, 1962.

Benton, A. (Ed.) *Contributions to neuropsychology*. Chicago: Aldine, 1969.

Benton, A. L. Development of a multilingual aphasia battery: Progress and problems. *Journal of the Neurological Sciences*, in press.

Benton, A. L., & Van Allen, M. W. Impairment of facial recognition in patients with cerebral disease, *Cortex*, 1968, **4**, 344–358.

Berger, L., Bernstein, A., Klein, E., Cohen, J., & Lucas, G. Effects of aging and pathology on the factorial structure of intelligence. *Journal of Consulting Psychology*, 1964, **28**, 199–207.

Beyn, E. S., Zhirmusnskaya, E. A., & Volkov, V. N. Electroencephalographic investigations in the process of recognizing images of objects during their tachistoscopic presentation. *Neuropsycholgia*, 1967, **5**, 203–217.

Brain, W. R. *Speech disorders*. London: Butterworth, 1961.

Burn, J. M. Concept identification: Post feedback variation in the brain damaged. Unpublished doctoral dissertation, University of Oklahoma, 1967.

Buschbaum, M., & Fedio, P. Visual information and evoked responses from the left and right hemispheres. *Electroencephalography and Clinical Neurophysiology*, 1969, **26**, 266–272.

Butter, C. M. *Neuropsychology, the study of brain and behavior*. Belmont, Calif.: Brooks/Cole, 1968.

Butters, N., & Brody, B. A. The role of the left parietal lobe in the mediation of intra- and cross-modal associations. *Cortex*, 1968, **4**, 328–343.

Canter, A. BIP Bender test for the detection of organic brain disorder: Modified scoring method and replication. *Journal of Consulting and Clinical Psychology*, 1968, **32**, 522–526.

Carmon, A., & Benton, A. L. Tactile perception of direction and number of patients with unilateral cerebral disease. *Neurology*, 1969, **19**, 525–532.

Chapman, L. F., & Wolff, A. G. The cerebral hemisphere and the highest integrative functions of man. *Archives of Neurology*, 1959, **1**, 19–86.

Cohen, B. D., Noblin, C. D., & Silverman, A. Functional asymmetry of the human brain. *Science*, 1968, **162**, 475–477.

Corkin, S. Tactually guided maze learning in man: Effects of unilateral cortical excision and bilateral hypocarnipal lesions. *Neuropsychologia*, 1965, **3**, 339.

Critchley, M. *The parietal lobes*. Baltimore: Williams & Wilkins, 1953.

Davidoff, R. A., & McDonald, D. G. Alpha blocking and autonomic responses in neurological patients. *Archives of Neurology*, 1964, **10**, 283–292.

Delgado, J. M. R., Mark, V., Sweet, W., Ervin, M. D., Weiss, G., Bach-Y-Rita, G., & Hagiwara, R. Intracerebral radio stimulation and recording in completely free patients. *Journal of Nervous and Mental Disease*, 1968, **147**, 329–340.

Dennerll, R. D. Prediction and unilateral brain dysfunction using Wechsler Test scores. *Journal of Consulting Psychology*, 1964, **28**, 278–284.

De Renzi, E. Nonverbal memory and hemispheric side of lesion. *Neuropsychologia,* 1968, **6,** 181–189.

De Renzi, E., & Faglioni, P. The comparative efficiency of intelligence and vigilance tests in detecting hemispheric cerebral damage. *Cortex,* 1965, **1,** 410–429.

De Renzi, E., & Faglioni, P. The relationship between visuo-spatial impairment and constructional apraxia. *Cortex,* 1967, **3,** 327–342.

De Renzi, E., Faglioni, P., Savoiardo, M., & Vignolo, L. A. The influence of aphasia and of the hemispheric side of the cerebral lesion on abstract thinking. *Cortex,* 1966, **2,** 399–420.

De Renzi, E., Pieczuro, A., & Vignolo, L. A. Ideational apraxia: A quantitative study. *Neuropsychologia,* 1968, **6,** 41–52.

De Renzi, E., & Scotti, G. The influence of spatial disorders in impairing tactual discrimination of shapes. *Cortex,* 1969, **5,** 53–62.

Doehring, D. G., & Reitan, R. M. Concept attainment of human adults with lateralized cerebral lesions. *Perceptual and Motor Skills,* 1962, **14,** 27–33.

Efron, R. Temporal perception, aphasia and deja vu. *Brain,* 1963, **86,** 403–424.

Eichenwald, H., & Fry, P. C. Nutrition and learning. *Science,* 1969, **163,** 644–648.

Fitzhugh, K. B., & Fitzhugh, L. C. WAIS results for Ss with longstanding chronic, lateralized and diffuse dysfunction. *Perceptual and Motor Skills,* 1964, **19,** 735–739.

Furth, H. G. *Thinking without language.* New York: Free Press, 1966.

Garmezy, N. The prediction of performance in schizophrenia. In P. H. Hoch & J. Zubin (Eds.), *Schizophrenia.* New York: Grune & Stratton, 1965.

Gazzaniga, M. S. Psychological properties of the disconnected hemisphere in man. *Science,* 1965, **150,** 372.

Gazzaniga, M. S., Bogen, J. E., & Sperry, R. W. Dyspraxia following division of the cerebral hemisphere. *Archives of Neurology,* 1967, **16,** 606–612.

Geschwind, N. The paradoxical position of Kurt Goldstein in the history of aphasia. *Cortex,* 1964, **1,** 214–224.

Geschwind, N. Disconnexion syndromes in animals and man. Parts I & II. *Brain,* 1965, **88,** 237–294 & 585–644.

Geschwind, N., & Levitsky, W. Human brain: Left-right asymmetries in temporal speech region. *Science,* 1968, **161,** 186–187.

Giannitrapani, D. Developing concepts of lateralisation of cerebral functions. *Cortex,* 1967, **3,** 353–370.

Goldstein, K. *Aftereffects of brain injuries in war.* New York: Grune & Stratton, 1942.

Goldstein, K. Functional disturbances in brain damage. In S. Arieti (Ed.), *American handbook of psychiatry.* New York: Basic Books, 1959. Pp. 770–796.

Goodglass, H., Quadfasel, F. A., & Timberlake, W. H. Phrase length and the type of severity of aphasia. *Cortex,* 1964, **1,** 133–153.

Gottlieb, Ann L., & Parsons, O. A. A coaction compass evaluation of Rorschach determinants in brain-damaged individuals. *Journal of Consulting Psychology,* 1960, **24,** 54–60.

Guertin, W. H., Ladd, C. E., Frank, C. H., Rabin, A. I., & Hiester, D. S. Research with the Wechsler Intelligence Scales for Adults, 1960–1965. *Psychological Bulletin,* 1966, **66,** 385–509.

Hall, M. M., Hall, G. C., & Lavoie, P. Ideation in patients with unilateral or bilateral midline brain lesions. *Journal of Abnormal Psychology,* 1968, **73,** 526–531.

Halstead, W. *Brain and intelligence.* Chicago: University of Chicago Press, 1947.

Haynes, J. R., & Sells, S. B. Assessment of organic brain damage by psychological tests. *Psychological Bulletin,* 1963, **60,** 316–325.

Head, H. *Aphasia and kindred disorders of speech.* Vol. 1, New York: Hafner, 1963.

Heilbrun, A. B. Psychological test performance as a function of lateral localization of cerebral lesion. *Journal of Comparative and Physiological Psychology,* 1956, **49,** 10–14.

Heilbrun, A. B. Issues in the assessment of organic brain damage. *Psychological Reports,* 1962, **10,** 511–515.

Helson, H. *Adaptation-level theory: An experimental and systematic approach to behavior.* New York: Harper & Row, 1964.

Herron, W. G. Abstract ability in the process-reactive classification of schizophrenia. *Journal of General Psychology,* 1962, **67,** 147–154.

Holloway, F. A., & Parsons, O. A. Unilateral brain damage and bilateral skin conductance levels in humans. *Psychophysiology,* 1969, **6,** 138–148.

Huse, M. M., & Parsons, O. A. Pursuit-rotor performance in the brain damaged. *Journal of Abnormal Psychology,* 1965, **70,** 350–359.

Kantor, R. E., & Herron, W. G. *Reactive and process schizophrenia.* Palo Alto: Science and Behavior Books, Inc., 1966.

Kimura, D. Functional asymmetry of the brain in dichotic listening. *Cortex,* 1967, **3,** 163–178.

Krech, D. Cortical localization of function. In L. Postman (Ed.), *Psychology in the making.* New York: A. A. Knopf, 1962. Pp. 31–72.

Lacey, J. I. Somatic response patterning and stress: Some revisions of activation theory. In M. H. Appley & R. Trumbull (Eds.), *Psychological stress.* New York: Appleton-Century-Crofts, 1967.

Lenneberg, E. H. *Biological foundations of language.* New York: Wiley, 1967.

Lenneberg, E. H. On explaining language. *Science,* 1969, **164,** 635–643.

Livanov, M. N. The application of electronic-computer techniques to the analysis of bioelectric processes in the brain. In M. Cole & I. Maltzman (Eds.), *A handbook of contemporary Soviet psychology.* New York: Basic Books, 1969. Pp. 717–734.

Lodge, Ann. Effects of facilitating, neutral and inhibiting instructions on perceptual tasks following brain damage. *Acta Psychologica,* 1966, **25,** 173–198.

Luria, A. R. *Higher cortical functions in man.* New York: Basic Books, 1966.

Luria, A. R., Sokolov, E. N., & Klemkowski, M. Towards a neurodynamic analysis of memory disturbances with lesions of the left temporal lobe. *Neuropsychologia,* 1967, **5,** 1–11.

Maher, B. *Principles of psychopathology.* New York: McGraw-Hill, 1966.

Majumder, R. Cognitive and central nervous system factors in psychophysical judgment. Unpublished doctoral dissertation, University of Oklahoma, 1966.

Meyer, V. Critique of psychological approaches to brain damage. *Journal of Mental Science,* 1957, **103,** 80–109.

Millikan, C. H., & Darley, F. L. *Brain mechanisms underlying speech and language.* New York: Grune & Stratton, 1967.

Milner, B. Laterality effects in audition. In V. B. Mountcastle (Ed.), *Interhemispheric relations and cerebral dominance.* Baltimore: Johns Hopkins Press, 1962.

Milner, B. Visual recognition and recall after right temporal lobe excision in man. *Neuropsychologia,* 1968, **6,** 191–209.

Monk, Ruth Ann. The role of verbal cues and practice in improving concept formation. Unpublished NIMH Medical Student Fellowship Report. University of Oklahoma Medical Center, 1965.

Mountcastle, V. B. *Interhemispheric relations and cerebral dominance.* Baltimore: Johns Hopkins, 1962.

Newcombe, F., & Russell, W. R. Dissociated visual, perceptual and spatial deficits in focal lesions of the right hemisphere. *Journal of Neurology, Neurosurgery, and Psychiatry,* 1969, **32**, 73–81.

Obrist, W. D., Ingvar, D. H., Chivian, E., & Cronqvist, S. Regional cerebral blood flow in senile and presenile dementia. *Gerontologist,* 1968, **8**, 18.

Paoletti, P., Vandenheuvel, F. A., Fumagalli, R., & Paoletti, R. The Sterol Test for the diagnosis of human brain tumors. *Neurology,* 1969, **19**, 190–197.

Parsons, O. A. Psychological responses, brain-damage and performance. Paper given at AAAS Meeting, Dallas, Texas, December 29, 1968.

Parsons, O. A., & Chandler, P. J. Electrodermal indicants of arousal in brain damage: Cross-validated findings. *Psychophysiology,* 1969, **5**, 644–659.

Parsons, O. A., & Klein, H. P. Concept identification and practice in brain-damaged and process-reactive schizophrenic groups. NINDS Progress Report NB 05359. April 1969. University of Oklahoma Medical Center, Oklahoma City, Okla.

Parsons, O. A., Majumder, R. K., & Chandler, P. J. Impaired flicker detection in visual fields subserved by non-damaged hemispheres. *Cortex,* 1967, **3**, 307–316.

Parsons, O. A., & Stewart, K. D. Effects of supportive versus disinterested interviews on perceptual-motor performance in brain-damaged and neurotic patients. *Journal of Consulting Psychology,* 1966, **30**, 260–266.

Parsons, O. A., Vega, A., & Burn, J. Different psychological effects of lateralized brain-damage. *Journal of Clinical and Consulting Psychology,* 1969, **33**, 551–557.

Penfield, W., & Roberts, L. *Speech and brain mechanisms.* Princeton: Princeton University Press, 1959.

Piercy, M. The effects of cerebral lesions on intellectual function: A review of current research trends. *British Journal of Psychiatry,* 1964, **110**, 310–352.

Pribram, K. H. Interrelations of psychology and the neurological disciplines. In S. Koch (Ed.), *Psychology: The study of a science.* Vol. IV. New York: MrGraw-Hill, 1962. Pp. 119–157.

Redlich, F. C., & Freedman, D. X. *The theory and practice of psychiatry.* New York: Basic Books, 1966.

Reitan, R. M. Investigation of the validity of Halstead's measures of biological intelligence. *A.M.A. Archives of Neurology & Psychiatry,* 1955, **73**, 28–35. (a)

Reitan, R. M. Certain differential effects of left and right cerebral lesions in human adults. *Journal of Comparative and Physiological Psychology,* 1955, **48**, 474–477. (b)

Reitan, R. M. The significance of dysphasia for intelligence and adoptive abilities. *Journal of Psychology,* 1960, **50**, 355–376.

Reitan, R. M. Psychological deficit. *Annual Review of Psychology,* 1962, **13**, 415–444.

Reitan, R. M. Psychological deficits resulting from cerebral lesions in man. In J. M. Warren & K. A. Akert (Eds.), *The frontal granular cortex and behavior.* New York: McGraw-Hill, 1964.

Reitan, R. M. Problems and prospects in studying the psychological correlates of brain lesions. *Cortex,* 1966, **2**, 127–153.

Reitan, R. M. Psychological changes associated with aging and cerebral damage. *Mayo Clinic Proceedings,* 1967, **42**, 653–673.

Russell, W. R. *Brain, memory learning.* New York: Oxford Univ. Press, 1959.

Russo, M., & Vignolo, L. A. Visual figure-ground discrimination in patients with unilateral cerebral disease. *Cortex,* 1967, **3**, 113–127.

Satz, P. A block rotation task: The application of multivariate and decision theory analysis for the prediction of organic brain disorder. *Psychological Monographs,* 1966, **80**, 1–29.

Satz, P., Fennell, E., & Reilly, C. The predictive validity of six neurodiagnostic tests: A decision theory analysis. *Journal of Consulting and Clinical Psychology,* 1970, **34**, 375–381.

Satz, P., Richard, W., & Daniels, A. The alteration of intellectual performance after lateralized brain injury. *Psychonomic Science,* 1967, **7**, 369–370.

Schuell, H., Jenkins, J. J., & Jimenez-Pabon, E. *Aphasia in adults.* New York: Harper & Row, 1965.

Semmes, Josephine. Hemispheric specialization: A possible clue to mechanism. *Neuropsychologia,* 1968, **6**, 11–26.

Semmes, Josephine, Weinstein, S., Ghent, L., & Teuber, H. *Somatosensory changes after penetrating brain wounds in man.* Cambridge: Harvard Press, 1960.

Shure, G. H., & Halstead, W. C. Cerebral localization of intellectual processes. *Psychological Monographs,* 1958, **72**(12, Whole No. 465).

Simpson, C. D., & Vega, A. Brain-damage and patterns of age-corrected WAIS subtest scores. Paper presented at Southwestern Psychological Association Meeting, Austin, Texas, April, 1969.

Smith, A. Ambiguities in concepts and studies of "brain damage" and organicity. *Journal of Nervous and Mental Disease,* 1962, **35**, 311–326.

Smith, A. Verbal and nonverbal test performances of patients with "acute" lateralized brain lesions (tumors). *Journal of Nervous and Mental Disease,* 1966, **141**, 517–523.

Smith, A. Nondominant hemispherectomy. *Neurology,* 1969, **19**, 442–445.

Sokolov, E. N. *Perception and the conditioned reflex.* New York: Macmillan, 1963.

Sperry, R. W. Hemispheric deconnection and unity in conscious awareness. *American Psychologist,* 1968, **23**, 723–733.

Spreen, O., & Benton, A. Comparative studies of some psychological tests for cerebral damage. *Journal of Nervous and Mental Disease,* 1965, **140**, 323–333.

Stein, K. B. The effect of brain damage upon speed, accuracy and improvements in visual motor functioning. *Journal of Consulting Psychology,* 1961, **25**, 171–177.

Stern, J. A. Towards a developmental psychophysiology: My look into the crystal ball. *Psychophysiology,* 1968, **4**, 403–420.

Stern, J. A., & Plapp, J. M. Psychophysiology and clinical psychology. In C. D. Spielberger (Ed.), *Current topics in clinical and community psychology.* Vol. 1. New York: Academic Press, 1969.

Sternlof, R. E. Differential perception in paranoid schizophrenia and depression as a function of structure and content. Unpublished doctoral dissertation, University of Oklahoma, 1964.

Stevens, S. A metric for the social consensus. *Science,* 1966, **1151**, 530–541.

Sullivan, P. L., & Welsh, G. S. A technique for objective configural analysis of MMPI profiles. *Journal of Consulting Psychology,* 1952, **16**, 383–388.

Talland, G. A. Psychology's concern with brain damage. *Journal of Nervous and Mental Disease,* 1963, **136**, 344–359.

Talland, G. A. *Deranged memory.* New York: Academic Press, 1965.

Teuber, H. L., & Weinstein, S. General and specific effects of brain lesions. *American Psychologist,* 1955, **10**, 408–409.

Teuber, H. L., & Weinstein, S. Ability to discover hidden figures after cerebral lesions. *Archives of Neurology and Psychiatry,* 1956, **76**, 369–379.

Tyler, H. R. Defective stimulus exploration in aphasic subjects. *Neurology,* 1969, **19,** 105–112.

Vaughan, H. S., & Costa, L. D. Performance of patients with lateralized cerebral lesions II: Sensory and motor tests. *Journal of Nervous and Mental Disease,* 1962, **134,** 237–243.

Vega, A. Use of Purdue Pegboard and Finger Tapping Performance as a rapid screening test for brain damage. *Journal of Clinical Psychology,* 1969, **25,** 255–258.

Vega, A., & Parsons, O. A. Cross-validation of the Halstead-Reitan tests for brain damage. *Journal of Consulting Psychology,* 1967, **31,** 619–625.

Vega, A., & Parsons, O. A. Relationship between sensory motor deficits and WAIS Verbal and Performance Scales in unilateral brain damage. *Cortex,* 1969, **5,** 229–241.

Vega, A., Parsons, O. A., & Chandler, P. J. Localization of brain lesions by flicker perimetry: A quantitative method. *Cortex,* 1966, **2,** 213–221.

Warrington, E. K., & James, M. Disorders of visual perception in patients with localized cerebral lesions. *Neuropsychologia,* 1967, **5,** 253–266.

Wechsler, D. *The measurement of adult intelligence.* Baltimore: Williams & Wilkins, 1944.

Wechsler, D. *The measurement and appraisal of adult intelligence.* Baltimore: Williams & Wilkins, 1958.

Weinstein, S. Deficits concomitant with aphasia or of either cerebral hemisphere. *Cortex,* 1964, **1,** 154–169.

Wheeler, L., Burke, C. J., & Reitan, R. M. An application of discriminant functions to the problem of predicting brain damage using behavioral variables. *Perceptual and Motor Skills,* 1963, **16,** 417–440 (Monogr. Suppl. 3-V16).

Wheeler, L., & Reitan, R. M. Discriminant functions applied to the problem of predicting cerebral damage from behavioral tests: A cross-validation study. *Perceptual and Motor Skills,* 1963, **16,** 681–701 (Monogr. Suppl. 6-V16).

Wyke, M. The effect of brain lesions in the performance of an arm-band precision task. *Neuropsychologia,* 1968, **8,** 125–134.

Yacorznski, G. K. Organic mental disorders. In B. B. Wolman (Ed.), *Handbook of clinical psychology.* New York: McGraw-Hill, 1965. Pp. 653–688.

A Sequential System for Personality Scale Development[1]

Douglas N. Jackson
Department of Psychology
University of Western Ontario
London, Canada

If one were to survey current opinion among psychologists of the prospects for personality testing, the evaluations would be, at best, mixed. A sizable proportion would hold quite pessimistic views. They might point, for example, to the frequent failures of widely used personality tests to demonstrate either convergent or discriminant validity (Campbell & Fiske, 1959), or to the literature on response sets; or they might challenge the theoretical relevance of many of the traits assessed. These attitudes are not specific to particular tests; they have often generalized to the field as a whole. A good many psychologists have

[1] Certain portions of this chapter were presented in an Invited Address sponsored by the Division of Personality and Social Psychology at the annual meetings of the American Psychological Association, September, 1966. Its present extended form has benefited considerably from the editorial assistance of Eyde Smythe and Merilee Trott. John A. Neill and Lee Ruggles carefully supervised major portions of the data analyses of the studies reported. The author gratefully acknowledges the support of the Ontario Mental Health Foundation, Research Grant No. 151.

expressed their disillusionment with even the *possibility* of valid measurement of personality.

It is the author's opinion that such attitudes reflect both an insufficient faith in the cumulative nature of psychological knowledge, and a lack of appreciation for the very real advances made in the vigorously emerging research discipline of personality assessment. Rather than attempt to challenge these negative attitudes by appealing to the increasing use of formal test theory in assessment, or to important measurement applications of personality theory, the writer believes that it is incumbent upon the personality assessment specialist to translate some of the research progress into viable and valid measurement. Indeed, such a translation might well contribute to furthering personality research. Having faith in the proposition that personality can be measured at least as well as most of the attributes encountered in psychology, the writer set forth on a venture that was to take a number of years, the development of the *Personality Research Form* (PRF) (Jackson, 1967a). This work was aided immeasurably by a number of talented research assistants. It also benefited substantially from collaborative research over the years with Samuel Messick and with Lee Sechrest.

The Personality Research Form is the result of a research program whose principal aim was the application of recent developments in the areas of personality assessment and test theory to personality test construction. The hope guiding these efforts was that by a careful application of modern conceptions of personality and of psychometric theory and computer technology more rigorous and more valid assessment of important personality characteristics would result. In this program of research, careful attention was paid to the problem of devising an instrument which would combine concise, manageable scales with the qualities of high reliability and validity.

I. Some Principles of Personality Scale Construction

The construction of the Personality Research Form was unique primarily by virtue of the application of a sequential strategy for scale development. A number of methods were used in an orderly sequence to decide the question of how items should be selected to form constituent scales. The question has sometimes been asked (e.g., Hase & Goldberg, 1966), "Which of the alternative methods for personality scale construction, like empirical item selection or rational methods, yields the highest validity?" Such a question is meaningfully investigated only to the extent that these alternatives are mutually exclusive; that the use of one prevents the use of a second and a third. But, particularly with the aid of modern computer technology, it is entirely feasible to employ a number of strategies simultaneously or sequentially to capitalize upon the advantages of each. Some of the methods used in developing the PRF are well known; others are unique, still others are used in unique combinations.

But before going into detail about the particular methods used, it is important to describe the principles that guided the choice of strategy. There are four interrelated principles essential to a program of personality test development. These are, first, the overriding *importance of psychological theory;* second, *the necessity for suppressing response style variance;* third, *the importance of scale homogeneity, as well as generalizability;* and fourth, *the importance of fostering convergent and discriminant validity* at the very beginning of a program of test construction. The formulation of these principles has been greatly influenced by the work of others, but particularly by the already classic works of Loevinger (1957) and of Cronbach and Meehl (1955) on the importance of theory, and of Campbell and Fiske (1959) on the necessity of demonstrating both convergent and discriminant validity. Also influencing this work was much recent work on response style and test theory.

The importance of theory in personality test construction cannot be overemphasized. There is no substitute in the creative task of defining dimensions and of preparing personality items for a sound grasp of formal personality theory and research, and for a more informal sensitivity to the diverse ways in which psychological tendencies can be revealed in behavior. Often we psychologists are excessively modest in recognizing the strides we have made in understanding personality. But the enormous research and theoretical productivity of the past twenty years has greatly changed the complexion of our knowledge. No longer is it necessary, or even desirable, to take refuge from our psychological ignorance by relying on an external criterion, and *ad hoc* procedures like empirical item selection, as Paul Meehl (1945) advocated more than two decades ago. In short, a great deal of importance has been learned about personality, and such knowledge ought to be applied in the formulation and measurement of personality characteristics.

A concern for theory has important implications for the nature of the variables we undertake to measure. Theoretically relevant scales are likely to bear on constructs of some import. Purely empirical methods, on the other hand, can and frequently do generate a heterogeneous hodgepodge of items comprising scales of a most trivial nature, temporally and situationally specific, with little generality, and even less theoretical substance and "surplus value." A second virtue of theory in scale construction is the requirement it places upon one to be explicit about what one is measuring. It is a chastening experience to specify in detail how one defines a construct, and in what manner it can be differentiated from related constructs. When, for example, the question of how Exhibition is distinguished from Need for Social Recognition is answered, the definition of each has been sharpened. A third advantage of theory is that it permits a broader empirical evaluation of both the personality scales developed and the constructs they represent. Thus, a personality scale of Achievement can be evaluated in terms of what is hypothesized about such a construct from other sources. Confirmation of hypotheses would add confidence both in the theory and in its representation within a particular personality scale.

It is not necessary to dwell at length upon the importance of suppressing stylistically determined consistencies in responding (Jackson & Messick, 1958). While a few intrepid investigators (Block, 1965; Rorer, 1965) have attempted to defend the proposition that such response styles are unimportant, the evidence is now overwhelming (cf. Jackson, 1967b, 1967c; Jackson & Messick, 1965; Messick, 1967; Trott & Jackson, 1967) that these tendencies, if uncontrolled, may override hoped-for content consistencies. It is true that some response styles, like the tendency to respond desirably, may contain valid variance (Jackson & Messick, 1958); but if they are strongly represented in every scale it is difficult to succeed in an attempt to measure several unique traits. Response styles often will determine major portions of the variance, causing content scales to be much more highly correlated than they should be, thus interfering with attempts to distinguish reliably among persons on the basis of correlated, although distinct dimensions. For example, the high correlations among MMPI scales, partly as a function of their sharing response style variance, cause the reliability of differences between scales to be very low. This in turn makes it extremely difficult to engage in accurate, refined differential diagnosis. Clearly, reducing the impact of stylistic response determinants would contribute to an attempt to identify unique substantive personality traits.

There is one further mode of response which can be conceived of as stylistic in nature, that of nonpurposeful or pseudorandom responding (Sechrest & Jackson, 1963; Bentler, 1964). Rather than introducing large and consistent factors into personality scores, nonpurposeful responding adds an element of chaos into attempts to make sense out of personality.

In the history of personality assessment, surprisingly little attention and even less research effort has been focused on such a source of unreliability. We do not know, for example, the circumstances under which pseudorandom responding is due to carelessness, lack of ability, negativism, or other motives. But my hunch was that this troublesome source of variance was encountered more frequently than often suspected. A means for reliably assessing nonpurposeful response tendencies and for appraising their effects in trait measurement was considered an urgent research requirement.

To argue that personality scales should demonstrate both homogeneity and generalizability suggests an apparent contradiction. Homogeneity implies that items measure the same underlying dimension, to which all of the items ideally share a relation, and that all other characteristics measured by each individual item be uncorrelated from one time to the next (Green, 1954). It thus emphasizes the sameness of the items. Generalizability (Cronbach, Rajaratnam, & Gleser, 1963), on the other hand, represents the degree to which items purporting to measure a given trait sample adequately the universe of situations in which the trait may be manifested. Consider a scale appraising Order. Such a scale might be developed based entirely on items having to do with keeping one's personal effects and papers in their proper places. Such a scale will demonstrate high statistical homogeneity, but lack representativeness in that it has failed to sample adequately the variety of situations in which Order might be manifested. Such a scale would prove to be both an incomplete exemplar of a broader construct of Order and an inconsistently valid measure in predicting related behavior.

The Campbell and Fiske (1959) article on convergent and discriminant validity focused on the important requirement that a test should not only relate to conceptually similar measures, but *should not* correlate highly with theoretically unrelated constructs. Although Campbell and Fiske highlighted the *evaluation* of already developed tests, we may note that their explication of this important problem has most profound implications for test *development*. An investigator who postpones his concern about convergent and discriminant validity until after a test has been constructed may find he has waited too long. By then it is too late to do much about the problem. This phase of test validation, like those outlined above, implies a program of test construction wherein successive attempts are made to approach a specified variety of optimal properties, rather than leaving the outcome entirely to capricious nature. Thus, in addition to other considerations in the construction of the PRF, it was considered important to undertake positive steps to insure a degree of convergent and discriminant validity.

II. The Substantive Definition of Personality
Scale Content

The methods used in the development of the Personality Research Form will be outlined to illustrate the particular pathways chosen to put into practice the above principles. Because sequential strategies are involved, wherein one stage rests on the results of a previous stage, a chronological order in describing its evolution is convenient.

A. THE CHOICE OF APPROPRIATE CONSTRUCTS

The first step in constructing a personality test is to decide what to measure. This is a most serious matter, having implications for theoretical cogency, practical utility, reliability, validity, and cultural generality. Should one, for example, undertake to assess a general trait such as aggression, or should one subdivide it into components like physical and verbal aggression, overt and covert aggression, or aggression toward authority and aggression toward subordinates? Should one seek to define entirely new constructs, or direct one's efforts only at the measurement of constructs having approved research pedigrees? What is the proper balance between constructs which are primarily cognitive or intrapsychic in nature, and those involving interpersonal consistencies in behavior? In the absence of knowing specific goals of assessment, one cannot supply dogmatic answers to all of these questions, but from the experience of developing the PRF, many decisions were found to be rather compelling.

Two significant considerations influence the outcome of most questions about test construction. The first can be summarized under the concept of *cost*, a term introduced into testing by Cronbach and Gleser (1964). If cost (e.g., the total time allotted for testing) is finite, then there is an inevitable conflict between bandwidth and fidelity. Since reliability is a function of the number of items (Gulliksen, 1950), a constraint on the total number of items in a test requires a decision as to the number and the length of scales. Fewer traits can be measured more reliably, or more traits less reliably. Thus, one might be constrained from attempting to assess several different kinds of aggression unreliably in favor of a better assessment of general aggression. Such a general definition of aggression would have considerably more validity generalization, but for certain kinds of predictions, a more specific scale might be better.

A second consideration in test construction is the available theoretical and empirical support which can be invoked in defining a construct. For several reasons it seems a more prudent strategy to develop sets of scales about which a good deal is already known. Such scales are more likely to be useful to a number of research workers; it is easier to prepare large numbers of items for dimensions whose correlates are well established; and the methodological portion of a research program designed to appraise techniques of personality scale construction is better undertaken using well-founded dimensions of personality.

The system of Variables of Personality developed many years ago by Henry Murray and his colleagues (Murray, 1938) at the Harvard Clinic was selected for study. These had the triple advantages of covering broadly, if not exhaustively, the spectrum of personality needs, states, and dispositions, of possessing carefully worked out published definitions, and of having a good deal of theoretical and empirical underpinning. We found that not all of the definitions were equally satisfactory for our purposes. For example, the necessity of defining traits into exclusive sets and of defining both poles of dimensions revealed a few places where revisions were required. But, on the whole, the decision to proceed with the careful measurement of these traits proved to be a most fortunate choice.

Before writing any items it was necessary to develop mutually exclusive, specific definitions of each variable. Thus, at the very first stage in the program, the question of convergent and discriminant validation demanded our attention. The research literature was reviewed for evidence bearing on the nature of each of the variables. In short, this effort was a conscious attempt to undertake the foundation for the substantive component of validity (Loevinger, 1957). A special effort was made to map out the area covered by the potential item universe by establishing a grid of situations and behavior sequences. This procedure proved to be helpful later in generating items of sufficient quality and quantity, while at the same time reducing the biases inevitably cropping up when an item writer depended solely on his own intuition for ideas.

B. THE DEVELOPMENT OF SUBSTANTIVELY DEFINED ITEM SETS

The next task was the most difficult of all—the creation and editing of the item pool of some three thousand items, comprising the set from which PRF scales were finally developed. Many informal rules evolved about what constituted a good item. Subsequently, this large item pool with known characteristics has proved to be a good source of material upon which to draw for experimental purposes (cf. Trott & Jackson, 1967), so that it should soon be possible to report with some hard data on optimum item characteristics. One of the findings that has already emerged from this work is the superiority of short items and of items high in content saturation. More subtle variables, individually and in inter- action, are currently under investigation. In the editing process items comprising each dimension were evaluated for a number of charac- teristics. These included (*a*) their conformity to the definition of the scale for which they were written; (*b*) the adequacy of the negative instances of the trait; (*c*) their clarity and freedom from ambiguity; (*d*) their judged freedom from extreme levels of desirability bias; (*e*) their judged discriminating power and popularity levels when adminis- tered to appropriate populations; and (*f*) their judged freedom from various forms of content bias, and their representativeness as a set. I refer in particular to an item's freedom from bias toward particular populations like college students, or males. In avoiding bias it was con- sidered advantageous to have two editors, one male and one female, scrutinize each set. Not only did this facilitate the identification of sex specific activity, like crocheting or football, but it aided in spotting more subtle biases in phrasing.

Finally, items were judged not only in terms of the degree to which they conformed to the definition of the scale for which they were written, but in terms of their fortuitous convergence with irrelevant constructs, particularly those which were to be included in the PRF. Again, this concern about eliminating irrelevant items was based upon the aim of developing a finished set of scales possessing both convergent and dis- criminant validity. In judging items it proved to be the case that con- vergent and discriminant aspects of content were not necessarily com- plementary, nor would an item writer always be sensitive to discriminant aspects while focusing on the convergent substantive definition of a construct. It was necessary in editing these items to judge them explicitly in terms of their conceptual distinctiveness from each irrelevent trait, as well as in terms of their substantive convergence.

C. A MULTIDIMENSIONAL SCALING EVALUATION OF SUBSTANTIVE ITEM SELECTION

Those with an empirical bent in personality assessment, with little experience in bringing human judgment to bear upon item selection, will be naturally skeptical of such heavy reliance upon rationality. For- tunately, it is possible to demonstrate empirically how this process can work in item selection. A modern multivariate judgment scaling tech- nique, multidimensional successive intervals scaling, provides informa- tion both in regard to the number of dimensions along which stimuli, such as personality items, are perceived to differ, and in regard to the scale value of each stimulus on each of the dimensions (Torgerson, 1958; Jackson & Messick, 1963). A number of studies have been undertaken (e.g., Boyd & Jackson, 1966) in which judges (given a set of descriptions of hypothetical people) have been asked to rate the probability that these hypothetical people would endorse certain personality items. This was done to appraise the degree to which each item could be considered relevant to a hypothetical item universe.

To illustrate how multidimensional scaling might facilitate the explication of PRF content dimensions, six descriptions of hypothetical people were prepared, designed to represent opposite poles of three PRF scales, Autonomy, Impulsivity, and Dominance. The following is one such person description, written to reflect low Autonomy.

Alex Reed
   Alex Reed works in the public relations office of a large insurance company. Although he is responsible for the advertising displays for his company, he constantly seeks the advice of his fellow workers and his superiors before coming to a decision. Typically, he will hold a meeting in which everyone can talk over advertising plans and come to a group decision which he will take to his superiors for approval. Alex derives special pleasure in organizing his office as a "team," where individuals work together and cooperate in all phases of the work.
   Alex has always been very close to his family. He recently bought a home near that of his parents so he would be able to visit them more often. He also has a number of brothers and sisters who regularly join him in family gatherings. Alex and his wife and children are all very close. Together they plan activities in which the whole family can share.
   Alex's friends describe him as cooperative, conventional, and agreeable.

In addition, three statements were selected from those defining each pole of the three hypothesized dimensions. Thus, each of the three scales was defined positively by a person description and three items; the respective negative poles were each defined by three different items, and by a different hypothetical person. Judgments of mutual probability of endorsement were obtained for each of the possible pairs of stimuli, either statements or person descriptions, from 59 judges, Officer Candidates in the Royal Canadian Air Force. These judgments of psychological distance were subjected to the analytical procedures of multidimensional successive intervals scaling, including the solution of interval boundaries, determining an additive constant and converting relative distances to absolute distances, obtaining scalar products of these distances from which characteristic roots and vectors are derived, and finally, rotating axes to a normalized varimax criterion of analytic simple structure.

Multidimensional scaling results yielded three large dimensions, readily interpretable as Dominance, Impulsivity, and Autonomy. Hypothesized person descriptions and items loaded their respective dimen-

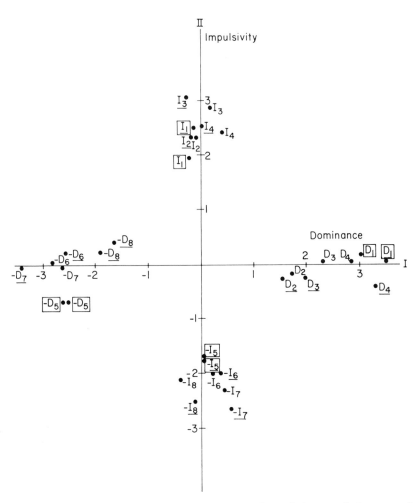

FIG. 1. The two largest replicated dimensions derived from multidimensional scaling of person descriptions and PRF items (only projections $> \pm 1.5$ plotted).

sions highly and without exception. No nonpredicted persons or items were salient on any of the three dimensions. The two largest dimensions, Dominance and Impulsivity, are represented in Figure 1. Note that persons, shown as squares in Figure 1, fall in their proper place, and that the items are clearly separated from each other along orthogonal axes.

Persuasive evidence for the consistency of these judgments may be obtained from an examination of scaling results based upon independent samples. When the total sample was divided randomly into two groups and their judgments separately and independently analyzed by completely objective methods and then independently analytically rotated, the resulting scale values as shown in Figure 1 are extremely close. In Figure 1, the results for Group I are not underlined, while those for Group II are underlined. The correlations between respective projections on the axes defining Dominance, Impulsivity, and Autonomy as independently derived for Group I and Group II were .98, .99, and .99. These dramatic findings might convince even the most empirically oriented skeptic of the potential value of rational judgment methods in item selection.

D. Empirical Evaluation of Homogeneity of Postulated Item Content

After preparing substantial sets of theoretically defined items, the next step was an empirical evaluation of their structural properties. Provisional scales were administered to a number of groups of respondents, all university students. The administration of the items was divided into more than a dozen sessions with four different booklets of items given to groups totaling over a thousand. There was approximately an equal division between males and females. Particular care was exercised in collecting these data. For example, filler tasks were provided for subjects when they completed the items so as to avoid the disturbances caused by persons leaving while others were still working, and to eliminate any temptation on the part of respondents to rush through the items so that they might leave early.

Prior to undetaking an elaborate set of strategies for item selection, it was considered important to review carefully the degree to which the larger item sets comprising each scale conformed to the hypothesized structural homogeneity model implicit in our approach. Item selection might not be justified on an initially inadequate item pool. Figure 2 provides a frequency distribution of the lower-bound Kuder-Richardson formula 20 estimates of reliability. Note that the distribution of reliability estimates is skewed, with more than half falling in the range of .92 to .94. The median was .925. The highest reliability obtained was .94 for six of the scales, Aggression, Endurance, Exhibition, Harmavoidance, Order, and Social Recognition. These are among the highest KR-20 reliabilities reported for any true-false personality scale. If the number of true and false keyed items in each scale had not been balanced, these reliabilities would have been even higher, although spuriously. When only true keyed items were considered in the Aggression scale the KR-20 was .97. The lowest reliability estimate (.80) was for the Defendence scale. This is not at all surprising, since defensive people might be less

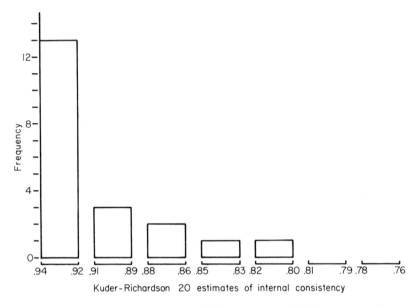

Fig. 2. Frequency distribution of reliability estimates of PRF content scales.

willing to admit defensiveness consistently. It is a safe observation that longer scales defined substantively in the manner outlined conformed very well to expectations of structural homogeneity. This was an important finding, particularly because the application of further item selection, as, for example, in suppressing desirability variance, would be unlikely to increase reliability, and could substantially decrease it.

III. A Sequential Strategy in Scale Construction

An elaborate series of sequential strategies were employed in scale construction in the PRF. Item analysis typically has been used to contribute to a single desired property of a test, such as homogeneity or validity, but rarely has it been employed to satisfy a number of requirements, although, in principle, such a procedure is entirely possible. It is analogous to applications of decision-making in personnel selection (Cronbach & Gleser, 1964), although in the present instance sequential strategies are recommended to construct a test rather than to enhance validity of personnel decisions in relation to cost. Of course, cost is an important consideration in test construction as well. If it is possible to identify a small set of items which will approximate the properties of a much larger set, the time gained may be used to obtain broader information about different personality variables. Until the advent of the digital computer, elaborate item selection programs were rarely possible. The heroic capacity of the modern computer for tireless decision-making permits one to demand much in the way of refinement. For example, the computer made more than 50,000 decisions in the various stages of PRF item analysis. A single individual would be hard pressed to complete a similar task in a lifetime.

Essentially, there were seven steps in scale construction after the provisional theoretically constructed PRF content scales had been administered to subjects and individual item responses keypunched. Items had to survive each of the following hurdles: (a) evaluation to determine whether the proportion of subjects endorsing the item was within an acceptable range—items with a p value below .05 or above .95 were eliminated as too weak in informational value; (b) evaluation for convergent and for discriminant validity—if an item correlated higher with any content scale total score than the one for which it was written, it was eliminated; (c) evaluation of the degree to which the item elicited tendencies to respond desirably; (d) evaluation of the item's saturation as indicated by the magnitude of its correlation with the total scale; (e) evaluation of the item's content saturation in relation to its desirability bias as revealed by a specially devised Differential Reliability Index; (f) assignment of items to strictly parallel forms on the basis of item and scale statistical properties; (g) final substantive review to evaluate generalizability and representativeness of scale content. Discussion of each of these steps, together with their respective rationales, is now in order.

A. Evaluation of Items for Infrequency

The elimination of infrequently endorsed items is an obvious first step in a program of scale development. An item which only a small percentage of respondents endorse—or one which almost everyone endorses—will have a very small variance, and will fail to add appreciably to scale reliability and validity. Items with extreme p values represent excess baggage in a test, and should be replaced with items yielding more information about respondents. Furthermore, as will be seen, such items tend to elicit stylistic tendencies to respond deviantly or nonpurposefully. When scored in terms of content, they may actually attenuate construct validity by virtue of the fact that in a proportion of cases they have been endorsed for the wrong reasons. An additional reason for the rejection of such items is that estimates of item-scale correlation cannot be determined reliably. The computer program therefore con-

TABLE 1

ILLUSTRATION OF ITEM ANALYSIS OF ENDURANCE SCALE FROM THE PRF

Item	Endorsement frequency	Endurance	Desirability	Biserial correlations with total scale					
				Exhibition	Social recognition	Abasement	Sentience	Play	Harm-avoidance
1. I put tireless effort into almost everything I do	23.1	.69	.41	.04	−.09	.13	.08	−.24	.07
2. I am more concerned with finishing what I start than the average person is	54.6	.72	.40	−.01	−.14	.20	.04	−.28	.05
3. If other people give up working on a problem, I usually quit too	71.2	.86	.24	.03	−.44	.13	.13	−.11	−.16
4. I would enjoy the challenge of long-distance swimming	47.3	.39	.15	.25	−.06	.05	.21	−.01	−.40

tained a provision for printing the message "UNRELIABLE" next to an infrequently endorsed item, instructing us to consider it no further.

B. Evaluation of Items for Convergent and Discriminant Content Saturation

The introduction of an empirical means for evaluating the degree to which an item was saturated with appropriate content was also considered essential, for, as already observed, a necessary precondition for obtaining empirical evidence for discriminant validity is to build it in at the initial stages of test construction. For example, consider the data in Table 1, which presents correlations of four of the 118 Endurance items with their own scale and with a number of related scales. In the first column are the percentages of people endorsing each item in the keyed direction. In the next column are the correlations between each item and the total Endurance scale. In each of the succeeding columns are correlations with other scales, namely, Desirability, Exhibition, Social Recognition, Abasement, Sentience, Play, and Harmavoidance. Note that the correlations with each of the first three items and the Endurance scale are high and positive, and exceed the correlations with all of the other scales, including Desirability, by a very comfortable margin. Such items were selected for the final scale. Now consider the fourth item, "I would enjoy the challenge of long-distance swimming." While the correlation with Endurance is moderately high, .39, note that it correlates $-.40$ with Harmavoidance. Presumably, long-distance swimming is dangerous, and therefore would be rejected frequently by respondents who were interested in maintaining personal safety. This item was rejected as having failed to yield evidence for possessing sufficient discrimination within the internal structure of the scales, and was thus excluded from further consideration. Items which correlated highly with a scale other than the one for which they were written were never rekeyed, even though on statistical grounds they might have indicated good discrimination, because they were considered to have failed to provide empirical evidence consistent with our evaluation of their substantive validity.

C. Evaluation of Desirability: The Differential Reliability Index

A third consideration in item selection was the relative degree to which items avoided eliciting tendencies to respond desirably. This was a three-stage process. As already indicated, an item was automatically eliminated from further consideration if it correlated more highly with a heterogeneous set of items keyed for desirable and undesirable responding than it did with its own scale. But the evidence for the pervasiveness

TABLE 2
Comparison of Differential Reliability of Three Hypothetical Items

Item	Item-scale correlation r_{is}	Item-desirability correlation r_{id}	Differential reliability index $(r_{is}^2 - r_{id}^2)^{1/2}$
A	.60	.60	.00
B	.60	.30	.52
C	.60	.00	.60

of desirability bias on other personality questionnaires provided an impetus for seeking further means for reducing its impact. Consider the illustration contained in Table 2. It offers a contrast between three hypothetical items: note that Item A correlates as highly with the Desirability Scale as it does with its own scale. Thus, even though it correlates .60 with its own scale, it is practically worthless if the goal in measurement is the identification of a number of unique dimensions upon which respondents can be placed. A number of scales comprised entirely of such items would load highly a single common factor of desirability. It would be difficult, if not impossible, to obtain evidence of discriminant validity for scales so constituted. Items B and C show progressive improvement in this situation. Even though the correlation between the item and its total scale does not change, the degree to which it is free from desirability variance does. Hence the items improve as an inverse function of their correlation with desirability. Ideally, it would seem that an item completely free of desirability variance, yet highly correlated with its own scale, is the item with which to build good scales. Such items are, however, rarely present in sufficient number, even in the most carefully written set of items. Indeed, the distribution of desirability scale values has been found to be bimodal in a very large pool of items (Edwards, 1966), indicating that more often than not, items possess a positive or negative evaluative component. This is particularly true for scales which are themselves evaluative in some degree, like Achievement or Aggression.

The question then arose as to the best method for obtaining an optimal relationship between the relative saturation of content and of desirability variance. There are, literally, an infinite number of solutions to this problem. One could, for example, carry the suppression of desirability to an extreme, selecting only items with negligible loadings on a desirability factor. But such items may be difficult to come by, and such a strategy might unduly restrict the variables to those less interesting ones in the neutral range of desirability. An even more important reason for being wary of such a strategy is that one runs the risk of eliminating a good deal of potentially valid variance from the scale by failing to consider items showing some correlation with desirability (Scott, 1963).

From the standpoint of convergent and discriminant validity, it is equally hazardous to go to the other extreme and completely ignore the problem of desirability bias. The solution becomes one of finding some reasonable compromise. Samuel Messick collaborated in developing a solution which involved considering a number of possible alternatives, particularly variance ratio procedures (Gulliksen, 1950). Finally, the Differential Reliability Index was selected, which simply reduces the variance in the item associated with content by that associated with desirability. It yields a numerical index which may be interpreted as the item's content saturation with the effects of desirability removed. Note that this index does not require the final set to have any predetermined level of correlation with content or desirability, only that content saturation be *relatively* high in comparison with desirability. Thus, an item might be chosen because of only a moderately high content saturation, if desirability variance was quite low. If desirability variance were moderately high, on the other hand, the item might still be chosen, if its correlation with content were very high. Thus, the hypothetical items in Table 2 are distinguished very well on the basis of the Differential Reliability Index, even though their respective biserial correlations with the total scale provide no basis for differentiation.

A further illustration of the method of item analysis is provided in Table 3, which presents the results from four of the 120 items from the Exhibition Scale. Again, the first column shows the p value of the item, the proportion of responses in the keyed direction. The second column contains the estimate of content saturation, the item-total biserial with the Exhibition Scale. The third and fourth columns report the correlation with the Desirability Scale and Differential Reliability Index, respectively. The remaining columns contain correlations with related but irrelevant scales. Note that the first three Exhibition items listed in Table 3 have very substantial correlations with Exhibition, and only minimal relationships with desirability. The fourth item, "I have trained myself to speak in clear and well-modulated tones," correlates .31 with Exhibition, but .35 with desirability. It is possible that a concern for speaking in well-modulated tones shares with the desirability scale an interest in impression management. In any event, even though this item might be judged to be relevant to Exhibition, and indeed does in fact correlate moderately with it, it was discarded as being too highly saturated with desirability variance.

The screening of items on the basis of their correlations with an

TABLE 3

ILLUSTRATION OF ITEM ANALYSIS OF EXHIBITION SCALE FROM THE PRF

Item	Endorsement frequency	Exhibition	Desirability	Differential reliability index	Biserial correlations with total scale					
					Social recognition	Endurance	Abasement	Sentience	Play	Harmavoidance
1. I like to be in the spotlight	.38	.85	.04	.85	.47	-.10	-.32	.26	.32	-.10
2. I am more of a listener than a talker	.40	.67	-.01	.67	.21	-.13	-.26	.09	.33	-.12
3. At a party I enjoy entertaining others	.44	.64	.15	.63	.11	.08	-.12	.24	.34	-.25
4. I have trained myself to speak in clear and well-modulated tones	.41	.31	.35	.00	.05	.28	-.06	.20	-.10	.05

Note: KR-20 = .94; 118 items, N = 260.

TABLE 4

MEDIAN ABSOLUTE CORRELATION BETWEEN ABASEMENT ITEMS AND RELEVANT AND
IRRELEVANT SCALES

	Abasement scale	Irrelevant scale
20 Retained items	.48	.28
* 20 Discarded items	.24	.42

* Higher correlation with an irrelevant scale than with abasement scale.

irrelevant content or desirability scale might be expected to contribute
to the "purity" with which each content dimension is measured by the
items surviving this test. Thus, the relative proportion of total item
variance associated with its own scale should be increased in relation to
the variance associated with irrelevant content. Table 4 illustrates this
in the case of the Abasement Scale. Items selected because they correlate
more highly with the appropriate scale of necessity will be more homogeneous, and suffer less from the intrusion of irrelevant content variance.

The fact that every item is considered in terms of its correlation with
a desirability scale placed heavy demands upon the desirability scales
used in these analyses in terms of reliability and heterogeneity of content.
The provisional desirability scale was therefore developed carefully by
first scaling a heterogeneous pool of over four hundred items for desirability, and then randomly selecting items from the extremes of the
distribution so that an equal number of desirable items (keyed true) and
undesirable items (keyed false) appeared on the scale. Even though
items were chosen randomly in this way, the scores for this scale had
substantial reliability, the KR-20 estimates ranging from .76 to .83 in four
samples.

What effects would this suppression of desirability be expected to
have on the properties of content scales? There should be three major
effects. First, scale intercorrelations should in general be reduced. This is
so because the correlation between each scale and a desirability factor
would be lowered. This proved to be the case empirically. A second
expected effect of suppressing desirability is that correlations with a
desirability scale should not be as substantial as they might otherwise be.
Table 5 illustrates the effect of suppressing desirability variance on the
Defendence Scale. Note how the average item correlation with desirability drops after application of the Differential Reliability Index to item
selection. When all scales are considered, the application of this method
of item analysis resulted in a set of scales reflecting desirability variance
as only a relatively minor proportion of the total scale variance. On a
cross-validational sample, the median absolute correlation with desir-

TABLE 5

EFFECTS ON MEAN ITEM-DESIRABILITY SCALE CORRELATION OF SCREENING ITEMS
FOR DESIRABILITY: DEFENDENCE SCALE

	Average biserial correlation with desirability
20 Retained items	.17
20 Discarded items*	.43

* Higher correlation with desirability scale than with defendence scale.

ability was but .20. Figure 3 shows the distribution of correlations between PRF content scales and the Desirability Scale. Note the absence of extremely high correlations. While individual differences in level of desirable or undesirable responding have not been completely eliminated as a response determinant, factor analytic results confirm that the major factors are free from potential definition in terms of desirability scales.

A third expected effect of desirability suppression might be that certain influences attributable to desirability might no longer be prominent. One such influence is the well-established tendency of test scores to move in a more desirable direction as a function of repeated testings (Windle, 1955). Table 6 gives the means of 135 subjects for PRF scales on two occasions separated by a one-week interval in a study by Bentler (1964). Note that these means are very similar. None of the differences between means for the two occasions approached significance.

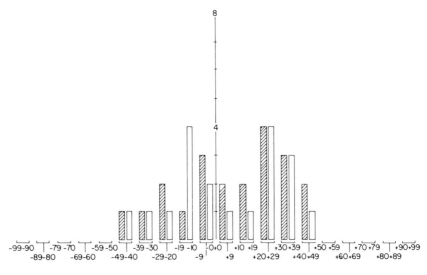

FIG. 3. Distribution of correlations of PRF scales with Desirability.

TABLE 6
TEST-RETEST MEANS—PRF FORM A[a]

	Occasion			Occasion	
	One	Two		One	Two
Affiliation	15.2	14.9	Endurance	10.9	11.3
Order	10.9	11.1	Aggression	7.2	6.8
Exhibition	10.4	10.2	Change	12.2	12.2
Defendence	7.9	8.0	Social recognition	11.7	11.5
Impulsivity	10.3	10.1	Abasement	7.1	6.8
Succorance	8.7	8.7	Cognitive structure	10.5	10.5
Sentience	15.8	16.0	Nurturance	13.7	13.3
Dominance	9.9	10.0	Harmavoidance	8.1	8.3
Play	11.6	11.8	Achievement	12.2	12.5
Autonomy	8.2	8.6	Desirability	15.3	15.6
Understanding	12.2	12.6	Infrequency	.8	.6

Note: N = 135.
[a] From Bentler (1964). One week separated the two administrations.

D. THE DEVELOPMENT OF MEASURES OF RESPONSE STYLE

It is appropriate to turn next to a discussion of the development of measures of two response styles, infrequency (Sechrest & Jackson, 1963) and desirability. It might appear a bit surprising, after going to some lengths to remove items which elicit such tendencies from the content scales, to return to these items for the development of purified scales of response style. But there is nothing anomalous in such an aim. Homogeneity of the content component of personality scales is abetted by the reduction of intruding response style variance. Furthermore, well-founded scales of response style may provide invaluable means for detecting invalid records, as well as providing much useful research data.

The attempt to construct a pure Infrequency Scale was begun by preparing a set of items which *prima facie* reflected extremely rare forms of behavior, but which were not highly evaluative. A rational rather than purely empirical approach was preferred because experience with empirical selection, as with the MMPI *F* scale, has indicated that items so chosen confound pure infrequency response style with purposeful deviation and psychopathology. Most of the items which came to mind were too bizarre or too ludicrous for use. Thus, an item like "When I go upstairs, I usually do so walking on my hands" had to be discarded. But it was possible to identify a number of items which fitted our purposes, such as "I learned to repair watches in Switzerland," or "I have visited the Republic of Samoa during the past year." Sixty-five such items were administered to 305 respondents and subjected to the regular item analysis procedures used for the content scales. It was a matter of considerable interest as to whether or not a scale so constructed would manifest properties similar to those revealed by content scales. In spite of a highly skewed distribution and a restricted range, the lower Infrequency Scale had a reliability of .52. The average p value of the items when keyed for infrequency was less than 2 per cent. When these items were correlated with their own total scale, as well as with a number of content scales, the majority of them were found to relate most highly to the Infrequency Scale. It was thus possible to perform an item analysis to select the best items for the final Infrequency Scale in the same manner as that used for the content scales, except, of course, the restriction on extreme p values was suspended.

Subsequently, this scale has proved to be of considerable benefit in interpreting other scales and in understanding the nature of nonpurposeful responding. It has been possible to identify individuals who have, for reasons of noncooperation or carelessness, shown elevated Infrequency Scale scores. The scale has also aided in identifying errors in keypunching, scoring, and data analysis. Most important, however, is the insight it is providing about the nature of unreliability associated with people in contrast to the more traditional view of test theory (Gulliksen, 1950) which attributes unreliability to imperfect measures. In a study of response variability by Bentler (1964), the Infrequency Scale accounted for more than half of the variance of the PRF content scale score changes over two occasions of administration. More recently, Bentler has collaborated with the writer on a study of the test-retest reliability of PRF scales

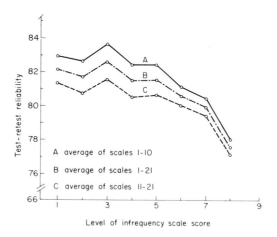

Fig. 4. Mean PRF scale retest stability as a function of Infrequency scale.

as a function of increasing levels of infrequent responding. Figure 4 illustrates some preliminary results. There is a consistent drop in reliability on PRF content scale scores as Infrequency Scale scores increase. This implies that subjects, as well as tests and testing conditions, should be examined for a complete understanding of reliability.

The construction of the final Desirability Scale was similar to that of the content scales. A large number of heterogeneous items previously scaled for desirability were carefully edited, revised, and administered. Those items showing the highest correlation with the total scale were selected; items correlating more highly with a content scale were eliminated. In deciding upon the final set, care was taken to avoid a heavy representation of the broad dimension of psychological disturbances so well represented on the MMPI. The resulting Desirability Scales were characterized by independence of specific content consistency, while retaining a substantial degree of statistical homogeneity. Figure 5 presents the results for the two parallel Desirability Scales from PRF Forms A and B of a recent factor analytic study by Jackson and Lay (1968). In this study, four content dimensions were determined by items from four PRF scales. A fifth factor was well defined by virtue of the fact that

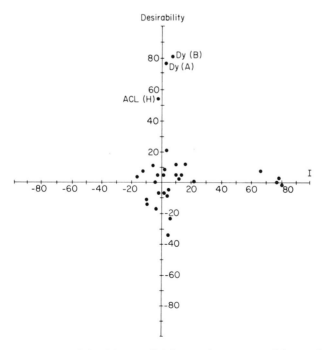

Fig. 5. Factor defined by parallel forms of PRF Desirability scale.

both PRF Desirability Scales had similar very high loadings, and a desirability scale comprised of heterogeneous adjectives was also strongly represented on this factor.

E. Development of Parallel Forms

Because of the many occasions when an investigator may wish to undertake repeated testing of the same respondent, parallel forms were considered advantageous. Rigorously parallel forms were therefore prepared so that one could with confidence state that each form measured "the same thing" both psychologically and statistically. The first step in this venture was to obtain the endorsement proportions and biserial correlations with the total scale for every item. Next, following a procedure recommended by Gulliksen (1950), these items were paired in

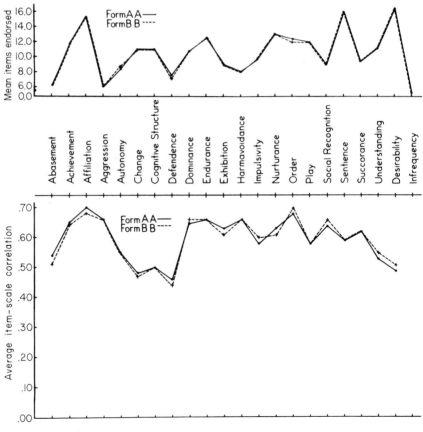

FIG. 6. Comparison of parallel forms.

terms of the similarity of these two characteristics in combination. Making use of the enormous capacity of the computer for routine iteration, a program was written with the able consultation of Lee Ruggles which would continue to reassign each member of the paired items to alternate forms until these forms were maximally similar in summary statistics, namely, mean and content saturation. Figure 6 provides an indication of the success of this venture. Note the extremely similar pattern of means and average item reliability indices. The initial results were even closer, but a final evaluation of the scales revealed that a few very similar items appeared on the same scales. So that substantive generality might be enhanced, these items were replaced by different items having similar statistical properties. The value of having at hand a large pool of items cannot be overemphasized.

IV. The Appraisal of the Structural Component of Validity

Loevinger (1957) recommends that a test, if it is to be considered as an instrument of psychological theory, must, among other things, be evaluated in terms of the degree to which the responses which it elicits conform to a particular hypothesized structural model. The structural model preferred is the classical one of homogeneity, with the important addition that this homogeneity be primarily attributable to content rather than to response style. The method of item analysis employed was designed to provide optimal levels of homogeneity. Table 7 illustrates the item-total biserial correlations obtained for five scales for items retained in the final scales, and for items rejected as failing to meet criteria. Note that average content saturation is much higher in the selected items. Over all PRF content scales, average item-total correlation is approximately .60.

TABLE 7
MEAN CONTENT SATURATION OF RETAINED AND DISCARDED PRF ITEMS

Scale	Item-total scale biserial correlation	
	20 Retained items	20 Discarded items
Achievement	.65	.20
Aggression	.71	.24
Dominance	.69	.19
Order	.74	.17
Social recognition	.66	.22

The presence of highly saturated items in the final form of the PRF had the effect of preserving much of the high reliability noted for the initial long scales. When the reliabilities for the forty best items were compared with the initial scales on the original sample, it was found that median reliability decreased only slightly from .925 to .91, even though the scales were reduced to roughly one third of their original length. When evaluated on a new sample median odd-even reliability of forty-item scales remained above .86, indicating only moderate shrinkage. The forty-item scales represent the combinations of Forms A and B into a single total score. Thus, an investigator who wishes to maximize reliability may use these combined scales. If testing time is at a premium, an investigator may prefer to use either Form A or Form B separately, reducing the length of the task by one half with reliability reduced somewhat.

Some psychologists have challenged the importance of homogeneity and content saturation in structured personality inventories, arguing that criterion-oriented validity is what counts. Criterion-oriented empirical item selection, of course, exemplifies this point of view, but fails to provide any guarantee that resulting scales will be homogeneous. Rather

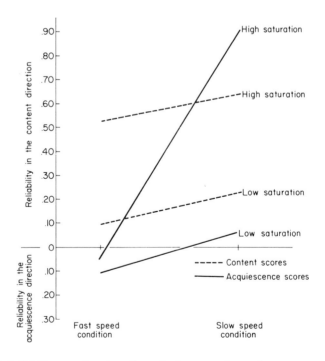

FIG. 7. Reliability as a function of speed of presentation and content saturation.

than advancing only theoretical argument to support the importance of content saturation, it is now possible to present the results of carefully controlled experimental research. Figure 7 shows how acquiescence is affected by content saturation. Trott and Jackson (1967) varied content saturation by including both retained and discarded PRF items in a carefully designed experiment in which they also varied item exposure time, scale content, and item length. Note that for items low in saturation, reliability is predominantly in the acquiescence direction. That is, true and false keyed subscales generally correlated negatively when keyed for content. On the other hand, with high saturation, reliability is in the content direction and is substantial. Similar evidence may be educed from Figure 8, containing results from the Jackson-Lay study mentioned earlier. PRF Exhibition items were presented in four subscales, positively worded original (P), positively worded reversal (R), negatively worded original (PN), and negatively worded reversal (RN). Unlike earlier factor analytic studies of personality inventories, true and false keyed and positively and negatively stated items of the same PRF scale loaded their appropriate content dimensions without exception. Only a small acquies-

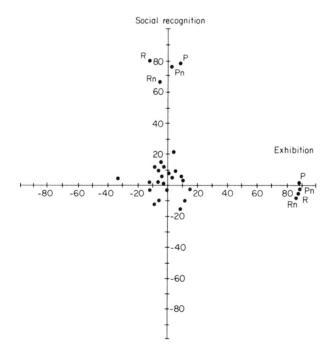

Fig. 8. Dimensions defined by true and false keyed Exhibition and Social Recognition subscales. Data from Jackson and Lay (1968).

cence factor was identified, defined primarily by acquiescence scales from the MMPI and California Psychological Inventory (CPI), with only very small loadings from homogeneous PRF scales.

V. Evaluation of the External Component of Validity

To appraise external validity, a four-hour battery of assessment techniques was prepared and administered to groups of paid volunteers living in housing units at Stanford University and well acquainted with one another. These procedures included: Forms AA and BB of the Personality Research Form, a set of behavior ratings of 20 variables relevant to the 20 PRF content scales, and 600 adjectives measuring the same 20 traits relevant to each of the 20 scales. Subjects responded true or false to each of the 600 adjectives as self-descriptive, and later judged the desirability of each of them in other people. This latter task was included to appraise the hypothesis that a person's point of view about the desirability of a trait would tell us something valid about his own personality (Jackson, 1964; Stricker, Messick, & Jackson, 1968).

An examination of correlations between PRF scales and appropriate criterion measures revealed that there was substantial convergent and discriminant validity associated with PRF scales. The median correlation between PRF scales and the corresponding behavior rating was .52, with the trait-descriptive adjectives, .56, and with the judgments of desirability, .38. Only one scale, Abasement, failed consistently to yield evidence of significant convergent and discriminant validity, correlating more highly with behavior ratings associated with the absence of aggression than with those thought to indicate abasement.

A question might arise about the method employed to suppress desirability. Some critics might argue that too much desirability variance was removed; that the baby—valid variance—might have been lost with the bath water. Others will undoubtedly suggest that since a few significant correlations with desirability remain, too little desirability variance was removed. It is possible, fortunately, to examine these potential criticisms with the validity data already reported. To evaluate the effect of removing additional desirability variance, partial correlations were computed between each of the PRF scales and the appropriate criterion behavior rating. The general result of this analysis was that with the effects of desirability statistically eliminated there was no overall improvement in validity. In fact the validity coefficients changed very little. The mean absolute discrepancy between validity coefficients before and after statistically removing desirability was less than .01. The median validity remained at .52. Thus the validity does not change appreciably with additional controls for desirability, at least under the conditions of testing evaluated.

In evaluating the possible validity of desirability variance, an interesting finding did emerge. A ranking of the scales in terms of their correlation with the Desirability Scale was obtained. Similarly, a ranking of the comparable behavior-rating criterion correlations with the Desirability Scale was obtained. The rank order correlation between these two sets of correlations was .74. This finding implies that there is a consensus about desirability such that traits responded to as desirable are also perceived as desirable when judged in other people. It might also suggest that those who are concerned with managing impressions on a personality test might also do so successfully in interpersonal situations. Whatever the basis for such a finding, the evidence would support the inference that there is some convergent validity associated with desirability response style (Jackson & Messick, 1958). However, the presence of very substantial desirability variance on a test will generally interfere with refined discriminant validation of a set of traits against multiple criteria. Therefore, it would be a mistake to permit desirability variance to remain uncontrolled in scale construction.

In considering the maze of correlations in the various validity studies, the potential importance of a simple, direct analytic technique for appraising convergent and discriminant validity in matrices in which a number of traits are appraised by different methods became apparent. There are a number of limitations in rule-of-thumb methods like searching for the highest correlation in each column. Similarly, traditional linear principal components factor analysis is often unsatisfactory because of a recurring interaction between trait and method factors recently noted by Campbell and O'Connell (1967). Method variance seems to cause a distortion and exaggeration of the factor pattern determined by trait relationships. A number of alternatives were explored and a technique was finally developed which considers only trait variance, eliminating completely from consideration variance unique only to a single method. Based on a rationale related to Tucker's (1958) interbattery method of factor analysis, only correlations between traits using different methods are factored, an identity matrix being substituted for the monomethod correlation matrices. Using this technique, termed multimethod factor analysis (Jackson, 1969), Jackson and Guthrie (1968) factored the correlations between PRF scales, self ratings and peer behavior ratings. Table 8 illustrates the salient loadings emerging from this analysis after rotation. Eighteen clearly defined factors appear for the 20 PRF scales,

TABLE 8
Multimethod Factor Analysis of Self Rating, Peer Rating, and Personality Research Form Scores

FACTOR I
82 Achievement-Sr
61 Achievement-Pr
83 Achievement-PRF

FACTOR II
76 Dominance-Sr
64 Dominance-Pr
60 Dominance-PRF

−52 Abasement-Sr
−38 Abasement-Pr
−56 Abasement-PRF

FACTOR III
84 Affiliation-Sr
69 Affiliation-Pr
64 Affiliation-PRF

FACTOR VII
79 Sentience-Sr
60 Sentience-Pr
60 Sentience-PRF

FACTOR VIII
73 Change-Sr
50 Change-Pr
35 Change-PRF

FACTOR IX
86 Harmavoidance-Sr
60 Harmavoidance-Pr
73 Harmavoidance-PRF

FACTOR X
74 Nurturance-Sr
44 Nurturance-Pr
64 Nurturance-PRF

FACTOR XIV
75 Impulsivity-Sr
44 Impulsivity-Pr
44 Impulsivity-PRF

36 Aggression-Sr
41 Aggression-Pr
53 Aggression-PRF

FACTOR XV
77 Exhibition-Sr
61 Exhibition-Pr
69 Exhibition-PRF

FACTOR XVI
85 Play-Sr
67 Play-Pr
60 Play-PRF

FACTOR IV	FACTOR XI	FACTOR XVII
79 Autonomy-Sr	83 Social Recognition-Sr	79 Understanding-Sr
66 Autonomy-Pr	52 Social Recognition-Pr	63 Understanding-Pr
55 Autonomy-PRF	74 Social Recognition-PRF	49 Understanding-PRF
FACTOR V	FACTOR XII	FACTOR XVIII
93 Order-Sr	76 Defendence-Sr	77 Succorance-Sr
84 Order-Pr	57 Defendence-Pr	23 Succorance-Pr
83 Order-PRF	54 Defendence-PRF	38 Succorance-PRF
FACTOR VI	FACTOR XIII	
78 Cognitive Structure-Sr	76 Endurance-Sr	31 Nurturance-Pr
23 Cognitive Structure-Pr	31 Endurance-Pr	29 Play-PRF
31 Cognitive Structure-PRF	70 Endurance-PRF	−46 Cognitive Structure-Pr
−30 Abasement-Pr	49 Achievement-Pr	
−28 Play-PRF		

Note: Factor loadings reported are the highest loadings obtained for each factor. Abbreviations used are as follows: Self ratings—Sr; Peer ratings—Pr; Personality Research Form—PRF. N = 202.

Douglas N. Jackson

with Impulsivity and Aggression loading one factor positively, and Dominance and Abasement defining a bipolar factor. Note how distinctly the parallel measures from the three domains are represented, and note too the substantial evidence for convergent and discriminant validity of PRF scales provided by this analysis.

A further study was recently undertaken using this analytic technique by Jackson and Skippon (1970). A Leaderless Group Discussion (LGD) situation was used to study the role of personality variables as assessed by PRF scales. An observer rated each interaction made by participants in terms of a number of categories similar to those designated by Bales (1951). Variance common to PRF scales and small group performance was subjected to multimethod factor analysis and rotated analytically. Figure 9 represents two of the four factors obtained, *Exhibitionistic*

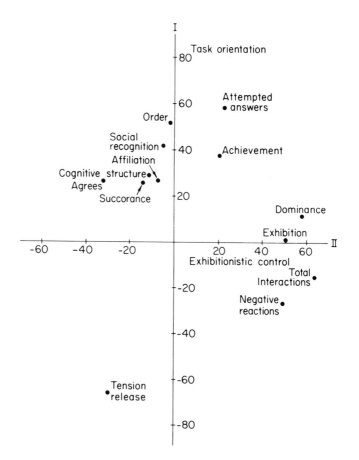

Fig. 9. Projections of personality traits and group rating categories on Factors I and II (values greater than ±.25 only).

Control, with prominent loadings for the Dominance and Exhibition scales from the PRF, and the LGD measures of Total Interaction and Negative Reactions. Similarly, the second factor, *Task Orientation,* was defined by high loadings on PRF scales for Order, Need for Social Recognition, and Achievement, and by LGD measures for Attempted Answers, Agrees, and negatively by Tension Release. These dimensions appear to reflect consistently a theoretically cogent link between small group performance and personality.

One additional study has been undertaken in an attempt to link personality measurement with a traditional area of assessment, occupational interests. Siess and Jackson (1970) used the multimethod factor analysis

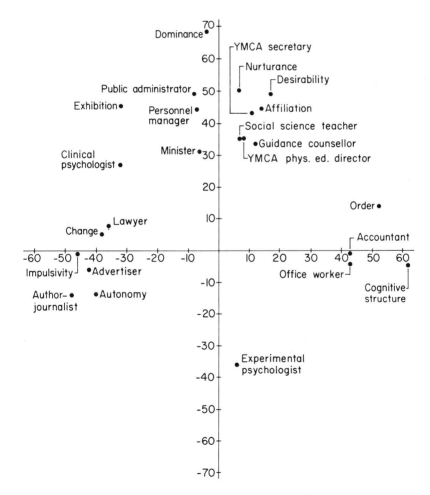

Fig. 10. Dimensions defined jointly by personality traits and vocational interests.

described above to appraise the common variance between PRF scales and the Strong Vocational Interest Blank. Seven quite distinctive factors appeared, two of which are presented on Figure 10. It is interesting that virtually all Strong scales reflecting social service are represented on the vertical axis together with PRF scales for Dominance, Nurturance, and Exhibition, among others. Experimental Psychologist stands alone in defining the opposite pole of this dimension. The horizontal axis identifies a factor which is defined at one end by the traditional literary-creative Strong scales of Lawyer, Advertising, and Artist and the PRF scales labeled Impulsivity and Change, and, at the other end, by Strong business detail interests like Accountant and Office Worker, and the PRF Order and Cognitive Structure scales. With this sort of evidence it should be easier to develop a theory of vocational interests which will go beyond the technology of testing, and be rooted in personality theory and development (Darley & Haganah, 1955).

The research to date with the Personality Research Form is sufficiently encouraging to permit a conclusion on a note of optimism, both for the present state of assessment methodology and for future prospects for scientific developments. With the advent of the computer, with the confidence of a vigorously growing empirical and theoretical foundation, and with the present realization that the techniques of an earlier generation have been outgrown, there is little doubt that developments in this field will continue at an accelerating pace. It is not an idle hope that this expanding knowledge will help to open new vistas before us that may serve to enrich man's understanding of himself and provide a fuller realization of his human potentialities.

REFERENCES

Bales, R. F. *Interaction process analysis.* Cambridge, Mass.: Addison-Wesley, 1951.
Bentler, P. M. Response variability: Fact or artifact? Unpublished doctoral dissertation, Stanford University, 1964.
Block, J. *The challenge of response sets.* New York: Appleton-Century-Crofts, 1965.
Boyd, J. E., & Jackson, D. N. An empirical evaluation of judgment and response methods in multivariate attitude scaling. *American Psychologist,* 1966, **21**, 718. (Abstract)
Campbell, D. T., & Fiske, D. W. Convergent and discriminant validation by the multitrait-multimethod matrix. *Psychological Bulletin,* 1959, **56**, 81–105.
Campbell, D. T., & O'Connell, E. J. Method factors in multitrait-multimethod matrices: Multiplicative rather than additive? *Multivariate Behavioral Research,* 1967, **2**, 409–426.
Cronbach, L. J., & Gleser, G. C. *Psychological tests and personnel decisions.* (2nd ed.) Urbana: University of Illinois Press, 1964.

Cronbach, L. J., & Meehl, P. E. Construct validity in psychological tests. *Psychological Bulletin*, 1955, **52**, 281–302.

Cronbach, L. J., Rajaratnam, N., & Gleser, G. C. Theory of generalizability: A liberalization of reliability theory. *British Journal of Statistical Psychology*, 1963, **16**, 137–163.

Darley, J. G., & Haganah, T. *Vocational interest measurement: Theory and practice.* Minneapolis: University of Minnesota Press, 1955.

Edwards, A. L. Relationship between probability of endorsement and social desirability scale value for a set of 2,824 personality statements. *Journal of Applied Psychology*, 1966, **50**, 238–239.

Green, B. F. Attitude measurement. In G. Lindzey (Ed.), *Handbook of social psychology.* Vol. 1. Cambridge, Mass.: Addison-Wesley, 1954.

Gulliksen, H. *Theory of mental tests.* New York: Wiley, 1950.

Hase, H. D., & Goldberg, L. R. Comparative validity of different strategies of constructing personality inventory scales. *Psychological Bulletin*, 1966, **67**, 231–248.

Jackson, D. N. Desirability judgments as a method of personality assessment. *Educational and Psychological Measurement*, 1964, **24**, 223–238.

Jackson, D. N. *Manual for the Personality Research Form.* Goshen, New York: Research Psychologists Press, 1967. (a)

Jackson, D. N. Acquiescence response styles: Problems of identification and control. In I. A. Berg (Ed.), *Response set in personality assessment.* Chicago: Aldine, 1967. Pp. 71–114. (b)

Jackson, D. N. Review of J. Block, *The challenge of response sets. Educational and Psychological Measurement*, 1967, **27**, 207–219. (c)

Jackson, D. N. Multimethod factor analysis in the evaluation of convergent and discriminant validity. *Psychological Bulletin*, 1969, **72**, 30–49.

Jackson, D. N., & Guthrie, G. M. Multitrait-multimethod evaluation of the Personality Research Form. *Proceedings of the 76th Annual Convention, American Psychological Association*, 1968, 177–178.

Jackson, D. N., & Lay, C. Homogeneous dimensions of personality scale content. *Multivariate Behavioral Research*, 1968, **3**, 321–338.

Jackson, D. N., & Messick, S. Content and style in personality assessment. *Psychological Bulletin*, 1958, **55**, 243–252.

Jackson, D. N., & Messick, S. Individual differences in social perception. *British Journal of Social and Clinical Psychology*, 1963, **2**, 1–10.

Jackson, D. N., & Messick, S. Acquiescence: The nonvanishing variance component. *American Psychologist*, 1965, **20**, 489. (Abstract)

Jackson, D. N., & Skippon, R. Personality factors in small group performance. London, Canada: University of Western Ontario, Research Bulletin, 1970, in preparation.

Loevinger, J. Objective tests as instruments of psychological theory. *Psychological Reports*, 1957, **3**, 635–694.

Meehl, P. E. The dynamics of "structured" personality tests. *Journal of Clinical Psychology*, 1945, **1**, 296–303.

Messick, S. The psychology of acquiescence: An interpretation of research evidence. In I. A. Berg (Ed.), *Response set in personality assessment.* Chicago: Aldine, 1967. Pp. 115–145.

Murray, H. *Explorations in personality.* Cambridge: Harvard University Press, 1938.

Rorer, L. G. The great response-style myth. *Psychological Bulletin*, 1965, **63**, 129–156.

Scott, W. A. Social desirability and individual conceptions of the desirable. *Journal of Abnormal and Social Psychology,* 1963, **67,** 574–585.

Sechrest, L. B., & Jackson, D. N. Deviant response tendencies: Their measurement and interpretation. *Educational and Psychological Measurement,* 1963, **23,** 33–53.

Siess, T. F., & Jackson, D. N. Vocational interests and personality: An empirical integration. *Journal of Counseling Psychology,* 1970, **17,** 27–35.

Stricker, L. J., Messick, S., & Jackson, D. N. Desirability judgments and self-reports as predictors of social behavior. *Journal of Experimental Research in Personality,* 1968, **3,** 151–167.

Torgerson, W. S. *Theory and methods of scaling.* New York: Wiley, 1958.

Trott, D. M., & Jackson, D. N. An experimental analysis of acquiescence. *Journal of Experimental Research in Personality,* 1967, **2,** 278–288.

Tucker, L. R. An inter-battery method of factor analysis. *Psychometrika,* 1958, **23,** 111–136.

Windle, C. Further studies of test-retest effect on personality questionnaires. *Educational and Psychological Measurement,* 1955, **15,** 246–253.

The Prediction of Violence with Psychological Tests

Edwin I. Megargee
Department of Psychology
Florida State University
Tallahassee, Florida

The traditional way of beginning a paper such as this one on the prediction of violence is to convince the reader of the importance of the topic. One time-honored approach is to turn to the FBI *Uniform Crime Reports* and cite statistics to show that the incidence of violent crime is increasing. We could point out, for example, that the rate of violent crimes[1] per 100,000 population has gone up 55% since 1962 (Hoover, 1968). Another opening gambit is to ignore the statistics and use anecdotes of horrifying crimes of violence. On the basis of his own experience, for example, the writer could have attempted to depict the scene at a county hospital when a deputy sheriff who had just delivered

[1] This includes murder, forcible rape, robbery, and aggravated assault.

97

a patient abruptly emptied his revolver into the social worker who was writing the intake summary. Or he could have described what it was like to crouch behind a wall for 90 minutes while a sniper shot 43 people on a university campus.

However such ploys are no longer necessary. No one who has lived through these troubled times needs to be convinced of the importance of the prediction of violence. If the reader has not had firsthand experience with violence, he probably knows someone who has. The very term "violence," which was once a technical term used only by a small group of people in the field, has now emerged into the popular lexicon. For example, a Presidential Commission for the Study of Law Enforcement was appointed in 1965. This was followed in 1967 by the convening of a Presidential Advisory Commission on Civil Disorder to investigate widespread rioting, and in 1968 by a Commission for the Study of Violence after the assassination of Senator Robert F. Kennedy.

The present chapter draws upon two reports prepared in 1969 for the Violence Commission, "The Assessment of Violence with Psychological Tests" (Megargee, 1968) and "The Psychology of Violence: A Critical Review of Theories of Violence" (Megargee, 1969b). In surveying the literature to prepare these reports, it became apparent to the writer that there are many problems in doing adequate research on violence and its prediction. Before reviewing the literature, some of these problems will be discussed.

I. Problems in Research on the Nature and Prediction of Violence

A. WHAT IS VIOLENCE?

The first problem that must be faced is that although everyone "knows what violence is," there is no completely adequate semantic or operational definition of the term. For the purpose of this review, we have adopted the working definition used by the President's Commission on Violence: "acts of violence mean the overtly threatened or overtly accomplished application of force which results in the injury or destruction of persons or property or reputation, or the illegal appropriation of property." This definition is better than most; nevertheless it has some serious drawbacks. The definition includes as violence such crimes as homicide, forcible rape, aggravated assult, robbery, arson, suicide, gang fights, mob violence, and lynchings. Thus far there is probably no quarrel with it. The definition also includes, however, other acts that some readers might not regard as violent. For example, by defining any acts which result in injury or destruction of persons, property, or reputation as violent, we include legal acts, such as executions and homicide in self-defense or by accident as well as any force which results in injury on the baseball diamond, the football field, or the basketball court. It also embraces the parent who physically punishes his child or the newspaper reporter who exposes graft at the expense of someone's reputation. One could even count among the violent the janitor who empties waste baskets and burns the contents in an incinerator. On the other hand, the man who plots a murder but is prevented from carrying it out by forces beyond his control would not be considered a violent person. The definition also excludes behavior by subhuman species.

Readers who are uncomfortable with one or more of the examples in the foregoing paragraph have had to confront two of the major problems in formulating a definition of violent behavior. The first of these is the issue of legality. The Commission's definition ignored legality and focused on the act. This has the drawback of categorizing legally sanctioned injuries to others as violent. The alternative, however, is to classify as nonviolent the legal behavior of the Nazi genocidists or Roman gladiators, to give but two examples.

The second issue is the question of intentionality. Intentionality by its very nature is something that cannot be observed. Psychologists know there is no hard and fast line between what is intended and what is not, for people can act on the basis of motives of which they are quite unaware. The man whose wife electrocutes herself plugging in an iron that he "accidentally" forgot to repair may never have consciously intended that any injury should befall her. Yet unconscious hostility may have caused this omission just as surely as repression might lead another person to forget a dental appointment. The present definition of violence includes unintentional injury of people or destruction of property. The inclusion of "accidental" violence will no doubt make some uncomfortable as will the exclusion of consciously intended violence that is not carried out.

Thus, despite the fact that everyone knows what violence is, on closer examination it is apparent that there can be considerable differences of opinion on what constitutes violent behavior. Differences in semantic definition naturally pave the way for differences in operational definition. As a result, different theorists and investigators who are all ostensibly studying the same phenomenon may in fact focus on quite different sets of behavior or use as subjects quite different samples of people or animals. It is natural that different theories as to the etiology and dynamics of violence should emerge and, given such diversity, that clinicians should differ on the test signs they believe to be indicative of violence.

B. Methodological Problems in Violence Research

In science, such differences of opinion are usually settled by recourse to empirical investigation. However, rigorous empirical investigation of the psychology of human violence is difficult. Ethical prohibitions rule out the straightforward experimental approach. It would be easy to make definitive causal statements if two matched groups could be exposed to two sets of conditions, one calculated to arouse violence and the other not, so that the resulting violence could be observed and measured. However, incitement to violence is both unethical and illegal.

Because the experimental method has been inappropriate for the investigation of human violence, scientists have had to resort to different strategies. One has been to apply the experimental method to milder forms of aggressive behavior in the hope that the principles derived could be extrapolated to violence without too much distortion on error. While the experimental investigation of mild aggression has afforded a number of valuable insights, it is obvious that the dynamics involved in such laboratory analogs could be substantially different from those involved in actual violence. It is one thing to deliver a mild electric shock to an unseen victim when told to by an experimenter who is committed to safeguarding his subjects from injury; it is another thing to pull the switch that will send a lethal dose of high voltage electricity to a condemned man in an electric chair.[2]

Another approach has been to fall back on the method of naturalistic observation. However, here too there are ethical problems. A psychologist who is making behavior ratings while observing incidents of aggressive behavior in a school playground should remain unobtrusive and not interfere with the ongoing behavior. However, if a squabble escalates to the point of violence so that serious injuries are possible, it is usually incumbent on the observer and other adults in the vicinity to intervene. Once this occurs the observations are no longer naturalistic.

Another tactic has been to attempt to reconstruct incidents in which violence actually erupted. This is generally done by interviewing people who observed or took part in the events. This procedure unfortunately has the drawback of relying on observers who are not only untrained but who may have reasons to distort events in order to justify their own behavior. The disturbances in Chicago at the time of the 1968 Demo-

[2] For a review of methods used in the assessment of aggression, see Megargee and Menzies, in press.

cratic National Convention were probably observed by more people (including members of the press who are trained to observe and report the facts) than any similar confrontation in our history. The plethora of differing accounts of the events which took place (D. Walker, 1968), not to mention the differing opinions of their causes, are good examples of the unreliability of this form of evidence for scientific purposes.

While naturalistic observation and the use of informants has been one of the principal techniques used by social psychologists, sociologists and anthropologists, some psychologists and psychiatrists interested in personality research have taken a somewhat different tack. In many studies they have relied on people who have participated in violence, not so much for information about the events that lead up to the violent confrontation but instead to obtain data about the personality structure of violent individuals. Of course, the subjects might be uncooperative; moreover judicial and correctional experiences may have altered their personality structure.

Another strategy which avoids some of the ethical dilemmas inherent in the investigation of human violence is the study of extreme aggressive behavior among infra-human species. This approach is particularly favored by those who seek innate causes of aggressive behavior. As with humans, ethical considerations prohibit laboratory procedures which might inflict severe pain or injury upon an animal. Therefore animal research has relied for the most part on field observations supplemented by laboratory studies of mild or moderately aggressive behavior.

As a result of these difficulties in doing rigorous research on human violence, there is as yet no way of adequately testing the various theories of violence that have developed to determine which formulations are accurate and which are in error. This naturally makes it difficult for the clinician who would attempt to predict or assess the potential for violent behavior in an individual. Lacking a well-establishing theory of the personality factors which result in violence, he must fall back on clinical experience, hunches, and intuition, all of which are notoriously fallible.

C. Factors Leading to Violence

While theories of violence are extremely diverse (Megargee, 1969b) there is at least some agreement on the broad factors that interact to determine whether or not a violent act will take place. These can be labeled "instigation," "inhibition," and "situational factors." "Instigation" refers to all the motivational factors which lead the individual toward violent behavior. Some theorists hold that man has an innate need for aggressive or violent behavior; others argue that these drives develop during childhood. Without attempting to arbitrate this dispute, suffice to say that violent behavior can be both an end in itself and also a means by which other ends might be accomplished. In assessing an individual's potential for violence, both sorts of instigation must be taken into account.

The second basic factor is inhibition, the forces within the individual which operate to block overt violence. Once again theorists have proposed a variety of innate and environmental causes for such taboos, and have given them a variety of names such as "conscience," "superego prohibitions," and the like (Megargee, 1969b; Megargee & Hokanson, 1970). But no matter what one's theoretical predilections, it is obvious that the strength of the inhibitory factors as well as of instigation must be measured and considered if accurate predictions are to be made.

The task of the clinician who would attempt to predict violence thus appears to be fairly simple. He should somehow measure the relative strength of instigation and of inhibition. When instigation exceeds inhibition, then he should predict violence; if inhibitions outweigh instigations, then no violence will result.[3]

One difficulty with this is that instigation and inhibition are not relatively fixed or permanent quantities like the amount of water in Lake Mead or the height of Boulder Dam. Instead they are quite variable. Not only do they vary as a function of time, but they also vary as a function of the target against which the aggressive instigation is felt. In most individuals there are more inhibitions associated with striking one's mother than with hitting one's child, for example. Similarly, the strength of inhibitions will vary from one aggressive act to another; physical assaults are less common than mild verbal reproofs because most individuals have stronger inhibitions against this extreme form of aggression. Consequently, extraordinarily high instigation is necessary to overcome these strong taboos (Megargee, 1969b). The fact that instigation and inhibition are so variable makes them more difficult to assess than relatively stable and enduring characteristics of the individual such as intelligence.

[3] Habit strength based on the frequency with which aggressive responses have been performed and rewarded in the past, is also very important. In the present formulation, habit strength is considered to be a factor influencing inhibitions: the stronger the habit strength, the lower the inhibitions. Some students, particularly those in the Hull-Spence tradition, may prefer to regard habit strength as a separate factor which, in addition to instigation and inhibition, determines the reaction potential of a given act.

Even if instigation and inhibition could be measured with ease, it would be foolish to expect that violence could then be predicted accurately. In the first place, people typically have a number of different needs and drives competing for expression at any given time. Often a response designed to satisfy one such need will frustrate a number of others. While a violent response usually cannot take place if inhibitions exceed instigation, the fact that instigation outweighs inhibition does not mean that violence will necessarily result. It merely means that a violent act is more probable. Before the organism can engage in violence the violent response must still compete with alternative incompatible responses. If some of these other responses satisfy more pressing drives or if they are better learned, they may be chosen instead. An infantryman on patrol may encounter an enemy soldier who is unaware of his presence. As a well-trained veteran combat soldier, his instigation toward shooting the enemy will probably exceed any inhibitions. However, by capturing the enemy he might be able to obtain important intelligence data. If the need for information is stronger than the need to injure the foe, then the nonviolent act may be selected. Thus, psychologists should assess not only the potential for violent action, but also the strength of competing nonviolent responses.

The situation becomes even more difficult and complex when we consider the third basic class of factors that help determine whether a violent response will take place, namely situational or stimulus factors— people or objects in the milieu that facilitate or impede the overt expression of violence. Violence by its very nature is a social phenomenon involving two or more people. Even in the simplest case involving an aggressor and his victim, violence usually comes about only after a complex scenario of interpersonal events involving moves and countermoves on the part of both individuals has taken place (Toch, 1969). In many cases it is the behavior of the victim rather than the offender which is the major factor in causing the encounter to culminate in violence (MacDonald, 1967; Toch, 1969; Wolfgang, 1957). The presence of weapons or other objects that might facilitate violence can be of crucial importance (Berkowitz, 1968; Berkowitz & LePage, 1967).

In the case of our soldier, seeing the enemy suddenly reach for a weapon might lead him to shoot instead of attempting to capture him alive. On the other hand, if the enemy soldier should start talking to several nearby buddies, then our infantryman might decide any aggressive action is too risky and go into hiding.

Although violence usually comes about through the interpersonal behavior of two or more people, and despite the fact that the stimulus situation can play a major role in shaping these transactions, the psychologist who would predict violence typically can evaluate only one actor in the potential scenario and he rarely has any accurate information about the stage setting. He is thus deprived of information about stimulus factors that might tip the scales toward or away from a violent resolution of an interaction. The result is poorer predictions.

D. Problems in the Assessment of Instigation and Inhibition

The preceding discussion indicated that the assessment of violence generally is based on the evaluation of one individual's instigation and inhibition. How are these constructs to be assessed? In choosing samples of behavior to measure these attributes, the clinical psychologist encounters some of the same ethical constraints faced by the scholar who would do research on violence. For example, one "test" of whether someone is likely to be violent would be for the psychologist to slap his face. If the client refrained from making a violent response to such arbitrary provocation, then the psychologist might reasonably infer that he would refrain from violence under other provocative circumstances as well. Obviously, no clinical psychologist, out of respect for professional ethics as well as his own safety, administers such a direct "test" of violence potential. Instead he might ask the individual to fill out a questionnaire which could include a question, "What would you do if someone for no reason at all slapped you in the face?" Whether or not this question provides an adequate assessment of the individual's behavior in such situations is, of course, difficult to say without data. Certainly it is much easier to disguise what one's behavioral response would be on a questionnaire than in a direct confrontation.

Similarly, in validating a test designed to predict violence, one straightforward procedure would be to select people with high and low scores on the test, and then frustrate or provoke them in some fashion to determine if the group tested as having more potential for violence did, in fact, lash out more readily. If ethical codes did not prohibit such tactics, experimenters' concerns for their own safety would. Psychologists who made a habit of inciting potentially homicidal subjects to violence would soon find it difficult to buy life insurance or, even worse, to hire graduate research assistants.

Therefore less direct criteria must be found. As in the case of research on the dynamics of violence, one approach has been to investigate how well tests can assess milder forms of aggression. The principal assumption which underlines this approach is that a test which can predict mild aggression can also predict violence. Unfortunately this assumption is not always correct.

Another tactic is to substitute *post*diction for *pre*diction. Instead of assessing people and then waiting for violence to occur, the investigator saves time and money by going to a prison or a psychiatric ward and testing people who have been violent in the past to determine whether their test scores differ from comparison groups who have not been violent.

Such an approach depends upon the care with which a nonviolent comparison group is selected. Residents of Death Row differ from college sophomores in so many ways that it is meaningless to compare their results. A study in which assaultive paranoid schizophrenics are contrasted with nonassaultive paranoid schizophrenics at the same hospital has greater potential value.

Even the best controlled postdictive study does not provide conclusive evidence of a test's potential for prediction. If differences are found, there is no way of knowing whether or not they would also have been found prior to the test. Test results are functions not only of enduring personality traits but also of the sets, defenses, and expectancies one brings into the testing situation (Murstein, 1961), and there is little doubt but that these could vary considerably from before to after a crime of violence. Failure to find differences is not conclusive either. The long-suffering husband who finally does in his wife may be measured as having little instigation to aggression simply because he has eliminated his chief source of frustration.

Postdictive research also has the effect of glossing over the base rate problem (Meehl & Rosen, 1955). We may be able to demonstrate that a certain cutting score on some test of violence identifies almost everyone in a sample of murderers while misclassifying only a few nonhomicidal convicts. Unfortunately, for violence predictors if not for the general public, the national homicide rate is "only" 6.1 per 100,000 population (Hoover, 1968). Let us assume that the incidence of murderers is about equivalent to the incidence of victims, although it is in fact likely to be somewhat lower. Before we undertake to use this test to identify all the murderous citizens in our communities, we should reflect that even if our false positive rate is only 1%, for every six murderers we correctly identify, we could erroneously label as homicidal 1000 other individuals. Obviously even such a paragon among tests would be useful only in a setting in which the incidence of violence was high enough to raise the base rate considerably.

The research consumer must also be wary of overgeneralizing from either positive or negative findings. The fact that a test has been found to be successful in a certain population does not guarantee that a similar degree of accuracy will be found in other settings. An instrument that has proved to be useful in inpatient psychiatric settings may not discriminate among criminals and vice versa.

While the problems associated with such gross overgeneralization are fairly obvious, there is a subtler problem of overgeneralization and oversimplification that cripples much research in the area of violence. Many different types or kinds of people can engage in violence, and failure to differentiate among these types can lead to erroneous conclusions. For example, Megargee (1964a, 1965a, 1966d, in press; Megargee, Cook, & Mendelsohn, 1967) has proposed that two quite different personality types can be found among those who engage in extreme acts of violence. One type, which Megargee terms the Undercontrolled or Habitually Aggressive, is characterized by minimal inhibitions against the expression of aggression; as a result he freqently lashes out when provoked. The other type, termed the Chronically Overcontrolled Assaultive, is just the opposite. This type is characterized by excessive, rigid inhibitions against the expression of aggression under any circumstances.

While the Undercontrolled Aggressive type can be readily identified on the basis of his police record or reports of associates, the violence of the Chronically Overcontrolled type is much more difficult to predict in advance. Sometimes, as a result of repeated provocations and frustrations, the Chronically Overcontrolled person's instigation to aggression may accumulate to the point where it overwhelms even his rigid inhibitive defenses, and he may then engage in an act of extreme violence. It is possible for the clinician to assess someone as being overcontrolled, but not all overcontrolled individuals eventually engage in violent behavior (Megargee, in press).

Unfortunately, in the validational literature on psychological tests little or no allowance is made for the fact that the dynamic and personality factors associated with violence can differ dramatically from type to type. This could hamstring a test validational study from the outset. For example, assuming Megargee's typology to be valid, if both of his types were included in the same criterion group of violent individuals, their differences in aggressiveness and control could cancel each other out so that the violent group, *on the average*, would appear no different from a nonviolent group on the test in question. Indeed, in cross-validating his MMPI scale of assaultive tendencies, Megargee made this very error and erroneously concluded the scale was invalid. Several years later, after the typology had been established, he returned to the abandoned scale and cross-validated it again using separate samples of Overcontrolled and Undercontrolled murderers. By adding this refinement, he found the scale could detect the Overcontrolled type but not the Undercontrolled (Megargee et al., 1967).

Similarly, many studies fail to differentiate between "instrumental" aggression and "angry" aggression. According to Buss (1961), instrumental aggression is not motivated by anger or the desire to injure someone, but involves violence as a means to some other end.

Included within this group are individuals who commit assaults in connection with strong-arm robberies, rapes, or in an effort to escape from the scene of a crime. Such individuals are undeniably violent, but it is likely that their personality dynamics differ significantly from persons who engage in violence simply to kill or injure their victim. However both types are often lumped together in the same violent criterion group. If a psychological test is sensitive to a personality dimension which is present in one type of violent person but not in another, its true effectiveness will be masked when extremely heterogeneous criterion samples are used. One major criticism which Wolfgang (1967, p. 152) levels against the psychological assessment literature is:

With few exceptions, the psychometric studies of homicides have failed to distinguish between different types of homicides. They have neglected to make use of control groups, they use inadequate statistical analyses and often they do not emerge from testable hypotheses. Most of the studies on the differential psychology of homicide are of an exploratory, tentative nature.

E. Problems of Establishing Test Validity

In the preceding pages we have discussed a number of problems that psychologists who would do research on the nature or the prediction of violence must somehow cope with. In addition to these problems peculiar to violence research, they must also face all the problems that beset anyone who is rash enough to study test validity. These problems are well known to clinical psychologists so there is no need to describe them in detail. The ever present problem of finding an adequate criterion, the base rate problem, and the problem of determining predictive validity have been discussed already. In addition to these difficulties, most studies attempt to validate individual scales, while in practice the interpretation of a test indicator varies as a function of the context. Interexaminer unreliability can cause different examiners to obtain different test protocols, lead different scorers to produce diverse scores for the same test responses, and induce different psychologists to arrive at different interpretations for a given protocol. Furthermore, many tests do not readily lend themselves to quantification. The adverse effects of these and other similar complications will be apparent in the literature to be reviewed below.

It can be seen that adequate research on the prediction of violence requires considerable expertise in such diverse areas as theories of aggression and violence, test theory and validation, and statistics and experimental design. Unfortunately such a combination of skills is rare; as a result many studies display considerable sophistication in one or two areas only to be crippled by naiveté in a third.

II. The Assessment of Violence with Structured Personality Inventories

Personality tests are generally divided into two broad classifications: structured tests and projective tests. Structured tests, which are discussed in the present section, are generally paper and pencil self-report inventories consisting of a number of statements or questions which the respondent is asked to mark "true" or "false," or "agree" or "disagree." The main advantages of these instruments are that they can be administered to large numbers of people at a sitting and scoring is highly reliable and objective. Indeed, scoring can often be carried out completely by automated methods, or by low-paid clerical personnel. This ease and convenience of administration and scoring, as well as the relatively low cost involved, make structured tests particularly useful in screening situations. They also have the added effect of encouraging research for, unlike the time-consuming projective techniques, large amounts of data on structured instruments can easily be obtained.

In describing the objectivity of structured techniques, however, it is easy to overlook the subjectivity which is also involved. Once normative and validational data have been collected on a scale it often appears that the construct it assesses is not exactly what the test author had in mind. Because of this, it is impossible to interpret a scale simply on the basis of the name the author originally assigned to it. Interpretation of its meaning requires a skilled clinical psychologist who is familiar with the research literature pertaining to the scale.

Most of the structured tests in common use in the United States today are multiphasic inventories: that is they contain questions and statements that are scored simultaneously on a number of different scales. Typically the test was originally published with about a dozen scales, but, in many instances, notably that of the Minnesota Multiphasic Personality Inventory (MMPI), subsequent researchers have used the original item pool to construct other specialized scales. Over 200 additional scales have been constructed for the MMPI alone.

Most scales in multiphasic inventories cannot be interpreted accurately out of context. Their meaning will vary as a function of the scores on other scales. For example an individual whose MMPI scores indicate strong hostility might be expected to turn that hostility outward against others if he also has a high score on the Paranoia scale. On the other hand, he may turn that hostility inward against himself in a suicidal fashion if he has a high score on the Depression scale. Hence most inventories are interpreted by means of profile analysis in which the psychologist looks beyond the individual scale scores to the configurations of the scales relative to each other. Thus while the structured tests are easy to administer and to score, their interpretation requires as much clinical acumen and skill as do projective tests.

Research on these tests, however, often ignores the clinician and examines the first-order correlation between a particular scale and some criterion of overt aggression or violence. While such procedures can provide important data regarding the construct validity of the scale, they may underestimate the degree to which a skilled clinician using a configurational analysis and a battery of tests is able to assess an individual's potential for violence.

A. THE MINNESOTA MULTIPHASIC PERSONALITY INVENTORY (MMPI)

The Minnesota Multiphasic Personality Inventory was constructed by Hathaway and McKinley in the 1940's to provide an instrument that would assist in psychiatric diagnosis. As usually administered, it consists of 566 statements printed in a test booklet with the respondent limited to true and false answers. The 10 clinical scales are particularly good for the assessment of psychopathy and psychoneurosis; they are less valid for the assessment of psychotic disorders. In addition to the standard scales, researchers have used the MMPI item pool to construct a variety of other scales. While many of these newer scales were also constructed by the method of empirical item analysis, others were based on the rational method of item selection. A number of the newly devised scales are aimed at the assessment of aggression, hostility, and hostility control—traits which should bear a relation to violence.

In the sections which follow, the literature on the assessment of violence using the standard MMPI clinical scales, as well as the newer scales, will be reviewed. Many of the validational studies of these scales correlate the MMPI measures with other test measures which purport to assess aggression or violence. In the present review these studies will not be summarized; instead only studies wihch use an overt behavioral criterion will be considered. Within that category the emphasis will be on studies that have attempted to determine the relation of the MMPI to violence. Those studies which have examined the relationship between the MMPI and milder aggressive tendencies will be referred to only in passing.

1. *The Assessment of Violence with the MMPI Clinical Scales*

The MMPI has shown itself to be a valuable aid in individual diagnosis. As with any clinical instrument it should be employed in conjunction with other sources of information such as interviews and case histories, as well as other psychological tests (see Megargee, 1966c, Ch. 12). The *Pd* scale, which discriminates people with antisocial tendencies, has been found to be particularly useful. The *Pa* scale, when highly elevated, often indicates hostility toward others. Elevations on the *Sc* scale can indicate alienation from society, while an elevated *Ma* scale can indicate impulsivity. Elevations on these scales do not have any one-to-one relationship to violence. However, among individuals with very high scores (particularly on *Pd*, *Pa*, and *Sc*), it is likely that the incidence of violence will be substantially higher than among people with "normal" profiles. Thus while the MMPI cannot point with unerring accuracy at one individual and label him violent, it can be used to separate *groups* of people among whom there is a greater likelihood of violence, such as psychopaths or paranoid schizophrenics, from a normal population.

We previously noted that violence is, in part, an outcome of situational factors, and that the MMPI can only assess personality. However, among deviant personality groups we can predict that, given stressful environmental circumstances, particularly extremely frustrating or threatening events, the likelihood that they would resort to acting out or to aggression as a defense is considerably higher than in the normal population (see Butcher, 1969; Dahlstrom & Welsh, 1960; Hathaway & Monachesi, 1953; Wirt & Briggs, 1959).

Most of the above conclusions were based on the clinical experience of the writer and on the research literature relating the MMPI to criminality, delinquency, and psychosis (Butcher, 1969; Dahlstrom & Welsh, 1960). As a general rule these studies have not focused primarily on the issue of violence. There are some studies, however, which have examined the relationship between the standard clinical scales and aggressive or violent behavior. Shipman and Marquette (1963) correlated scores on the *Pd*, *Pa*, and *Sc* scales with ratings of verbal hostility, physical hostility, and hostile attitude that were made on the basis of the case records of patients in treatment at an outpatient psychiatric clinic. They found no significant correlations between any of these scales and their ratings of hostility.

On the basis of peer ratings and teacher ratings Butcher (1965) divided a sample of 234 eighth grade students into high, medium, and low aggression groups. He found more deviant MMPI scores in the high and low group than in the middle. The high aggressive group had higher elevations on the *Hy* and *Pd* scales than did the medium and low groups. Their elevations on the *Hs*, *Sc*, and *Ma* were also higher than those of the middle aggressive group.

Erikson and Roberts (1966) administered the MMPI to two matched groups of institutionalized delinquent boys. One group consisted of boys who broke the rules, caused trouble in the dormitories, and were frequently found fighting and making general nuisances of themselves. The other group generally conformed to the rules and regulations of the training school. Comparing the two groups' MMPI profiles, they found that the unruly group had a significantly higher elevation on the *Pd* scale than did the conforming group. When the study was replicated, however, no significant differences were found on any of the standard MMPI clinical scales. The investigators concluded:

On the basis of the results of this study and the results of previous studies in this general area, it is concluded that the MMPI has questionable value in discriminating between different levels and types of delinquents. On the other hand, it seems to have been consistently successful in the differentiating between delinquents and nondelinquents. Possibly the differences among delinquent groups is not large enough to be measured by the MMPI [Erikson & Roberts, 1966, p. 165].

Megargee and Mendelsohn (1962) compared the MMPI scale scores of the following four groups: (*a*) 14 extremely assaultive men referred to a probation department clinic after conviction of murder, manslaughter, mayhem, or assault with a deadly weapon; (*b*) 25 moderately assaultive men referred after conviction for battery; (*c*) 25 nonviolent criminals referred after thefts and other nonassaultive crimes; and (*d*) a group of 46 normals with no known criminal records. The use of two different assaultive groups increased the likelihood of a test being found valid if it was sensitive to only the Overcontrolled or Undercontrolled type. The use of both normal and nonviolent criminal contrast groups enabled the authors to determine whether a scale simply detected criminality, or if it specifically measured violence with criminality controlled. They found that while a number of the standard MMPI scales discriminated the three criminal groups from the noncriminal group, no scale was able to discriminate the violent criminal groups from the nonviolent criminals.

Megargee and Mendelsohn (1962) also evaluated two experimental indices of aggressive behavior, the Active Hostility Index (Welsh & Sullivan, 1952) and the Frustration Tolerance Index (Beall & Panton, 1957) which combines the scores on several MMPI clinical scales in such a way as to maximize their ability to assess aggressive tendencies. They found that scores on these indices were not related to violence when criminal tendencies were controlled. Thus, on the basis of this study it would appear that the MMPI can differentiate between criminal and noncriminal groups, but the standard scales cannot separate the assaultive criminal from his nonviolent cell mate. This of course would lessen the test's utility in a prison setting or in a probation department in which all of the clients are criminals, and where it is necessary to sort the dangerous from the less dangerous inmates. This study was subsequently replicated and the same results were obtained (Megargee, Cook, & Mendelsohn, 1967).

One drawback to these studies is that they relate individual MMPI scales to the behavioral criteria. As we noted earlier, the MMPI is typically used configurationally, with a global interpretation made by a skilled clinical psychologist. The first-order relationships examined in these two studies do not indicate whether or not a clinician who has the full profile available would be able to discriminate between the violent and the nonviolent criminals.

2. The Assessment of Violence with MMPI Scales of Hostility and Control

Since its original publication, a number of additional scales that purport to measure traits that seem relevant to violence have been derived from the MMPI item pool. These scales will be reviewed in the order of their derivation. The literature for each scale indicating its relation to violence will also be described.

a. The Iowa Hostility Inventory. Moldawsky (1953) selected 100 MMPI items that appeared to measure aggressiveness. These items were then submitted to a group of judges and the 45 items on which they agreed were selected to comprise the inventory. Dinwiddie (1954) related scores on the Iowa Inventory to ratings of the aggressiveness of male psychiatric clinic patients. According to Buss (1961, p. 161), Dinwiddie found a positive correlation of .59 with therapists' ratings of hostility, and of .67 with the patients' self-ratings of hostility. Both of these correlations were significant, and suggested to Buss that the inventory ". . . has moderate validity." Charen (1955), however, correlated the Iowa inventory with nurses' ratings of hostility in tubercular patients and found no significant positive correlation.

Several studies have investigated the relationship between the Iowa Inventory and violence. Buss, Durkee, and Baer (1956) interviewed psychiatric patients and, allowing for patient bias, rated them on seven types of aggressive behavior. One category was assaultiveness which they defined as acts of violence against people or objects. The Iowa Inventory had a positive correlation of .36 with the ratings of assaultiveness in men, and of .41 with the ratings for women. A correlation of .37 was required for statistical significance at the .05 probability level; therefore the ratings for women were statistically significant but those for men fell just short of acceptable limits.

Shipman (1965) found no correlation between the Iowa Inventory and ratings of verbal or physical hostility in a sample of 120 neuro-psychiatric outpatients. A significant positive correlation of .31 was found with a hostile attitude, however. The findings of these studies suggest that while the Iowa Inventory does bear some relationship to aggressiveness, the correlations are generally small and too unreliable for it to be used successfully for the prediction of violence in the individual case.

b. Hostility (Ho). Like the Iowa scale, the Cook and Medley (1954) Hostility scale involved a combination of rationally and empirically derived items. The original pool consisted of items which discriminated between Minnesota teachers who were rated in the top and bottom 8% of the teachers in the state. Of the discriminating items, five judges selected 50 as measures of hostility.

Two studies have tested the relationship of the *Ho* scale with aggressiveness. Snoke (1955) found that college men who were high on the *Ho* scale were more likely to miss appointments for participation in an experiment than were men who were low. McGee (1954) found a significant positive correlation between the *Ho* scale and the extent to which subjects attributed hostility to photographs. While both studies supported the construct validity of the scale, the evidence was rather tangential.

Two studies have investigated the relationship of the *Ho* scale with violence. Megargee and Mendelsohn (1962), in their comparison of extremely assaultive criminals, moderately assaultive criminals, nonviolent criminals, and normals, found no significant differences on the *Ho* scale. They also failed to find any differences between groups in their replication study (Megargee *et al.*, 1967). Shipman (1965) found no significant correlations between the *Ho* scale and ratings of verbal and physical hostility, and ratings of hostile attitude in a sample of psychiatric outpatients. Thus, the *Ho* scale does not appear to be useful in the prediction of either aggressiveness or violence.

c. Overt Hostility (Hv) and Hostility Control (Hc). These two scales were both empirically derived by Schultz (1954) on the basis of therapists' ratings of 119 Veterans Administration patients. For the Overt Hostility scale, the protocols of patients in the top and bottom quartiles on ratings of the frequency of expression of overt hostility were used; on the Hostility Control scale the same procedure was used except the ratings were based on the adequacy of the methods which the patients used to deal with hostility. The initial scales were later cross-validated on the basis of therapists' ratings in a college sample.

Butcher (1965) studied the relation of the *Hc* scale to aggressive behavior in his eighth-grade sample. He found no significant differences between those who were rated by their teachers or peers as being high and low in aggression. Boys who were in the middle group on the aggressiveness ratings were significantly lower on the *Hc* scale which Butcher interpreted as indicating that individuals at the extremes have more difficulty with aggression. While this interpretation may be correct, the fact that both highly aggressive and relatively nonaggressive individuals obtained high scores on this scale would make for difficulties in predicting violence on the basis of this measure.

Megargee and Mendelsohn (1962) and Shipman (1965) studied the relationship of both of Schultz's scales to the criteria of violence used in their respective studies. No significant relationships were found between the criteria and the *Hv* scale in either study, and Shipman (1965) also found no significant differences for the *Hc* scale. Megargee and Mendelsohn found that *Hc* discriminated criminals from noncriminals, but did not discriminate the violent from the nonviolent criminals.

d. Ego Overcontrol (Eo), Neurotic Undercontrol (Nu), and Bimodal Control (Bc). Block (1955) derived these three scales to reflect different aspects of impulse control. Megargee and Mendelsohn (1962) investigated whether or not the scales would discriminate between their samples of extremely violent, moderately violent and nonviolent criminals and normals. The *Eo* scale was able to differentiate the criminal samples from noncriminal samples; however, contrary to expectations, the criminals' scores were significantly higher than those of the noncriminals. No significant differences were found between the violent and nonviolent criminals.

e. Inhibition of Aggression (Hy-5). The *Hy-5* is a rationally derived subscale of the MMPI *Hy* scale. It consists of those items on the *Hy* scale which Harris and Lingoes (1955) believed to measure inhibition of aggression. Megargee and Mendelsohn (1962) included *Hy-5* in their study and found it to be the only scale of those they studied which discriminated assaultive criminal groups from nonviolent criminals. Since the scale discriminated in a reverse direction, with the assaultive criminals assessed as higher than the nonviolent criminals on "inhibition of aggression," Megargee and Mendelsohn attributed this finding to chance. Their interpretation was borne out in the replication of the original study which showed no significant differences among their four groups (Megargee *et al.*, 1967).

f. Judged Manifest Hostility (Jh). The Siegel (1956) Manifest Hostility scale, or, as it was retitled by Dahlstrom and Welsh (1960), "Judged Manifest Hostility," has engendered more research than most of the scales which we have discussed thus far. The scale was rationally derived; 110 items deemed to indicate hostility were submitted to five judges who chose those items which they felt reflected manifest hostility. Any item on which four of the five judges agreed was included in the scale.

Shipman and Marquette (1963, p. 104) have summarized the early validational literature on this scale as follows:

The evidence for the validity of the scale, other than the method of selection, was that high scorers on the California F scale obtained high scores on the MHS. In the same study, however, it was found that the correlation of the MHS with the Elizur hostility score for the Rorschach approached zero. Four articles on the MHS can be found in the literature. Siegel, Spilka, and Miller (1957) showed that reliable subscales for extropunitive, intropunitive, and projected hostility could be drawn from the MHS and they had small correlations in the predicted directions with the Rosenzweig P-F scores. Feldman and Siegel (1958) and Siegel and Feldman (1958) reported no effect on the scores by combining anxiety and hostility items in a single scale. Swickard and Spilka (1961) showed that delinquents from minority groups had a higher mean MHS score than did other delinquents.

There have been several investigations of the validity of the Manifest Hostility Scale among violent individuals. Miller, Spilka, and Pratt (1960) compared 26 criminally insane paranoid schizophrenics, most of whom were murderers, with 26 noncriminal paranoid schizophrenics. The two groups were matched for age, length of time in the hospital, and intelligence. The investigators found no significant differences in the Manifest Hostility Scale scores for these groups, or in the extropunitive, intropunitive, and projected hostility scales which Siegel *et al.* (1957) had earlier derived.

Shipman and Marquette (1963) correlated the MHS scores of 94 neuropsychiatric outpatients with ratings of verbal hostility, physical hostility, and hostile attitudes based on their clinical records. The correlations with verbal hostility and hostile attitudes were not significant: the correlation of $r = .29$ with physical hostility was significant. They pointed out (1963, p. 105): "While the Physical Hostility correlation is significantly different from chance at the .05 level of confidence, it reflects only a small relationship." In a later study, Shipman (1965) once again correlated the MHS with ratings of these attributes in a new sample of 120 patients. In this later study no significant correlations were obtained. Similarly, Megargee and Mendelsohn (1962) found no significant differences on the MHS for their samples of violent and non-violent criminals and normals. Thus, the Siegel scale does not appear to be a valid or useful tool for the prediction of violence.

g. Adjustment of Prison (Ap). This scale was empirically derived by Panton (1958) to measure adjustment to prison; maladjustment was operationally defined as fighting, assaulting a guard, or refusing to obey orders. It would appear, therefore, that the *Ap* scale might have some potential for the assessment of violence. Megargee and Mendelsohn (1962) included it among the scales tested in their investigation. While it was able to discriminate the criminal samples from the noncriminal group, it did not prove capable of differentiating violent from nonviolent criminals. The same pattern was found in their replication study.

h. Impulsivity (Im). While the Impulsivity scale is included in Dahlstrom and Welsh's (1960) compendium of MMPI scales, it is not in fact an MMPI scale. Instead it is a scale which Gough (1960a) derived for the California Psychological Inventory, an instrument that has many items in common with the MMPI. Because of these overlapping items, some psychologists score the MMPI for CPI scales using the items which are common to both tests. While this procedure works fairly well in the case of some scales, research has shown that this is rather questionable in the case of the Im scale (Megargee, 1966a). In any case, because its designation suggested that the scale might be related to violence, Megargee and Mendelsohn (1962) included it in their investigation. They found no significant differences among their groups. It would seem, therefore, that the MMPI version of this scale is not useful in the assessment of violence. It should be pointed out however that this finding has no relevance to the *Im* scale in its usual context of the CPI.

i. Overcontrolled Hostility (O-H). The reader who has followed the discussion of the MMPI scales thus far will have noticed that few significant relations have been found between MMPI hostility scales and behavioral criteria of violence. Because of this Megargee, Cook, and Mendelsohn (1967) undertook to derive a violence scale for the MMPI. As noted above, previous research had indicated that violent individuals could be divided into Undercontrolled Aggressive and Chronically Overcontrolled subtypes who differed in their inhibitions against the expression of overt aggression. Megargee *et al.* (1967) hoped to derive a unidimensional scale for assaultiveness or violence. However, failing this, they were hopeful that a scale for the identification of the Overcontrolled type might be developed. This type presents greater diagnostic difficulty than does the Undercontrolled Aggressive type, who can usually be recognized by a long history of acting out. On the basis of a complex series of empirical item analyses of the MMPI protocols of extremely assaultive, moderately assaultive, and nonviolent criminals, as well as noncriminals, several experimental scales were constructed. On the basis of preliminary data, one of the scales was selected for further validational work. Additional research soon indicated that this scale was not a unidimensional violence scale, but it did appear to offer promise in the assessment of the Overcontrolled Assaultive type.

Subsequent validational work has focused on the relationship of the *O-H* scale to violence in criminal samples and to control in both criminal and noncriminal samples. Cross-validational studies showed that samples of extremely assaultive applicants for probation obtained *O-H* scores significantly higher than samples of moderately assaultive applicants or nonviolent criminals. As would be expected if the scale was assessing the Overcontrolled type, no differences between the moderately assaultive and nonviolent criminals were found. Another cross-validational study compared the scores of Overcontrolled and Undercontrolled assaultive Texas prisoners most of whom had been convicted of murder. It was found that the Overcontrolled sample had *O-H* scores significantly higher than the Undercontrolled sample. Other studies have related the *O-H* scale to various measures of control in normal samples and have found, as expected, a positive relationship with measures of control.

In a more recent study, Megargee (1969a) hypothesized that a group of conscientious objectors who were incarcerated for refusal to comply with the Selective Service Act of 1948 would have *O-H* scores significantly higher than a random sample of Federal prisoners. This hypothesis was confirmed. Not only did the conscientious objectors have a higher mean *O-H* score but the incidence of extreme scores was significantly higher in this group.

An unpublished study by Carol Spencer of the California Department of Corrections, cited by Megargee *et al.* (1967, p. 528) provided additional data:

In an as yet unpublished study, Spencer compared the O-H scores of 285 young men committed to the California Youth Authority for nonviolent offenses with the scores of 161 offenders committed for assaultive crimes in which injury to the victim was the primary motive. The assaultive Ss had a mean score of 14.94 and the nonviolent offenders a mean of 13.78, a difference which was statistically significant ($p < .001$).

More recently, White (1970) found that Federal prisoners with high *O-H* scores engaged in less aggressive verbalization than did those with low *O-H* scores.

However, Fisher (1970) divided adult felons into three groups: undercontrolled violent, overcontrolled violent, and nonviolent, and failed to find the expected differences on the *O-H* scale. He noted that his undercontrolled group tended to be predominantly Negro and the overcontrolled group white; since the *O-H* scores of Negroes tended to be higher than those of whites, Fisher suggested that race should be taken into account in interpreting the O-H scale. Subsequent research by Haven (1969) has confirmed that there is a small but significant difference between the O-H scores of whites and Negro prisoners.

The fact that preliminary work with the O-H scale has been promising suggests that assessment of violence might proceed better through the development of specialized instruments to measure different violent subtypes and the factors associated with violence, rather than through attempts to construct global scales of violence.

B. The Assessment of Violence with Other Structured Tests

While the MMPI is only one of many structured tests in the clinical psychologist's armament, more research has been done on its relation to violence than with other instruments. Several additional structured tests which show promise for the assessment of violence will be briefly described below; however until more research is undertaken their validity for the prediction of violence, either alone or in combination with other measures, is an open question.

1. The Buss-Durkee Inventory

Potentially, one of the most valuable aspects of the Buss-Durkee (1957) Inventory is that instead of attempting to derive a single overall hostility or aggression score, the test authors have constructed scales to measure several different kinds of hostile-aggressive behavior: assaultiveness, indirect aggression, irritability, negativism, resentment, suspicion, and verbal aggression. In addition they provide a scale to assess guilt over the expression of hostility. Thus the Buss-Durkee Inventory is based on a sounder conception of aggression than most other instruments.

Another valuable feature of the inventory is the attention that was given to item-writing. Not only was an effort made to overcome the influences of social desirability but the items were expressed in an idiomatic fashion which corresponds more closely with everyday language usage than do most test items. Work on the test has proceeded along traditional lines with efforts to determine the reliability of the subscales, their intercorrelations, and the factorial structure of the test. Factor analyses seem to indicate that most of the variance is accounted for by two major factors which have been identified as reflecting hostility and aggression (Buss, 1961), although some investigators prefer to label them overt and covert hostility (Bendig, 1962). Normative research has also been undertaken with data collected from several college and neuro-psychiatric samples (Buss, 1961).

A recent study by Leibowitz (1968) investigated the relationship between the Buss-Durkee Hostility Inventory scales and physical aggression as measured by the Buss Aggression Machine, a device which a subject believes inflicts a painful shock on a fellow subject. None of the correlations between the Buss-Durkee subscales and the scores on the aggression machine attained statistical significance. Of course an instrumental laboratory task such as this only tangentially related to violence if indeed there is any relationship.

More relevant is the study by Miller *et al.* (1960) who included the Buss-Durkee Inventory in their investigation of the differences in test scores between a sample of criminally insane (homicidal) paranoid schizophrenics and a matched sample of noncriminal paranoid schizophrenics. Their data showed that the Buss-Durkee total scores for violent and nonviolent groups overlapped almost exactly, with identical medians and similar ranges. There was a slight tendency for the violent group to have a higher mean score, but the differences between the two groups were not statistically significant.

A study by Buss, Fisher, and Simons (1962) was slightly more encouraging. They correlated the Buss-Durkee scores of 96 neuropsychiatric patients with behavior ratings made by their psychiatrists. While significant correlations were obtained for some subscales, the Assault scale was not one of them. Relatives of the patients were interviewed and, on the basis of these interviews, the investigators rated the patients' behavior. Although Assault scale scores did not correlate significantly with the ratings of aggressive behavior for male patients, a moderate but significant positive correlation ($r = .31$) was obtained for females. Thus the Buss-Durkee Inventory does not appear to be consistently related to violent behavior in neuropsychiatric samples.

2. California Psychological Inventory

Gough's (1960a) California Psychological Inventory (CPI), like the MMPI, is a multiphasic inventory with scales reflecting 18 behavioral dimensions. While the MMPI focuses on psychopathology, the CPI attempts to measure personality traits more relevant to everyday life. A number of the CPI scales assess dimensions such as "socialization," and "self-control," which appear potentially relevant to overt aggression.

The usefulness of the CPI for assessing delinquency has been shown in several different cultures. The CPI Socialization Scale has been particularly useful in this regard. According to Gough, Wenk, and Rozynko (1965, p. 434):

In particular, the So (Socialization) scale (Gough, 1960b; Gough & Peterson, 1952) which rests on an international or role-taking theory of delinquent behavior (Gough, 1948), has proved to be valid for forecasting asocial behavior among children

(Scarpitti, Murray, Dinitz, & Reckless, 1960), incidence of delinquency among military personnel (Datel, 1962), rate of delinquency among military personnel (Knapp, 1963), severity of asocial behavior (Gough, 1960a), delinquency in other cultures (Gough & Sandhu, 1964), and even such specific criteria as cheating on course examinations in college (Hetherington & Feldman, 1964).

Since delinquents are more prone to violence than most groups, the CPI, like the MMPI, is thus useful in discriminating groups of people within which there is likely to be a higher than average incidence of violent behavior. This of course does not indicate the usefulness of the CPI for the assessment of violence in the individual case. Some tangential evidence can be gleaned from a study by Megargee (1966d) who attempted to test implications derived from his hypothesis that both Overcontrolled and Undercontrolled personality types are to be found among extremely assaultive delinquents and criminals. He tested a sample of extremely assaultive juvenile delinquents on a number of projective and structured tests and compared their scores with those obtained by groups of delinquents detained for moderate assaults, incorrigibility, and property offenses. Megargee hypothesized that the extremely assaultive sample, if it indeed included Overcontrolled individuals, would be assessed as being generally better controlled, more conforming, and less aggressive as a group than the others. The CPI was administered as part of the battery and it was hypothesized that the extremely assaultive group would be significantly higher than the others on the Self-Control scale. There was a tendency in this direction, but it did not obtain acceptable levels of significance. Megargee did note, however, that the extremely assaultive group also obtained scores significantly higher than the others on the Responsibility, Well Being, Tolerance, Achievement by Independence, Intellectual Efficiency, and Flexibility scales.

Mizushima and DeVos (1967) compared the CPI scores of 18 Japanese property offenders with those of 14 other Japanese reformatory inmates convicted of "more violent antisocial activity." The property offenders were found to be significantly higher on the Femininity scale and significantly lower on the Social Presence and Self-Acceptance scales. Unpublished research by Gough and Wenk (Gough, 1968, personal communication) suggests that incarcerated murderers may be identified by using deviation scores on the Socialization scale in conjunction with other CPI scales. These findings suggest that the CPI has the potential capacity to discriminate certain types of violent and nonviolent offenders from one another. However, the exact diagnostic patterns must yet be determined.

The CPI appears to be a promising instrument for differentiating certain types of violent from nonviolent criminals. Findings which have emerged from attempts to use the CPI to predict parole success (Gough *et al.*, 1965) and academic achievement (Gough, 1964) suggest that the approach most likely to be successful in predicting different types of violence is to derive a weighted combination of CPI scales, along with other criteria such as scores from other tests and demographic data. Attempts to obtain a single CPI measure which relates to "violence" as if violence were a unidimensional phenomenon are overly simplified and seem unlikely to succeed. Differentiating subtypes of violent or aggressive individuals and then using a number of different predictor variables appears to offer a much higher likelihood of success. At present such research has not been undertaken either with the CPI or any of the other structural tests.

3. The Zaks and Walters Aggression Scale

Zaks and Walters (1959) and Walters and Zaks (1959) have reported the derivation and preliminary validation of a scale for the measurement of aggression. The initial item pool consisted of 33 items regarding aggressive behavior. This set of items along with a number of buffer items was administered to 19 assaultive Negro prisoners and their answers were compared with those of 60 adult noncriminals. Nineteen items discriminated the two groups significantly; of these seven failed to discriminate when control subjects more comparable in socioeconomic status were used, and deletion of these items left a 12-item scale. Preliminary validational work has focused on studies with graduate students, normal and delinquent adolescents, and narcotics addicts. Further research is necessary to determine whether or not this scale relates to violence when criminality and race are controlled.

III. The Assessment of Violence with Projective Techniques

Like structured tests, the so-called "projective techniques" provide the clinician with a sample of behavior which he can use to estimate the likelihood of violence. In this sense, there is no essential difference in the clinical task whether projective or structured techniques are used. However, the nature of the behavior sampled by the projective technique differs in certain salient respects.

Projective tests typically yield rich, complex, and varied responses. Indeed, this is their chief asset for through their very complexity projective tests have the potential to reveal the full richness of the individual's personality dynamics. However, this complexity makes it difficult to treat the resulting data psychometrically. A complex TAT story is hard to reduce to a set of quantitative measurements. The more it is quantified, the more its richness is lost. This has proved to be a major handicap in research that has used projective techniques. Because of the fact that no scoring system is completely satisfactory many investigators have been inspired to attempt to produce better scoring schemes. As a result a variety of scoring systems are available and in common use for most of the major projective techniques. This has the disadvantage of decreasing the generality of results from a study using the scoring methods of one school to a study which may have used the methods of another.

Not only is there disagreement about the optimal method of scoring projective responses, but there is also considerable controversy about how to interpret the resulting data. To cite the most dramatic example, one school of thought holds that aggressive responses on the TAT indicate a propensity for overt aggressive behavior (Atkinson, 1958) while another group maintains just the opposite—namely that aggressive TAT responses may contraindicate the occurrence of overt aggressive behavior (Lazarus, 1961).

Such disagreements stem in part from differences in opinion regarding the determinants of projective responses. Classical projective theory maintains that the projective test stimulus, such as a Rorschach inkblot or a sentence completion stem, are so unstructured and ambiguous that the resulting response is determined only by the respondent's personality patterns. However, Murstein (1963) and others have pointed out that the projective testing situation is really much more structured than it appears; while the examiner may think there are no guidelines, the testing situation provides a great deal of structure even though the immediate stimulus may be ambiguous. The way in which the test is administered and the personality of the examiner can influence projective responses. For example, Lord (1950) found that the method of administration and personality of the examiner could influence the scores obtained on the Rorschach test, while Sanders and Cleveland (1953) demonstrated that the examiner's own hostility influenced the hostility scores obtained by the subject. However, given a standardized administration procedure which is rigorously adhered to, even relatively inexperienced examiners can obtain reliable results on projective tests (Megargee, Lockwood, Cato, & Jones, 1966).

One principle on which every projection tester agrees, however, is the holistic nature of projective tests. While certain hypotheses can be made about how this aspect of a story relates to personality or how that aspect relates to behavior, such hypotheses are always suggestive and clinicians agree that the overall context determines how a particular aspect of the protocol is to be interpreted. Thus the interpretation of projective tests, like that of structured tests, depends upon the skills of a trained and experienced clinician.

As was the case with the structured tests, one of the problems in the projective test literature on violence is the large number of studies which have attempted to relate a single test sign to an overt behavioral criterion. While this is a simple and strightforward validational technique, and indeed one which the present writer has often used, it still represents a distortion of the way the test is used in actual practice. While such single-sign studies are useful, they need to be supplemented by more representative investigations in which a clinician interprets the total test protocol. This is particularly true in the case of projective techniques which may tap deeper levels of the personality, for one part of the test protocol may relate to covert or unconscious tendencies whereas another aspect may be quite accessible to consciousness and reflected in overt behavior (see Rosenzweig, 1950).

These problems of validating projective tests compound the many basic difficulties in predicting violence that we have already discussed. In the pages which follow we shall explore some of the research which has been done on the assessment of violence with the major projective techniques. As with the structured tests, we shall not discuss the literature that relates scores on one projective test to scores on some other test, and we shall deal only briefly with those studies which have correlated test responses to relatively mild forms of aggressive behavior.

A. THE ROSENZWEIG PICTURE-FRUSTRATION STUDY

The Rosenzweig Picture-Frustration Study (*P-F*) was designed to assess the nature and direction of aggressive responses to frustration. The most interesting *P-F* scale to investigators in the field of aggression is the Extrapunitiveness (*E*) scale which indicates aggression directed outward against others. A number of studies have been performed to determine the extent to which this scale relates to overt criteria of aggression and violence. Megargee (1964a, p. 20) summarized the early literature on this issue as follows:

A number of studies on aggression have been made using the Extrapunitiveness (*E*) score of the Rosenzweig Picture-Frustration study. Albee and Goldman (1950), Walker (1951) and Holzberg and Posner (1951) found no significant relationships between the E score and various criteria of aggressive behavior in samples of hospital patients and student nurses. Towner (1950) and Holzberg and Hahn (1952) using mildly delinquent boys and anti-social aggressive psychopathic delinquents respectively found no significant differences between them and appropriate normal control groups.

Kaswan, Wasman and Freedman (1960) studied the relation between the E score and 22 other measures of aggression in a sample of 121 male State prisoners, including 40 aggressive offenders. Only a few relationships were found to be significant and there was no apparent pattern among them.

Three studies, however, have consistently found E% to be lower among people who act out. Angelino (1950) using children classified as disciplinary cases by their teachers found they had a lower E score and higher Impunitiveness (M) score than did children classified as "nonproblem cases," "well adjusted" or "behavior problems." Deming (1960) found that delinquents detained in Juvenile Hall for aggressive offenses had E scores significantly lower than the published norms for the test. While it may be that such cases are indeed intrapsychically less extrapunitive despite their overt behavior . . . it is equally likely that they consciously inhibit anti-social responses on the fairly transparent P-F study when tested in a custodial setting. . . .

Weinberg (1953) . . . used three groups differing in aggressiveness. The first consisted of State prison inmates who could be considered Extremely Assaultive since they were convicted of Assault With a Deadly Weapon, Felonious Assault or Assault with Intent to Kill. His second group consisted of non-assaultive inmates (forgers), and his third group of normals matched for occupation, age, and education. Group I had a mean E score of 7.8, Group II a mean score of 8.6 and Group III a score of 10.4. The E scores of both criminal groups were significantly lower than the normals, as might be expected if they tended to suppress anti-social responses. However, the Extremely Assaultive group was also significantly lower than the non-assaultive criminal group.

Megargee (1964b) studied the P-F scores of four groups of delinquents that differed in overt aggressiveness. The first group consisted of delinquents detained for extremely assaultive crimes such as assault with a deadly weapon and murder; the second group was detained for moderately assaultive offenses such as battery; the third group consisted of delinquents detained for verbally aggressive offenses such as incorrigibility and the fourth group were property offenders. Megargee found no significant differences between the four groups of delinquents. As in the earlier investigators' studies, the delinquents' scores on the E scale all fell below those of the published norms for high school students. To test the hypothesis that dissimulation or distortion of the test responses accounted for the low E scale scores observed, Megargee correlated them with the CPI Good Impression scale, a measure of test-taking defensiveness. He obtained a significant correlation of —.46 which he interpreted as indicating that a defensive test-taking attitude probably accounted for the results. Megargee also correlated the E scale scores with observations of overt verbal and physical aggression; all of the correlations were of a zero order.

A more extreme comparison was made by Mercer and Kyriazis (1962) who compared the scores of physically assaultive prisoners with a group of matched normals. They obtained no significant differences. According to Wolfgang (1967), Rizzo (1961) examined 50 murderers and 30 thieves with the *P-F* Study and found no significant differences. One of the few positive studies was conducted by Peterson, Pittman, and O'Neal (1962) who, on a sample of 19 cases, found assaultive and violent offenders to have higher scores.

Rosenzweig (1950, 1963) has pointed out that an individual can respond to the *P-F* Study at a number of different levels. He may respond: (a) in accord with social expectations, (b) at the overt level, indicating through his responses how he himself would respond in such a situation or (c) at the projective level at which unconscious determinants may come to the fore. All three levels may be used during the course of a test. This of course makes the interpretation of the *P-F* Study much less straightforward than it would appear at first glance. The generally negative results obtained in the studies reviewed above, as well as the frequent findings that the scores for delinquent groups are lower than those obtained by normal groups, suggest that social desirability may well influence these responses as Megargee (1964b) has suggested. Whether or not this is the case, the overall trend of the data in these studies is consistent with Megargee's (1964b) conclusion that the *P-F* Study has relatively little usefulness for the prediction of violence.

B. The Thematic Apperception Test (TAT)

It would be difficult to find a literature more complex and contradictory than that on the Thematic Apperception Test and its relation to overt aggressive behavior. One problem with the TAT literature is that the test is rarely given in a uniform fashion. The TAT was originally designed to be given on two consecutive days with 10 cards administered the first day and 10 on the second. This is rarely done in clinical practice. Most clinicians select from the total set of pictures available a few which they think will be fruitful. Some researchers even devise special TAT-like cards to be used in their studies. Thus "the TAT" refers, in fact, to a loosely related family of tests rather than a single well-defined instrument. Since the nature of the cards strongly influences the types of relationships which are obtained, it is small wonder that contradictory findings have been reported.

Another problem is that the TAT can be analyzed in a number of different ways and at a number of different levels. The most common method of analysis is to identify the central figure in each story and analyze the motives manifested in his behavior in the story. However, it is also possible to simply classify stories for the presence or absence of certain types of content, or to focus on the behavior of the respondent as he answers the stories. Thus "aggression on the TAT" can mean that the central figure in the story engaged in aggressive behavior, or that some figure in the story engaged in aggressive behavior, or that the subject told the story in an insolent fashion. Obviously the differences in the sample of behavior which are chosen for analysis can also influence the results that are obtained.

It was originally hoped by Murray (1943) that the TAT would relate to aspects of the personality which the individual would not, or could not, express in overt behavior. According to this view, material found in the TAT stories would be inversely related to the individual's overt behavior (Lazarus, 1961; Symonds, 1949; Tomkins, 1952). Other workers have challenged this view and argued that the relationship is direct—that is, scenes depicted in the stories are likely to be found in the individual's everyday life (Atkinson, 1958).

Before we review the TAT literature on the assessment of violent tendencies, we should briefly examine some of the factors which have been found to influence the nature of this relationship. A major factor is the nature of the scenes depicted on the different TAT cards. Murstein, David, Fisher, and Furth (1961) have found major differences in the "hostility pull" of the pictures. On some cards it is unusual for a person *not* to tell a story dealing in some way with aggression, while for others aggressive stories are extremely rare.

There is some disagreement in the literature about how such differences in hostility-pull might influence the relationship between apperceptive and overt aggression. Murstein (1963, 1965) is of the opinion that cards which strongly suggest hostility are relatively useless in differentiating overtly hostile subjects from nonaggressive subjects. He suggested that, "When . . . a card is highly unambiguous with regard to hostility, it compels a hostile response not through projection of personal perceptions or attitudes but rather because of respect for the reality consideration of what is obviously there in the picture" (1965, p. 47). On an ambiguous card which does not immediately suggest an aggressive story, however, the presence of an aggressive story can be attributed to the individual's personality dynamics.

Starr (1960) obtained data consistent with Murstein's formulation. He found that overtly hostile neuropsychiatric patients were discriminated from nonhostile patients on the medium- and low-pull cards but not on the high-pull cards. Kaplan (1967), however, found that it was the high-pull cards which best differentiated his samples of high and low hostile students. Similar findings had been obtained by Kagan (1956).

We have noted earlier that overt aggression is the result of both aggressive drives and of inhibitions against the expression of these drives. While it may be, as Murstein suggested, that high-pull cards are relatively ineffectual in measuring aggressive instigation, it could be that these cards differentiate individuals on the basis of inhibitions. As Kagan (1956) and Saltz and Epstein (1963) have suggested, perhaps differences in response to highly suggestive cards are a function of inhibitions or guilt against the expression of aggression and possibly such inhibitions would apply to overt behavior as well. Thus it may be that the low-pull cards measure instigation but the high-pull cards relate to inhibitions. Evidence consistent with this formulation has been obtained by Megargee (1967). Much research remains to be done on this issue. In particular, studies that use overtly aggressive and criminal groups should be conducted to supplement the data collected on student samples.

The nature of the stimulus cards is only one of many factors that influence the relationship between TAT responses and overt behavior. In a sample of neuropsychiatric patients Dalack (1964) found that the relationship between the TAT themes and self reports of hostility was a function of psychiatric condition; there was a large discrepancy between the test measure and the behavioral report in schizophrenics, but the discrepancy was relatively slight in a normal sample. Lesser (1957) found that among boys whose mothers disapproved of overt aggression there was a correlation of −.41 between fantasy and overt aggression, but in another sample of 23 boys whose mothers supported or approved of aggressive behavior a correlation of +.43 was obtained.

Another problem in evaluating the literature is that a variety of criteria of overt aggressive behavior has been used in different studies. In one study an aggressive sample may consist of murderers; in another it may consist of college students who are rated low in friendliness. A study of delinquents' TATs by Megargee and Cook (1967) related four different methods of scoring the TAT for aggression to 11 different criteria of overt aggressive behavior, including self reports, rating by observers, and police records. They found that three of the four TAT scales were positively related to the criterion of school conduct but that no significant relationships were obtained with other criteria. Similar findings were obtained from the analysis of inkblot aggression scores, suggesting once again that aggression is not a unidimensional construct, and that the outcome of a particular study strongly depends on the particular criterion of aggressive behavior which the investigator selects.

Megargee and Cook (1967, p. 48) summarized this rather contradictory literature on the relationship between the TAT and overt aggression as follows:

1. Authorities differ as to the relationship which should be expected between projective test scores and overt behavior, some holding that it should be direct and others that it should be inverse.

2. Empirical studies have generally found either no significant relationships or significant direct ones. The notion of significant inverse relations between projective test measures and overt aggression has received little empirical support (Lindzey & Tejessey, 1956).

3. There is a great deal of diversity in the findings reported. A number of factors apparently influence the relation between projective tests and overt aggressive behavior. These include: a) internal inhibitions against the expression of aggression as measured by inhibitory forces within the test protocol (Mussen & Naylor, 1954; Pittluck, 1950) and by maternal attitudes toward aggressive behavior (Lesser, 1957; Weatherly, 1962); b) the guilt which the subject feels (Saltz & Epstein, 1963); c) social class differences (Mussen & Naylor, 1954); d) the degree to which the stimulus material "pulls" an aggressive response (Haskell, 1961; Kagan, 1956; Murstein, 1963, 1965); e) external factors in the testing situation which might influence the level of response (Megargee, 1964b; Rosenzweig, 1950); f) the criterion of aggression used (Haskell, 1961); g) whether the aggressive act is a product of excessive or inadequate controls (Megargee, 1966d).

Megargee and Cook might have added to this list the age of the subject and the nature of the population which is investigated, for these factors, too, could significantly influence the outcome of the study.

In the pages that follow we shall review some of the studies on the relationship between various TAT measures and overt aggressive and violent behavior. We shall first review studies which have focused on neuropsychiatric patients and, next, studies that have used juvenile delinquents or adult criminals in their subject pool. Studies that have focused on aggression in normal samples will not be covered in this review. Within each category we shall first examine studies which attempted to correlate some simple measure of TAT aggression to the criterion; then we will turn our attention to studies which have used more complex ratio scores, where forces within the protocol which contraindicate aggression are balanced against those forces which do suggest aggressive tendencies.

1. TAT Studies Using Neuropsychiatric Patients

Psychiatric patients have been a favorite source of subjects for investigations of the relationship between the TAT and overt aggressive behavior. Living in a controlled environment under constant observation, outbursts of overt violence are easily detected. Thus, it is often possible for nurses and ward attendants to make reliable and accurate ratings of the patients' propensities for violence. Since many patients are examined routinely with the TAT, test data are readily available. The disadvantage of using psychiatric patients is that results found on this specialized group may not be generalizable to normal groups who live in more typical circumstances.

The summary which follows is based in part on the excellent reviews of the earlier literature by Buss (1961) and Murstein (1963). For more detailed accounts of studies published prior to 1962, the reader is referred to these reviews or to the original articles. One of the earliest studies of the relationship between the TAT and overt violence was contributed by Scodel and Lipetz (1957) who compared violent and nonviolent schizophrenic patients. The stories were scored using the Stone Aggressive Content Scale (Stone, 1956) and no significant differences were found between the groups. A similar study was carried out by Ramachandra Rao (1964) who compared aggressive schizophrenics with a matched nonviolent group and found no significant differences in aggressive content on five TAT cards. Minuchin (1950) obtained a positive association between fantasy aggression and reports of spontaneous aggressive behavior on the wards in a sample of 72 psychiatric patients. However, he found it was necessary to consider the aggressive content in relation to modifying mechanisms such as the patient's rejection, denial, or justification of the aggression.

Other studies have employed more complex scoring systems for the TAT. One of the earliest was that of Pittluck (1950) who attempted to improve the prediction of aggressive behavior by computing the ratio of the number of punishment themes to the number of aggressive themes. She computed a large number of tests of statistical significance of which only a chance number attained respectable confidence limits. However this work has served as an inspiration to others to attempt more complex ratio scoring. One such study was that of Haskell (1961). He scored the TAT protocols of 38 hospitalized schizophrenics, using both simple aggression scores and the more complex ratio scores proposed by Pittluck. These scores were related to ratings of overt aggressive behavior. While the simple aggression scores did not correlate significantly with the criterion of overt aggressive behavior, the ratio scores did correlate with ratings based on the social history, and with the nurses' ratings of ward behavior.

MacCasland (1961) related similar TAT ratios to observers' checklists and ratings of overt aggressive behavior in a sample of 30 disturbed boys. She found a positive relationship between the TAT measures and the overt aggressive behavior.

Miller (1953) related the TAT aggression of a sample of disturbed adolescents in a summer camp to counselors' ratings of physical aggression. He found significantly more TAT aggression among boys who were high in overt aggressive behavior. The findings of this study must be accepted with reservations, however, since Miller accepted as significant a probability level considerably higher than that which is customary (12%).

Murstein (1963, p. 305) has. concluded that "the work with patients indicates first that the TAT is more sensitive to aggression displayed in a natural setting than in a controlled environment such as the hospital." He suggests that the failure to find more positive results may result from the fact that behavior ratings are often made by nurses, who are relatively unsophisticated observers, as well as the possibility that the administration of tranquilizing medication has diminished the amount of violence.

2. Studies of Juvenile Delinquents and Adult Criminals

Weissman (1964) compared the TATs of four groups of adolescents: aggressive juvenile delinquents, less aggressive juvenile delinquents, aggressive high school students, and less aggressive high school students. A number of TAT measures were employed. On the most typical measure, the number of aggressive stories, no significant difference was found between the aggressive and nonaggressive delinquents. However, a significant difference was found between the aggressive and the non-aggressive high school students and between the aggressive delinquents and the nonaggressive high school students. Some other TAT measures such as reaction time, verbal productivity and the like also attain significance in some of the comparisons which were performed.

Mussen and Naylor (1954) scored the TATs of lower class delinquents' aggressive themes and the ratio of punishment-aggression themes and related these scores to observations of overt aggressive behavior made by the counselors in a juvenile hall setting. Noting that a number of previous studies on middle class adolescents had failed to show any significant relationships between TAT and overt aggression, Mussen and Naylor reasoned that this might be because middle class subjects are too inhibited to express aggression overtly even though they may express it in fantasy material. By using a sample of lower class delinquents, they felt that they would be dealing with a less inhibited group in which a positive association between TAT and overt aggression might be found. Whether or not it was because of such social class differences, Mussen and Naylor did obtain the relationship which they had hypothesized. A significant positive association between TAT and overt aggressive behavior was found, but the relationship between overt aggression and the TAT punishment aggression ratio fell short of acceptable limits of significance.

Megargee and Cook (1967) as part of their study replicated the Mussen and Naylor investigation using the same scales for scoring the TAT stories that Mussen and Naylor had devised. As noted above, the Megargee and Cook investigation related the TAT scores to 11 different criteria of overt aggression. Included in these criterion measures were the same behavior checklists and ratings filled out by juvenile hall counselors that Mussen and Naylor had utilized. In addition there were other indices of aggression including ratings of school conduct, delinquency records and, most important, the violence of the offense for which the delinquent was confined. While Mussen and Naylor's subjects had all been detained for relatively minor offenses, Megargee and Cook's sample included groups detained for extremely assaultive homicidal offenses, as well as for moderately assaultive, verbally aggressive, and nonviolent offenses. The Megargee and Cook investigation failed to replicate Mussen and Naylor's findings. The Mussen and Naylor Aggressive Content scale failed to relate significantly to any of the 11 criteria used, including those based on the Mussen and Naylor investigation. Similarly the punishment-aggression ratio failed to relate to any of the criteria used.

Marquis (1960) also failed to find a positive association between a TAT measure of outwardly directed aggression and ratings of overt aggressive behavior in a sample of acting out youngsters with traumatic backgrounds. Indeed, he obtained a reverse relationship, with the TAT aggression score relating *positively* to constructive behavior and *negatively* to disruptive behavior. He noted that this might be a function of the particular sample which he was studying.

Marquis did obtain a significant positive relationship between overt aggression and a TAT measure which he labeled "resistance" which included failure to respond to the cards and failure to cooperate with the examiner who was administering the test. Obviously this sample of test behavior is much more similar to the criterion behavior. The finding is reminiscent of Jensen's (1957) study of the relationship between overt and fantasy aggression in high school students. He found that the usual measures of TAT aggression did not discriminate high school students who were high in overt aggressive behavior. However, a measure based on the amount of swearing during the test and the use of tabooed themes of sex, violence, and the like, did differentiate between the groups.

Stone (1953, 1956) studied the TAT protocols of three groups of military prisoners. The most aggressive group consisted of men convicted of murder and assault, all of whom had at least two prior offenses. The medium aggressive group consisted of men who had gone absent without leave (AWOL) or deserted at least three times, while the least aggressive group consisted of men who had gone AWOL or deserted while in combat. On the TAT the assaultive group had significantly more fantasy aggression on Stone's Aggressive Content scale than did either of the other two groups.

3. Conclusions Regarding the TAT

We stated at the outset that the TAT literature is complex and often contradictory. The fact that significant differences have been obtained in some studies suggests that the material elicited by the TAT is potentially capable of discriminating some types of violent people. Much more research needs to be done, however. It would help if this research could be of a programmatic type in which one study builds upon the results of a previous study. One of the major difficulties in arriving at general conclusions on the basis of the literature is that a variety of TAT-like stimuli have been used, and the resulting stories have been subjected to such a variety of different scoring systems and related to such diverse criteria. The more investigators can use commonly agreed upon procedures, the sooner a consistent and interpretable literature will accumulate. Unfortunately, too many investigators have engaged in "one shot" studies and left the field without following up on the results of their research.

It is clear from the research on stimulus characteristics that much closer attention must be paid to the nature of the pictures to which the subjects respond. It was suggested earlier that perhaps aggressive themes in response to "low-pull" cards reflect instigation, while a lack of aggressive themes in response to "high-pull" cards reflects inhibitions. The practicing clinical psychologist frequently interprets a protocol in this fashion, but as yet no research studies have been designed which adequately test this hypothesis. Some studies have looked at instigation and others have focused on guilt or inhibition, but as yet no studies have attempted to integrate the two in conjunction with the type of card used.[4]

Another problem with the literature is that, almost without exception, studies have examined the relationship between certain quantitative TAT scoring categories and overt aggression; few have examined the relationship between clinical interpretations of the TAT and violent behavior. In practice, however, it is the clinical interpretation of the TAT that is used to predict aggression, and it is this interpretation which needs to be validated. If it can be demonstrated that clinicians can predict violent behavior with the TAT plus other relevant tests and data, then the signs and cues which the clinicians are using can be determined. The studies by Marquis (1960) and Jensen (1957), for example, suggest that it is not the story content but the behavior and attitude of the individual while telling the stories which may be the most important sample of behavior elicited by the TAT.

[4] Some studies have globally examined ratios of inhibitory tendencies to excitatory themes. However the measures of inhibitory tendencies have not consisted of the *absence* of aggression themes to high-pull cards but of the *presence* of punishment themes.

C. The Assessment of Violence with Inkblot Techniques:
The Rorschach Test and Holtzman Inkblot Technique

A number of studies have investigated the relationships between inkblot perception and violent behavior. As was the case with the TAT, most studies have focused on neuropsychiatric patients and on criminal samples. Two broad aspects of inkblot responses and scores have been used: content scores and formal scores. We shall investigate each in turn.

1. *Inkblot Content Scores*

A number of investigations have focused on the relationship between aggressive or hostile content on the Rorschach and Holtzman Inkblots and various types of overt aggressive behavior. Most investigators have not been content with the scales devised by other investigators and consequently have devised their own adaptations of these scales. Most of the scales are based on the original hostility scale devised by Elizur (1949) and most of these systems are closely related. Megargee and Cook (1967) scored the HIT records of a sample of 76 male juvenile delinquents on five inkblot scales devised by Elizur (1949), Hafner and Kaplan (1960), Holtzman, Thorpe, Swartz, and Herron (1961), Murstein (1956), and Finney (1955). They found that the correlations between the different scales ranged from .55 to .94 with a median value of .77. The Hafner and Kaplan, Holtzman and Murstein scales were so alike as to be virtually interchangable. A factor analysis showed them all loading on the same factor with loadings ranging from .81 to .92. In short, while the scales are not identical, most of the inkblot scales which have been devised are sufficiently similar that we can treat this family of scales as a unit. It is unlikely that the substitution of one scale for another would lead to radically different results.

Buss (1961) has reviewed the literature in this area and reported on the relationship of some of these inkblot aggressive content scales to measures of aggressiveness in normal samples. Generally the criterion consisted of self-ratings or questionnaire measures. One study by Smith and Coleman (1956) did study physical aggression, and in this investigation of remedial reading students a positive contingency coefficient of .54 was found between hostile content on the Rorschach and physical aggressiveness.

Studies dealing with violence have generally used samples of either neuropsychiatric patients or delinquents. We shall investigate the studies on neuropsychiatric patients first. Using a modification of the Elizur scale, R. G. Walker (1951) correlated the hostility of the Rorschach responses of 40 Veterans Administration psychiatric patients with ratings of hostility made by their psychotherapists and obtained a significant positive correlation of .50. Wolf (1957) compared the scores of assaultive neuropsychiatric patients with a matched nonassaultive sample and found that the assaultive group had significantly higher scores. Using the Palo Alto Aggressive Content scale, Storment and Finney (1953) found a highly significant ($p < .001$) difference between the mean scores of assaultive and nonassaultive neuropsychiatric patients. In a subsequent study on a new sample (Finney, 1955) this difference shrank until it fell just short of significance at the .05 level. Townsend (1967) found that aggressive content did not differentiate between aggressive and non-aggressive boys in a residential treatment center. Wirt (1956) also studied the Palo Alto scale in an attempt to demonstrate that aggressiveness in Rorschach responses increases as a function of psychopathology. Unfortunately for his theory he found the neurotics scored higher than schizophrenics, who in turn scored higher than normals. Whether this indicates that the scale or the theory is invalid is, of course, impossible to say.

In another study using psychiatric patients Towbin (1959) devised three scales. The first, based on the Elizur scale, focused on both the content and on hostile remarks made during the test administration. His criterion of assaultiveness consisted of ward reports; patients who had at least two outbursts of violence in the preceding four months were included in the assaultive sample. Towbin found that the assaultive patients were significantly higher than a matched sample of nonassaultive patients on this scale. Towbin also used two other scales, one based on counting the number of perceived objects with an aggressive function, and another based on hostility directed from the card towards the test respondent. Neither of these scales significantly differentiated between assaultive and nonassaultive psychiatric patients.

By and large then, studies relating the Rorschach content scales to criteria of overt violence in hospitalized psychiatric patients have been encouraging. However, content scales are not difficult to distort if the respondent should want to dissimulate. Within a psychiatric setting, patients are often freer to indicate aggressive or pathological tendencies than is the case elsewhere. For this reason, we should not be too bold in generalizing from studies conducted in psychiatric settings to situations in which the respondent may be more motivated to conceal or disguise any evidence of possible disturbance.

Turning to studies of delinquents and criminals, the Elizur scale has also been used in this setting. Gorlow, Zimet, and Fine (1952) compared the scores of juvenile delinquents with a contrast group of nondelinquents. Despite the fact that the delinquents had fewer responses on the Rorschach, they had a significantly higher number of hostile responses.

A similar study by Megargee (1965b) compared the Holtzman Hostility scale scores of delinquents, many of whom were extremely assaultive, with the normative scores obtained by Holtzman *et al.* (1961) on samples of nondelinquent seventh and eleventh graders. While statistically significant differences were obtained on a number of HIT scales, there were no significant differences in hostile content. It is possible that this discrepancy between Megargee's study and that of Gorlow, Zimet and Fine is the result of differences between the Rorschach and the Holtzman Inkblot techniques.

Stone (1953) compared the Rorschach responses of the same three groups of army prisoners that he used in his TAT study. It will be recalled that Stone employed one group of extremely assaultive prisoners, another group of antisocial prisoners characterized by chronic AWOL and desertion, and a third group of relatively nonaggressive prisoners who went AWOL from a combat situation. He called these his high aggressive, medium aggressive, and low aggressive groups, respectively. When Stone compared the Rorschach content of the three groups, he found that the medium aggressive group had the highest scores, followed by the most aggressive group, with the least aggressive group being lowest. Stone had predicted that the highly aggressive group would score low, on the supposition that the recent expression of their aggressive impulses would lower their aggressive instigation. However the pattern of the data was not in line with either this hypothesis or with the hypothesis that there should be a linear relationship between the amount of aggression expressed in Rorschach content and that expressed in overt behavior.[5]

In a broad study Megargee and Cook (1967) scored the Holtzman Inkblot Technique protocols of 75 juvenile delinquents on five aggressive content scales. These included the Elizur scale, the Murstein scale, the Hafner and Kaplan scale, the Holtzman *et al.* scale and the Palo Alto Aggressive Content scale. These inkblot scales were related to 11 different criteria of overt aggressive behavior, including the offenses for which the boys were detained (which ranged from incorrigibility to murder), school conduct and attendance reports, the degree of delinquency as determined by the sentence imposed on each boy, reports of the incidence of overt verbal and physical aggression during detention, and ratings of self-reported aggression based on structured interviews with each boy. A number of significant relationships between some of the inkblot scales

[5] Stone's data (1953) cannot be accounted for on the basis of supposing that the most assaultive group might have contained Chronically Overcontrolled Assaultive prisoners, for the criterion of habitual violence which Stone used would have excluded such individuals.

and some of the criteria of overt aggression were obtained. The inkblot scales did not relate to the violence of the boy's present offense, nor to the disposition of his case, nor to ratings of school conduct and attendence prior to the offense. Significant positive relationships were obtained between the Hafner and Kaplan and the Murstein scales and the boys' self-reports of the amount of physical aggression they engaged in against peers and adults. While a *positive* relationship was obtained between these scales and self-confessed aggression, a significant *negative* relationship was obtained between several scales and observations of overt physical aggression in detention. The Elizur scale, the Holtzman *et al.* scale, and the Murstein scale all had an inverse relationship to the amount of overt physical aggression the boys engaged in while in detention.

Since the scales differed in the degree to which they related to the criteria of overt aggression, and since the nature of the relationships varied as a function of the criterion used, it would appear from Megargee and Cook's data that one reason for the diversity which has been noted in the literature is the variety of operational definitions of overt aggression and of test aggression which have been used. Megargee and Cook pointed out:

the results clearly show that "overt aggression" is hardly a unitary variable and that the relation of "fantasy" to "overt" aggression varied widely. Depending on the criterion measure used, this relationship could be significantly positive, significantly negative or non-existent; studies employing only one or two criteria could have obtained quite different results [1967, p. 58].

To summarize implications of this study which, as noted above, investigated four TAT aggression scales as well as the five inkblot scales, Megargee and Cook (1967, p. 58) concluded:

For the clinician who might wish to use these scales in the prediction of overt aggression in the individual case, the results are quite discouraging. The paucity of significant findings, the low order of those which were obtained, and the contradictory modes of relationship to the criteria all suggest that the task of behavioral prediction with these instruments is one to be approached with a great deal of caution.

This limitation should not be interpreted to mean that the TAT and HIT are useless when it comes to predicting aggression. It may be that in another setting with a less defensive clientele these scales could be useful predictors. Or, within a custodial setting, use of these tests in a global manner by a skilled clinician might show better results . . . or it is possible the use of determinant scores in addition to aggressive content as was done by Finney (1955), Haskell (1961) and Sommer and Sommer (1958) might prove a better approach. It remains for future research to determine if this is the case.

According to Buss (1961, p. 131) a scale devised by DeVos (1952) has been used in two unpublished doctoral dissertations investigating assaultive and nonassaultive prisoners. Kane (1955) found that assaultive male prisoners were significantly higher on the DeVos scale than a matched group of nonassaultive prisoners. Sjostedt (1955) obtained similar results comparing assaultive women prisoners with acquisitive women prisoners.

In addition to hostile content scales, two other types of content have been studied. The first is the so-called "Barrier" score which is supposed to reflect the individual's body image. Fisher and Cleveland (1958) indicated that subjects with high Barrier scores expressed their anger outwardly, yet Brodie (1959) noted that subjects with low Barrier scores tended to be more impulsive and angry. Megargee (1965c) attempted to resolve this difference by investigating the relationship between Barrier scores and violence in juvenile delinquents. Megargee (1965c) found a moderate but significant negative correlation ($r = -.23$) between Barrier scores and ratings of aggressiveness while in detention. He also found the less delinquent juveniles had significantly higher Barrier scores.

The incidence of anatomical content has also been suggested as possibly being related to overt aggression (Phillips & Smith, 1953). This hypothesis has been tested in three studies. Wolf (1957) found that the incidence of anatomical content did not differentiate assaultive from nonassaultive neuropsychiatric patients, and Megargee (1964a) found no significance or differences, or indeed trends, when he compared delinquents confined for extremely assaultive offenses, moderately assaultive offenses, property offenses, or incorrigibility. Similarly Townsend (1967) found no significant differences in samples of aggressive and nonaggressive boys tested in a residential treatment center. Thus there has been no support for the notion that anatomical content on inkblot tests is related to violence.

As we have noted at several points in this discussion, one of the drawbacks of focusing on content scales in inkblot examinations is that it is not too difficult for the patient to manipulate the content as he sees fit. Indeed this may be one reason for the discrepancies between the studies of psychiatric patients and those of criminals and delinquents. For this reason the formal scoring categories of inkblot tests may be more useful in differentiating violent from nonviolent criminals, if their validity can be established. Unlike the content scores, the perceptual determinants are extremely subtle and much less likely to be manipulated by the client. Several studies have dealt with the formal inkblot scores and we shall turn to them now.

2. Assessment of Violence Using Formal Rorschach Scores

Formal Rorschach scoring requires the services of a trained examiner and scorer. It is more difficult to use than the content schemes which have been proposed, most of which can be scored by a well-trained undergraduate. Moreover the different schools of scoring and interpretation that sprang up following Hermann Rorschach's premature death have produced subtle differences between the schemes used by different practitioners such as Klopfer and Beck. The fact that not all Rorschachers can agree on which is the best formal scoring system has tended to decrease the amount of research on the formal scoring and aggression.

Unlike the quantitative content scoring systems, formal Rorschach scoring does not easily lend itself to quantification. The "scores" which result are typically nothing more than frequency counts of the number of responses which fall into various categories. Unlike the content systems, there is very little in the way of differential weighting of responses. The scores which result are highly dependent upon the total number of responses in a record. For example, there will usually be more movement responses in a record that has 50 responses overall than there will be in a record containing only 10 or 12 responses. In interpreting the greater number of movement scores in the former record it is therefore problematical whether one is interpreting movement *per se* or simply productivity (Cronbach, 1949). Moreover, simply taking the percentage of movement responses does not solve this problem because typically there is a curvilinear relationship between certain scoring categories and the total number of responses (Holtzman *et al.*, 1961).

In an effort to overcome some of the psychometric inadequacies of the Rorschach test, Holtzman *et al.* (1961) have devised a new inkblot test, the Holtzman Inkblot Technique. On the HIT, a quantitative scoring system is used. Since the subject is limited to one response on each of the 45 cards, the influence of differences in number of responses is minimized. However, differences in the number of words uttered in response to any given card can still influence the test results considerably (Megargee, 1966b). A simplified and more objective administration system has served to decrease the interexaminer differences so often observed on the Rorschach (Megargee *et al.*, 1966).

Partly because of the psychometric inadequacies of the Rorschach technique, the literature on the relation of formal Rorschach scores to violence is not characterized by the rigor and attention to experimental methodology found in the literature on the content scales. In addition to the problems in statistical analysis, which might be expected on the basis of the difficulty in scoring the Rorschach, some studies also lack adequate contrast groups.

In the literature on the relationship of violence to formal Rorschach scores, attention has centered on three of the many Rorschach variables: color, movement, and human content. We shall examine the studies dealing with each of these aspects of the Rorschach in turn before turning our attention to two studies in which formal scoring characteristics are examined in conjunction with content variables.

a. Color Scores. One of the most important aspects of the individual's Rorschach protocol is the manner in which he deals with the chromatic cards. According to traditional Rorschach lore, relatively uncontrolled use of color is likely to be found more in individuals who tend to be impulsive. Thus we might expect such uncontrolled color to be more characteristic of violent individuals. Rabin (1946) reported a detailed Rorschach study of a single individual who committed murder and later suicide. This analysis later indicated that color was indeed one of the salient variables which marked the changes in his mood state as he approached violence. Wolfgang (1967) has reported on the results of a study by Rizzo and Ferracuti (1959) in which the Rorschach protocols of 40 thieves and 160 criminals who committed crimes against the person were compared with those of 400 normals. According to Wolfgang's report (1967, p. 156), "In 33 percent of the subjects who had committed murder or attempted murder, pure color and color-form responses were more frequent than form-color responses, while the percentage for the thieves was 25%." This predominance of color-dominated in contrast to the form-dominated responses would be consistent with Rorschach theory. Townsend (1967) compared formal Rorschach characteristics with ratings of overt aggressive behavior in a sample of 63 boys at a residential treatment center. She found significantly more records with two or more color-form responses in the more aggressive group.

Megargee (1966d) also examined the incidence of color responses in an effort to test his hypothesis that extremely assaultive juvenile delinquents would be more controlled as a group than would delinquents detained for moderately assaultive offenses, property offenses, or incorrigibility. This hypothesis was based on Megargee's theory that some extremely assaultive individuals are characterized by chronic overcontrol, and, as a result, aggressive instigation accumulates to the point where it overwhelms rigid defenses (Megargee, 1965a, 1966d). Since color is thought to be related to lack of control, Megargee hypothesized that the extremely assaultive group would have lower color scores and fewer pure color responses. The differences between the groups in the total color score were in the predicted direction, but were not statistically significant. However, the incidence of pure color responses was significantly lower in the extremely assaultive group as compared with the moderately assaultive group and there was a noteworthy trend in this direction when the extremely assaultive group was compared with the other three groups combined. Thus the results tended to bear out the interpretation that inkblot color scores are related to impulsivity and lack of control, assuming Megargee's theory to be correct. This also demonstrates that violence can stem from a number of different causes so that direct linear relations between test scores and violence are not to be expected. Among Undercontrolled assaultive individuals (who probably made up the samples tested by Townsend) we would expect a greater incidence of this sort of color response, while among the Overcontrolled Assaultive type we would expect a lower incidence. This demonstrates once again why the intervention of a skilled clinical interpreter is necessary if test data are to be translated into meaningful diagnostic statements.

b. *Movement Scores.* Another area of major interest to inkblot testers is the degree to which the subject describes his percepts as if they were alive or engaged in movement. This is thought to be related to the "introversive experience type" in which the individual is turned inward upon himself and relies more on inner imaginal resources than on external stimulation. One would expect movement scores to be lower among Undercontrolled assaultive individuals, but, according to Megargee's (1966d) theory, such scores should be higher in the Overcontrolled Assaultive type. The data are consistent with this view. Townsend (1967) found significantly less movement among her aggressive subjects. Megargee (1966d) hypothesized that his extremely assaultive group would have significantly more movement than his other samples of delinquents. There was an appropriate trend in the data but it failed to attain significance. However, introversion and extratension are best measured by the relative balance of movement and color in the record, according to traditional Rorschach theory. When Megargee (1966d) investigated the movement-color balance, he found a much higher predominance of movement in relation to color among the extremely assaultive delinquents than among the other groups of delinquents. He interpreted this as support for his notion that some extremely assaultive groups are overcontrolled. Thus movement also appears to be sensitive to differences in control and mode of emotional expression within criminal samples. However, different dynamic patterns can be associated with different types of aggressive individuals.

c. *Human Content.* It has been suggested in the literature that those who commit assaultive crimes of violence against others should have Rorschachs which indicate a lack of concern with people. This should be manifested by a relative absence of human content in the protocol. Several studies have investigated this hypothesis. Perdue (1961, 1964) reported normative data on 47 murderers and, later, on 100 murderers (including the first 47). These reports consisted primarily of reporting the average incidence of various signs in the sample. According to Perdue the records of murderers which he obtained were characterized by a relatively high amount of human content. This is discrepant with theory and with others' findings. The fact that Perdue apparently administered the Rorschachs as well as scored them, and the fact that no contrast or comparison groups were used, diminishes the reliability of this finding.

Wolfgang (1967) reported a study by Serebrinsky (1941) in which it was found that murderers produce only half the amount of human content found in other criminals.

d. Other Rorschach Categories. In a study already discussed, Storment and Finney (1953) investigated the differences in 26 formal Rorschach scores between 23 violent and 23 nonviolent Veterans Administration patients. They found no statistically significant differences on any of the formal scores, including color, movement and human content.

The literature on the use of formal Rorschach categories among violent and nonviolent criminals thus suggests that some of these formal content categories might be useful in discriminating violent from nonviolent offenders. However the need for further, better controlled quantitative research is obvious. It is apparent from the multiplicity of signs which have been suggested, as well as from the fact that assaultive offenders with different etiologies apparently have different sets of Rorschach signs associated with them, that the assessment of potential violence with projective tests requires the services of a skilled projective tester. It is unlikely that any simple actuarial formula can be devised that will accurately differentiate violent from nonviolent individuals.

The trend in the data also suggests that further research may show that content scales are more useful among psychiatric patients while formal scores are more useful among criminal samples. If this is borne out by further research, it could be because of different response sets operating in different settings. While the relatively transparent content scales may work well in a psychiatric setting where individuals may be less motivated to dissimulate, the subtler formal scores may be more useful in dealing with criminal samples. Evidence relevant to this hypothesis comes from a study by Pattie (1954) who administered the Rorschach to 14 undergraduates. He then hypnotized them and told them that they would wake up feeling hostile and angry. He retested them while they were in the hostile, angry mood state. This manipulation yielded a twofold increase in hostile content for eight of the subjects. However, there was no change in the color scores. Assuming that the posthypnotic suggestion resulted in a change in role-playing behavior, this demonstrated that content scores may be affected by role-playing but that the determinant scores such as color are less likely to be so distorted.

In the typical Rorschach or Holtzman examination, the psychologist does not interpret only the determinants or only the content, but instead integrates both into a dynamic formulation. Two studies have dealt with a combination of selected determinant and content variables, and both have demonstrated the increase in predictability which comes from such an integration. Piotrowski and Abrahamsen (1952) examined the records of 134 sex criminals and selected 100 in which there were adequate samples of movement responses. They then differentiated the protocols on the basis of whether the movement was expansive or non-expansive, that is whether the inkblot figure was acting on the environment or was relatively passive. In 84% of the cases examined, they found support for their hypothesis that expansive movement would be associated with aggressive behavior under the influence of alcohol. While this study should be replicated, it does demonstrate how the integration of several different variables, in this case formal Rorschach scores, Rorschach content, and the influence of alcohol, might be associated with overt aggressive behavior while simpler relationships cannot be found.

Another study was one conducted by Sommer and Sommer (1958). While Piotrowski and Abrahamsen have confided themselves to an examination of different types of movement responses Sommer and Sommer explored different types of color responses. Given that a response was determined by color, they differentiated those in which the color was of an explosive variety (i.e., of a volcano) and those in which the color was nonexplosive (i.e, ice cream). They found that the explosive color responses were significantly associated with violent behavior on the ward in their sample of neuropsychiatric patients. However, the relationship between these Rorschach categories and verbal aggressiveness was not significant. Once again this demonstrates how investigations which take into account the interactions between different aspects of the test, thereby more closely matching the holistic interpretation which takes place in clinical practice, show more potential for the possible prediction of violent behavior. Of course it should be pointed out that, as was the case with almost all the studies which we have examined, Sommer and Sommer were postdicting aggressive behavior and that successful *post*diction does not necessarily imply that *pre*diction is possible. Moreover the demonstration of significant group differences does not necessarily mean that accurate predictions can be made which will be satisfactory for use in the individual case. However the data which are available do indicate that the Rorschach and the Holtzman inkblot techniques provide data which apparently differs as a function of propensity to violence. Therefore with further research there is the potential of possibly deriving violence indicators using this raw material.

D. THE HAND TEST

The Hand Test is a recently developed projective instrument which shows considerable promise for the assessment of aggressive behavior. The test consists of nine drawings of hands and the examinee is asked to indicate what he thinks the hands are doing (Bricklin, Piotrowski, & Wagner, 1962). Research on the relationship between the Hand Test and aggressive or violent behavior has been stimulated by the fact that an objective scoring system has been provided for the Hand Test which purports to measure aggression and acting-out tendencies. Moreover, unlike many projective tests, the manual for the Hand Test reports normative and experimental data on populations of prison inmates and parolees.

Some of the initial normative data on the Hand Test suggests that it may be potentially useful in the study of violence. For example, Bricklin *et al.* (1962) reported that prison inmates have a higher proportion of aggressive responses in their records than do normal subjects. Moreover the mean "Acting Out Scores" (AOS) of prison inmates and of acting-out hospital patients were significantly higher than were the AOS scores of normals and nonacting-out hospital patients.

As we have seen, the most difficult discriminations are between different criminal groups. Some work has been done on the Hand Test in an attempt to differentiate between such groups. When comparing a group of 37 recidivists with a group of 37 nonrecidivists, Bricklin found the recidivists to have a significantly higher mean AOS. However, most of the other Hand Test scoring categories failed to differentiate between the two groups. Bricklin and his associates also investigated the relationship between the Hand Test and the nature of the last crime which had been committed by each subject. They reported:

The results were encouraging in this area. The highest mean acting out score of +5 was had by those men who committed rape, the next highest score (+3.2) was had by those men who committed armed robbery. Ranked in terms of third highest to lowest in acting out score, the list follows with: grand larceny, passing bad checks, burglary, breaking and entering, alcohlism, and last with a mean acting out score of −2.00, vagrancy and manslaughter (there was only one case of manslaughter). These figures will be seen to reflect the interpersonal (and aggressive) nature of the crimes. Rape, which is a highly aggressive and directly interpersonal crime, leads the list. Armed robbery follows. Grand larceny, bad checks, burglary, and breaking and entering, occupy mid-positions. Alcoholism and vagrancy are at the bottom of the list [Bricklin, Piotrowski, & Wagner, 1962, p. 41].

Wagner and Medredeff (1963) reported on an attempt to differentiate aggressive from nonaggressive undifferentiated schizophrencis on the basis of the Hand Test acting out score. They found that the AOS correctly classified 67% of the cases and that the differences between the two groups were significant ($p < .01$). In a subsequent study Wagner and Hawkins (1964) administered the Hand Test to 30 assaultive delinquents and 30 nonassaultive delinquents. There were no significant differences between the groups in age, number of convictions, and intelligence or social class. They found that the acting out score successfully differentiated 47 of the 60 subjects, a finding which are statistically significant ($p < .001$).

Hodge, Wagner, and Schreiner (1966) attempted to validate the aggression score by means of hypnotically inducing an aggressive state in seven college students. When this was done a significant increase in the aggression scores on the Hand Test was noted. Whether this finding indicates the validity of the Hand Test or whether it indicates it is susceptable to role-playing is an interesting question. It will be recalled that in a study of the Rorschach, Pattie (1954) found that the Rorschach aggressive content scales were influenced by hypnotically induced aggression but that the Rorschach determinant scores were not.

In another study of recidivism, Wetsel, Shapiro, and Wagner (1967) reported that the acting out scores significantly differentiated delinquent recidivists from nonrecidivists, correctly categorizing 66% of the subjects. The Hand Test aggression score also differentiated the two groups successfully. In evaluating this study, our earlier discussion of base rates should be recalled. This study, like many of the Hand Test studies, used equal numbers of recidivists and nonrecidivists. Given this base rate of 50%, it will be recalled that a test with even moderate validity can often achieve impressive results; however given a lower base rate, as is often the case in the prediction of violence, the same test might be considerably less useful.

Brodsky and Brodsky (1967) studied the relationship between the Hand Test acting out score and the offense type in a sample of 614 military prisoners. They found significant differences between the mean acting out score of prisoners who had committed offenses against people and against property, and between subjects who were later found to be model prisoners and those who were disciplinary offenders. While the mean differences were statistically significant, Brodsky and Brodsky noted considerable overlap in the distributions of the scores in the different anti-social groups. They concluded, "the acting out score was felt to be of questionable value in predicting individual anti-social behavior in confinement" (Brodsky & Brodsky, 1967, p. 39).

Drummond (1966) attempted to replicate the study which found the Hand Test to differentiate aggressive from nonaggressive schizophrenics using a sample of 66 undifferentiated schizophrenics in an English mental hospital. While the earlier investigations had reported that the Hand Test could differentiate between aggressive and nonaggressive schizophrenics, Drummond reported that the scores on his investigation were quite similar for both the aggressive and the nonaggressive groups.

The literature on the Hand Test is still too incomplete to come to any conclusions about its ability to predict violence. However, the studies which have been done suggest that it may have the potential to discriminate differences in aggressiveness within criminal samples. Certainly further research, hopefully attempting to differentiate types of violent offenders, should be carried out using this promising new instrument.

IV. Conclusions

Thus far no structured or projective test scale has been derived which, when used alone, will predict violence in the individual case in a satisfactory manner. Indeed, none has been developed which will adequately *post*dict, let alone *pre*dict, violent behavior. However, our review of the literature suggests that it might be possible to demonstrate that violence could be predicted using psychological tests if programs of research were undertaken that were more sophisticated than the studies done to date.

Most of the research thus far has attempted to relate test scores to violent behavior in a one-to-one fashion, neglecting the fact that in clinical practice predictions are made on the basis of the total configuration of test scores and life history data. The first step that should be taken is to determine whether experienced clinical psychologists accustomed to working with violent people can accurately discriminate between violent and nonviolent individuals when the total array of assessment data, including situational data, are available. If clinicians are able to make this differentiation, then their behavior should be studied to determine wht tests or signs are most important so other clinicians can be trained to emulate their behavior. If they cannot, then their failure should be studied to determine if, with appropriate feedback, their predictions can be improved. Meanwhile quantitative multivariate research should proceed in an effort to derive empirically configurations of clinical data that are reliably related to violent behavior. The clinical data in these predictor equations should include both structured and projective tests, life history information, and various types of situational stress to which the individual is frequently exposed. Relevant medical data, such as whether the individual is of the XYY chromosome type, should also be considered.

Instead of attempting to predict "violence" as if it was a unitary, homogeneous mode of behavior, efforts should be directed at differentiating meaningful subtypes or syndromes of violent individuals and then determining the diagnostic signs in the clinical data that will enable us to identify individuals of each type. For example, research has shown that one such subtype is composed of Overcontrolled individuals with high inhibitions and strong repressed hostility. The recently developed O-H scale for the MMPI may be helpful in differentiating such people. Another syndrome is the Undercontrolled Assaultive type; for the latter category, life history data are most useful and O-H has little relevance (Megargee, Cook, & Mendelsohn, 1967). Similarly, different combinations of test signs and anamnestic data should prove useful in discriminating individuals who are likely to become violent as a result of a paranoid process, as part of a psychotic depressive reaction, or as a result of deviant subcultural values and so forth.

In such a program of research, closer attention will have to be paid to the usefulness of tests in different populations. Instruments which accurately predict violence in psychiatric patients may be inadequate for use in prison settings and vice versa. The question of base rates will also have to be considered to a greater extent than it has been in the past. Instruments which are ineffectual in settings where violence is rare may be useful in settings where violence is fairly common.

Implicit in this discussion has been the fact that progress is the assessment of violence is dependent on progress in the understanding of violence. The sooner personality researchers can determine how personality traits and situational variables interact to instigate or inhibit violent behavior, the sooner clinical psychologists will be able to devise instruments to assess the relevant traits and improve their predictions. Such research should focus on identifying the relevant syndromes as noted above. Another approach which should be exploited more than it has in the past is to investigate nonviolence. By studying individuals or situations in which many of the ingredients for violence are present and yet violence does not take place, we may be able to determine the relative importance of various factors. Such as approach would be particularly helpful in identifying variables that suppress or inhibit violence.

The fact that significant, although low order, relationships have been found between violent behavior and test data in the relatively unsophisticated and crude research which has been done to date suggests that programs of sophisticated multivariate research should have an even greater possibility of eventual success. It must be remembered, however, that clinical assessment involves taking small samples of behavior to estimate other behavior, and that such a process inevitably involves error and inaccuracy. The clinician will never be able to single out any one individual and state positively that he will commit a violent act, any more than he can single out another individual and state that it is impossible that he could ever engage in violence. Instead, the clinician implicitly assigns people to classes about which he can make rough probability statements. If the assessment indicates that the individual belongs to a group of people who, given certain circumstances, commit violence about 90% of the time, then the clinician will report that under these conditions it is probable that this particular individual will resort to violence. If the assessment has been done accurately then the prediction of violent behavior should be correct in about 90% of the cases of this type whom the clinician examines. However, 90% accuracy is simply another way of describing 10% error. While errors and failures in assessment can and must be studied to determine whether any lessons can be drawn from them which might improve assessment, some inaccuracy is inevitable in the prediction of behavior. It is the task of research to reduce this error to the minimum.

REFERENCES

Albee, G. W., & Goldman, R. The Picture-Frustration Study as a predictor of overt aggression. *Journal of Projective Techniques,* 1950, **14**, 303–308.

Angelino, H. The validity of the P-F Study's children's form. Unpublished thesis, University of Nebraska, 1950. Cited in W. L. Weinberg, The relationship of the extrapunitive category of the Picture-Frustration Study to an independent criterion of aggression in prisoners. Unpublished Master's thesis, University of Oregon, 1953.

Atkinson, J. W. (Ed.). *Motives in fantasy, action, and society.* Princeton: Van Nostrand, 1958.

Beall, H. S., & Panton, J. H. Development of a prison adjustment scale (PAS) for the MMPI. Unpublished manuscript, Central Prison, Raleigh, North Carolina, 1957. Cited by W. G. Dahlstrom & G. S. Welsh (Eds.), *An MMPI handbook: A guide to use in clinical research and practice.* Minneapolis: University of Minnesota Press, 1960. P. 308.

Bendig, A. W. Factor analytic scales of overt and covert hostility. *Journal of Consulting Psychology,* 1962, **26**, 200.

Berkowitz, L. Impulse, aggression and the gun. *Psychology Today,* 1968, **2** (4), 18–22.

Berkowitz, L., & LePage, A. Weapons as aggression-eliciting stimuli. *Journal of Personality and Social Psychology,* 1967, **7**, 202–207.

Block, J. The development of an MMPI based scale to measure ego control. University of California, Berkeley, Department of Psychology, 1955. (Ditto)

Bricklin, B., Piotrowski, Z. A., & Wagner, E. E. The Hand Test. Springfield, Ill: Charles C Thomas, 1962.

Brodie, C. W. The prediction of qualitative characteristics of behavior in stress situations, using test-assessed personality constructs. Unpublished doctoral dissertation, University of Illinois, 1959.

Brodsky, S., & Brodsky, A. M. Hand Test indicators of antisocial behavior. Journal of Projective Techniques and Personality Assessment, 1967, 31 (5), 36–39.

Buss, A. H. The psychology of aggression. New York: Wiley, 1961.

Buss, A. H., & Durkee, A. An inventory for assessing different kinds of hostility. Journal of Consulting Psychology, 1957, 21, 343–348.

Buss, A. H., Durkee, A., & Baer, M. The measurement of hostility in clinical situations. Journal of Abnormal and Social Psychology, 1956, 52, 84–86.

Buss, A. H., Fisher, H., & Simmons, A. J. Aggression and hostility in psychiatric patients. Journal of Consulting Psychology, 1962, 26, 84–89.

Butcher, J. N. Manifest aggression: MMPI correlates in normal boys. Journal of Consulting Psychology, 1965, 29, 446–454.

Butcher, J. N. (Ed.) MMPI: Research developments and clinical applications. New York: McGraw-Hill, 1969.

Charen, S. The awareness of hostile feelings in patients by their nurses. Journal of Consulting Psychology, 1955, 19, 290.

Cook, W. W., & Medley, D. M. Proposed hostility and pharisaic virtue scales for the MMPI. Journal of Applied Psychology, 1954, 38, 414–418.

Cronbach, L. J. Statistical methods applied to the Rorschach: A review. Psychological Bulletin, 1949, 46, 393–429.

Dahlstrom, W. G., & Welsh, G. S. An MMPI handbook: A guide to use in clinical practice and research. Minneapolis: University of Minnesota Press, 1960.

Dalack, J. D. The relationship between TAT hostility and self-report hostility as a function of psychiatric condition. (Doctoral dissertation, Columbia University) Ann Arbor, Mich.: University Microfilms, 1964. No. 65-7348.

Datel, W. E. Socialization scale norms on military samples. Military Medicine, 1962, 127, 740–744.

Deming, R. W. Reactions to frustration of assaultive delinquents. Research Report No. 2, Alameda County Probation Department, December, 1960.

DeVos, G. A. A quantitative approach to affective symbolism in Rorschach responses. Journal of Projective Techniques, 1952, 16, 133–150.

Dinwiddie, F. W. An application of the principle of response generalization to the prediction of aggressive responses. Unpublished doctoral dissertation, Washington, D. C.: Catholic University of America, 1954.

Drummond, F. A failure in the discrimination of aggressive behavior of undifferentiated schizophrenics with the Hand Test. Journal of Projective Techniques and Personality Assessment, 1966, 30, 275–279.

Elizur, A. Content analysis of the Rorschach with regard to anxiety and hostility. Journal of Projective Techniques, 1949, 13, 247–284.

Erikson, R. B., & Roberts, A. H. An MMPI comparison of two groups of institutionalized delinquents. Journal of Projective Techniques and Personality Assessment, 1966, 30, 163–166.

Feldman, M. J., & Siegel, S. M. The effect on self description of combining anxiety and hostility items on a single scale. *Journal of Clinical Psychology*, 1958, **14**, 74–77.

Finney, B. C. Rorschach test correlates of assaultive behavior. *Journal of Projective Techniques*, 1955, **19**, 6–16.

Fisher, G. Discriminating violence resulting from overcontrolled versus undercontrolled aggressivity. *British Journal of Social and Clinical Consulting Psychology*, 1970, **9**, 54–59.

Fisher, S., & Cleveland, S. E. *Body image and personality*. Princeton: Van Nostrand, 1958.

Gorlow, L., Zimet, C. N., & Fine, H. J. The validity of anxiety and hostility Rorschach content scores among adolescents. *Journal of Consulting Psychology*, 1952, **16**, 73–75.

Gough, H. G. A sociological theory of psychopathy. *American Journal of Sociology*, 1948, **53**, 359–366.

Gough, H. G. *California Psychological Inventory Manual*. Palo Alto: Consulting Psychologists Press, 1960. (a)

Gough, H. G. Theory and measurement of socialization. *Journal of Consulting Psychology*, 1960, **24**, 23–30. (b)

Gough, H. G. Academic achievement in high school as predicted from the California Psychological Inventory. *Journal of Educational Psychology*, 1964, **55**, 174–180. Reprinted in E. I. Megargee (Ed.), *Research in clinical assessment*. New York: Harper & Row, 1966.

Gough, H. G., & Peterson, D. R. The identification and measurement of predispositional factors in crime and delinquency. *Journal of Consulting Psychology*, 1952, **16**, 207–212.

Gough, H. G., & Sandhu, H. S. Validation of the CPI socialization scale in India. *Journal of Abnormal and Social Psychology*, 1964, **68**, 544–547. Reprinted in E. I. Megargee (Ed.), *Research in clinical assessment*. New York: Harper & Row, 1966.

Gough, H. G., Wenk, E. A., & Rozynko, V. V. Parole outcome as predicted from the CPI, the MMPI, and a base expectancy table. *Journal of Abnormal Psychology*, 1965, **70**, 432–441.

Hafner, A. J., & Kaplan, A. M. Hostility content analysis of the Rorschach and TAT. *Journal of Projective Techniques*, 1960, **24**, 137–143.

Harris, R. H., & Lingoes, J. C. *Subscales for the MMPI: An aid to profile interpretation*. San Francisco: University of California School of Medicine, 1955. (Mimeo)

Haskell, R. J., Jr. Relationship between aggressive behavior and psychological tests. *Journal of Projective Techniques*, 1961, **25**, 431–440.

Hathaway, S. R., & Monachesi, E. D. *Analyzing and predicting juvenile delinquency with the MMPI*. Minneapolis: University of Minnesota Press, 1953.

Haven, H. Racial differences on the MMPI O-H (Overcontrolled Hostility) scale. *FCI Research Reports*, 1969, **1** (5), 1-9. Federal Correctional Institution, Tallahassee, Florida. (Mimeo)

Hetherington, E. M., & Feldman, S. E. College cheating as a function of subject and situational variables. *Journal of Educational Psychology*, 1964, **55**, 212–218.

Hodge, J. R., Wagner, E. E., & Schreiner, F. Hypnotic validation of two Hand Test scoring categories. *Journal of Projective Techniques and Personality Assessment*, 1966, **30**, 385–386.

Holtzman, W. H., Thorpe, J. S., Swartz, J. D., & Herron, E. W. *Inkblot perception and personality*. Austin: University of Texas Press, 1961.

Holzberg, J. D., & Hahn, S. The Picture-Frustration technique as a measure of hostility and guilt reactions in adolescent psychopaths. *American Journal of Orthopsychiatry*, 1952, **22**, 736–797.

Holzberg, J. D., & Posner, R. The relationship of extrapunitiveness on the Rosenzweig Picture-Frustration Study to aggression in overt behavior and fantasy. *American Journal of Orthopsychiatry*, 1951, **21**, 757-779.

Hoover, J. E. *Uniform crime reports for the United States: 1967*. Washington, D. C.: Department of Justice, 1968.

Jensen, A. Aggression in fantasy and overt behavior. *Psychological Monographs*, 1957, **71** (Whole No. 445).

Kagan, J. Measurement of overt aggression from fantasy. *Journal of Abnormal and Social Psychology*, 1956, **52**, 390–393. Reprinted in E. I. Megargee (Ed.), *Research in clinical assessment*. New York: Harper & Row, 1966.

Kane, P. Availability of hostile fantasy related to overt behavior. Unpublished doctoral dissertation, University of Chicago, 1955. Cited by A. Buss, *The psychology of aggression*. New York: Wiley, 1961. P. 131.

Kaplan, M. F. The effect of cue relevance, ambiguity, and self-reported hostility on TAT responses. *Journal of Projective Techniques and Personality Assessment*, 1967, **31** (6), 45–50.

Kaswan, J., Wasman, M., & Freedman, L. Z. Aggression and the Picture-Frustration Study. *Journal of Consulting Psychology*, 1960, **24**, 446–452.

Knapp, R. R. Personality correlates of delinquency rate in a Navy sample. *Journal of Applied Psychology*, 1963, **47**, 68–71.

Lazarus, R. S. A substitutive-defense conception of apperceptive fantasy. In J. Kagan and G. S. Lesser (Eds.), *Contemporary issues in thematic apperceptive methods*. Springfield, Ill.: Charles C Thomas, 1961. Pp. 51–71.

Leibowitz, G. Comparison of self-report and behavioral techniques of assessing aggression. *Journal of Consulting and Clinical Psychology*, 1968, **32**, 21–25.

Lesser, G. S. The relationship between overt and fantasy aggression as a function of maternal response to aggression. *Journal of Abnormal and Social Psychology*, 1957, **55**, 218–221. Reprinted in E. I. Megargee (Ed.), *Research in clinical assessment*. New York: Harper & Row, 1966.

Levy, S., Southcombe, R. H., Cramer, J. R., & Freeman, R. A. The outstanding personality factors among the population of a state penitentiary: A preliminary report. *Journal of Clinical and Experimental Psychopathology*, 1952, **13**, 117–130.

Lindzey, G., & Tejessey, C. Thematic Apperception Test: Indices of aggression in relation to measures of overt and covert behavior. *American Journal of Orthopsychiatry*, 1956, **26**, 567–576.

Lord, E. Experimentally induced variations in Rorschach performance. *Psychological Monographs*, 1950, **64**, No. 10 (Whole No. 316).

MacCasland, B. W. The relation of aggressive fantasy to aggressive behavior in children. (Doctoral dissertation, Syracuse University) Ann Arbor, Mich.: University Microfilms, 1961. No. 62-1110.

MacDonald, J. M. Homicidal threats. *American Journal of Psychiatry*, 1967, **124** (4), 61–68.

Madsen, J. C. *The expression of aggression in two cultures*. (Doctoral dissertation, University of Oregon) Ann Arbor, Mich.: University Microfilms, 1966. No. 66-12974.

Marquis, J. N. *Fantasy measures of aggressive behavior*. (Doctoral dissertation, University of Michigan) Ann Arbor, Mich.: University Microfilms, 1960. No. 61-1763.

McGee, S. Measurement of hostility: A pilot study. *Journal of Clinical Psychology,* 1954, **10**, 280–282.

Meehl, P., & Rosen, A. Antecedent probability and the efficiency of psychometric signs, patterns or cutting scores. *Psychological Bulletin,* 1955, **52**, 194–216. Reprinted in E. I. Megargee (Ed.), *Research in clinical assessment.* New York: Harper & Row, 1966.

Megargee, E. I. Undercontrol and overcontrol in assaultive and homicidal adolescents. (Doctoral dissertation, University of California, Berkeley) Ann Arbor, Mich.: University Microfilms, 1964. No. 64-9923. (a)

Megargee, E. I. The utility of the Rosenzweig Picture-Frustration Study in detecting assaultiveness among juvenile delinquents. Paper presented at the meeting of the Southwestern Psychological Association, San Antonio, April, 1964. (b)

Megargee, E. I. Assault with intent to kill. *Trans-action,* 1965, **2**, (6), 27–31. (a)

Megargee, E. I. The performance of juvenile delinquents on the Holtzman Inkblot Technique: A normative study. *Journal of Projective Techniques and Personality Assessment,* 1965, **29**, 504–512. (b)

Megargee, E. I. The relation between Barrier scores and aggressive behavior. *Journal of Abnormal Psychology,* 1965, **70**, 307–311. (c)

Megargee, E. I. Estimation of CPI scores from MMPI protocols. *Journal of Clinical Psychology,* 1966, **22**, 456–458. (a)

Megargee, E. I. The relation of response length to the Holtzman Inkblot Technique. *Journal of Consulting Psychology,* 1966, **30**, 415–419. (b)

Megargee, E. I. (Ed.), *Research in clinical assessment.* New York: Harper & Row, 1966. (c)

Megargee, E. I. Undercontrolled and overcontrolled personality types in extreme anti-social aggression. *Psychological Monographs,* 1966, **80** (3, Whole No. 611). (d)

Megargee, E. I. Hostility on the TAT as a function of defensive inhibition and stimulus situation. *Journal of Projective Techniques and Personality Assessment,* 1967, **31** (4), 73–79.

Megargee, E. I. The assessment of violence with psychological tests. Consultant's report to the Task Force on Individual Violence of the President's Commission on Violence. Unpublished manuscript, 1968.

Megargee, E. I. Conscientious objectors' scores on the MMPI *O-H* (Overcontrolled Hostility) scales. *Proceedings of the 77th Annual Convention of the American Psychological Association.* Washington, D. C.: APA, 1969. Pp. 507–508. (a)

Megargee, E. I. The psychology of violence: A critical review of theories of violence. In National Commission On the Causes and Prevention of Violence, Staff Study Series. Vol. 13. *Crimes of Violence,* Report of the Task Force on Individual Acts of Violence, 1969. Pp. 1037–1115. (b)

Megargee, E. I. The role of inhibition in the assessment and understanding of violence. In J. E. Singer (Ed.), *Cognitive and physiological factors in aggression.* Boston: Little, Brown, in press.

Megargee, E. I., & Cook, P. E. The relation of TAT and inkblot aggressive content scales with each other and with criteria of overt aggressiveness in delinquents.

Megargee, E. I., & Menzies, E. The assessment and dynamics of aggression. In P. McReynolds (Ed.), *Advances in Psychological Assessment.* Vol. 2, in press.

Journal of Projective Techniques and Personality Assessment, 1967, **31** (1), 48–60.

Megargee, E. I., Cook, P. E., & Mendelsohn, G. A. Development and evaluation of an MMPI scale of assaultiveness in overcontrolled individuals. *Journal of Abnormal Psychology*, 1967, **72**, 519–528.

Megargee, E. I., & Hokanson, J. E. (Eds.) *The dynamics of aggression: Individual, group and international analyses.* New York: Harper & Row, 1970.

Megargee, E. I., Lockwood, V., Cato, J., & Jones, J. K. Effects of differences in examiner, tone of administration and sex of subject on scores of the Holtzman Inkblot Technique. *Proceedings of the 74th Annual Convention of the American Psychological Association.* Washington, D. C.: APA, 1966. Pp. 235–236.

Megargee, E. I., & Mendelsohn, G. A. A cross validation of 12 MMPI indices of hostility and control. *Journal of Abnormal and Social Psychology*, 1962, **65**, 431–438. Reprinted in E. I. Megargee (Ed.), *Research in clinical assessment.* New York: Harper & Row, 1966.

Mercer, M., & Kyriazis, C. Results of the Rosenzweig P-F Study for physically assaultive prisoner mental patients. *Journal of Consulting Psychology*, 1962, **26**, 490.

Miller, L. Relationships between fantasy aggression and behavioral aggression. Unpublished doctoral dissertation, Harvard University, 1953.

Miller, L., Spilka, B., & Pratt, S. Manifest anxiety and hostility in "criminally insane" patients. *Journal of Clinical and Experimental Psychopathology*, 1960, **21**, 41–48.

Minuchin, P. P. The relation between aggressive fantasy and overt behavior. (Doctoral dissertation, Yale University) Ann Arbor, Mich.: University Microfilms, 1950. No. 64-11877.

Mizushima, K., & DeVos, G. An application of the California Psychological Inventory in a study of Japanese delinquency. *Journal of Social Psychology*, 1967, **71**, 45–51.

Moldawsky, P. A study of personality variables in patients with skin disorders. Unpublished doctoral dissertation, State University of Iowa, 1953.

Murray, H. A. *Thematic Apperception Test manual.* Cambridge: Harvard University Press, 1943.

Murstein, B. I. The projection of hostility on the Rorschach and as a result of ego threat. *Journal of Projective Techniques*, 1956, **20**, 418–428.

Murstein, B. I. Assumptions, adaptation level and projective techniques. *Perceptual and Motor Skills*, 1961, **12**, 107–125. Reprinted in E. I. Megargee (Ed.), *Research in clinical assessment.* New York: Harper & Row, 1966.

Murstein, B. I. *Theory and research in projective techniques (Emphasizing the TAT).* New York: Wiley, 1963.

Murstein, B. I. Projection of hostility on the TAT as a function of stimulus, background and personality variables. *Journal of Consulting Psychology*, 1965, **29**, 43–48.

Murstein, B. I., David, C., Fisher, D., & Furth, H. The scaling of the TAT for hostility by a variety of scaling methods. *Journal of Consulting Psychology*, 1961, **25**, 497–504.

Mussen, P. H., & Naylor, H. K. The relationships between overt and fantasy aggression. *Journal of Abnormal and Social Psychology*, 1954, **49**, 235–240. Reprinted in E. I. Megargee (Ed.), *Research in clinical assessment.* New York: Harper & Row, 1966.

Panton, J. H. Predicting prison adjustment with the MMPI. *Journal of Clinical Psychology*, 1958, **14**, 308–321.

Pattie, F. A. The effect of hypnotically induced hostility on Rorschach responses. *Journal of Clinical Psychology*, 1954, **10**, 161–164.

Perdue, W. C. A study of the Rorschach records of 47 murderers. *Journal of Social Therapy*, 1961, **7**, 158–167.

Perdue, W. C. Rorschach responses of 100 murderers. *Corrective Psychiatry and the Journal of Social Therapy*, 1964, **10**, 323–328.

Peterson, R. A., Pittman, D. J., & O'Neal, P. Stabilities and deviance: A study of assaultive and nonassaultive offenders. *Journal of Criminal Law, Criminology and Police Science*, 1962, **53** (1), 44–48.

Phillips, L., & Smith, J. G. *Rorschach interpretation: Advanced technique.* New York: Grune & Stratton, 1953.

Piotrowski, Z. A., & Abrahamsen, D. Sexual crime, alcohol and the Rorschach test. *The Psychiatric Quarterly Supplement*, 1952, **26** (Part 2), 248–260.

Pittluck, P. The relationship between aggressive, fantasy and overt behavior. Unpublished doctoral dissertation, Yale University, 1950.

Rabin, A. I. Homicide and attempted suicides: A Rorschach study. *American Journal of Orthopsychiatry*, 1946, **16**, 516–524.

Rader, G. E. The prediction of overt aggressive verbal behavior from Rorschach content. *Journal of Projective Techniques*, 1957, **21**, 294–306.

Ramachandra Rao, S. K. Studies with the TAT. *Transactions of the All-India Institute of Mental Health*, 1964, **4**, 24–32.

Rizzo, G. B. Il Rosenzweig P-F Study applicato ad un Gruppo di omcidi e ad un gruppo di autori di reati contro la proprieta. V Congresso Internazionale Rorschach, Freiburg: 1961. Cited by M. E. Wolfgang, Crimes of violence. Report for the President's Commission on Law Enforcement and Administration of Justice, 1967.

Rizzo, G. B., & Ferracuti, F. Impiego del test di Rorschach in criminologia clinica. *Rassegna di Studi Penitenziari*, 1959, **1**, 23–50. Cited by M. E. Wolfgang, Crimes of violence. Report for the President's Commission on Law Enforcement and Administration of Justice, 1967.

Rosenzweig, S. Levels of behavior in psychodiagnosis with special reference to the Picture-Frustration Study. *The American Journal of Orthopsychiatry*, 1950, **20**, 63–72. Reprinted in E. I. Megargee (Ed.), *Research in clinical assessment*. New York: Harper & Row, 1966.

Rosenzweig, S. Validity of the Rosenzweig Picture-Frustration Study with felons and delinquents. *Journal of Consulting Psychology*, 1963, **27**, 535–536.

Saltz, G., & Epstein, S. Thematic hostility and guilt responses as related to self-reported hostility, guilt and conflict. *Journal of Abnormal and Social Psychology*, 1963, **67**, 469–479.

Sanders, R., & Cleveland, S. E. The relationship between certain examiner personality variables and subjects' Rorschach scores. *Journal of Projective Techniques*, 1953, **17**, 34–50.

Scarpitti, F. R., Murray, E., Dinitz, S., & Reckless, W. C. The "good" boy in a high delinquency area: Four years later. *American Sociological Review*, 1960, **25**, 555–558.

Schultz, S. D. A differentiation of several forms of hostility by scales empirically constructed from significant items on the MMPI. *Pennsylvania State University Abstracts of Doctoral Dissertations*, 1954, **17**, 717–720.

Scodel, A., & Lipetz, M. E. TAT hostility and psychopathology. *Journal of Projective Techniques,* 1957, **21**, 161–165.

Serebrinsky, B. *El psicodiagnostico de Rorschach en los homicidas.* Cordoba, Argentina: Imprenta de la Universidad, 1941. Cited by M. E. Wolfgang, Crimes of Violence. Report for the President's Commission on Law Enforcement and Administration of Justice, 1967.

Shipman, W. G. The validity of MMPI hostility scales. *Journal of Clinical Psychology,* 1965, **21**, 186–190.

Shipman, W. G., & Marquette, C. H. The manifest hostility scale: A validation study. *Journal of Clinical Psychology,* 1963, **19**, 104–106.

Siegel, S. M. The relationship of hostility to authoritarianism. *Journal of Abnormal and Social Psychology,* 1956, **52**, 368–372.

Siegel, S. M., & Feldman, M. J. A note on the effect on self description of combining anxiety and hostility items on a single scale. *Journal of Clinical Psychology,* 1958, **14**, 389–390.

Siegel, S. M., Spilka, B., & Miller, L. The direction of manifest hostility: Its measurement and meaning. Paper presented at the meeting of the American Psychological Association, New York, September, 1957.

Sjostedt, E. M. A study of the personality variables related to assaultive and acquisitive crimes. Unpublished doctoral dissertation, Purdue University, 1955. Cited by A. Buss, *The psychology of aggression.* New York: Wiley, 1961. P. 131.

Smith, J. R., & Coleman, J. C. The relationship between manifestations of hostility in projective tests and overt behavior. *Journal of Projective Techniques,* 1956, **20**, 326–334.

Snoke, M. L. A study in the behavior of men students of high and low measured hostility under two conditions of goal clarity. Unpublished doctoral dissertation, University of Minnesota, 1955.

Sommer, R., & Sommer, D. T. Assaultiveness and two types of Rorschach color responses. *Journal of Consulting Psychology,* 1958, **22**, 57–62. Reprinted in E. I. Megargee (Ed.), *Research in clinical assessment.* New York: Harper & Row, 1966.

Starr, S. *The relationship between hostility-ambiguity of the TAT cards, hostile fantasy, and hostile behavior.* (Doctoral dissertation, Washington State University) Ann Arbor, Mich.: University Microfilms, 1960. No. 60-5352.

Stone, H. The relationship of hostile-aggressive behavior to aggressive content on the Rorschach and Thematic Apperception Test. Unpublished doctoral dissertation, University of California at Los Angeles, 1953.

Stone, H. The TAT aggressive content scale. *Journal of Projective Techniques,* 1956, **20**, 445–452.

Storment, C. T., & Finney, B. C. Projection and behavior: A Rorschach study of assaultive mental hospital patients. *Journal of Projective Techniques,* 1953, **17**, 349–360.

Swickard, D. L., & Spilka, B. Hostility expression among delinquents of minority and majority groups. *Journal of Consulting Psychology,* 1961, **25**, 216–220.

Symonds, P. N. *Adolescent fantasy.* New York: Columbia University Press, 1949.

Toch, H. *Violent men: An inquiry into the psychology of violence.* Chicago: Aldine, 1969.

Tomkins, S. S. *The Thematic Apperception Test: The theory and technique of interpretation.* New York: Grune & Stratton, 1952.

Towbin, A. Hostility in Rorschach content and overt aggressive behavior. *Journal of Abnormal and Social Psychology,* 1959, **58,** 312–316.

Towner, W. A comparison of the frustration reactions of delinquent and non-delinquent adolescent boys as measured by the Rosenzweig Picture-Frustration Study. Unpublished thesis, University of Washington, 1950. Cited in W. L. Weinberg, The relationship of the extrapunitive category of the Picture-Frustration Study to an independent criterion of aggression in prisoners. Unpublished Master's thesis, University of Oregon, 1953.

Townsend, J. K. The relation between Rorschach signs of aggression and behavioral aggression in emotionally disturbed boys. *Journal of Projective Techniques and Personality Assessment,* 1967, 31 (6), 13–21.

Wagner, E. E., & Hawkins, R. Differentiation of assaultive delinquents with the Hand Test. *Journal of Projective Techniques and Personality Assessment,* 1964, 28, 363–365.

Wagner, E. E., & Medredeff, E. Differentiation of aggression behavior of institutionalized schizophrenics with the Hand Test. *Journal of Projective Techniques and Personality Assessment,* 1963, **27,** 110–112.

Walker, D. *Rights in conflict.* Report submitted to the National Commission on the Causes and Prevention of Violence, 1968.

Walker, R. G. A comparison of clinical manifestations of hostility with Rorschach and MAPS tests performances. *Journal of Projective Techniques,* 1951, **15,** 444–460.

Walters, R. H., & Zaks, M. S. Validation studies of an aggression scale. *Journal of Psychology,* 1959, **47,** 209–218.

Weatherley, D. Maternal permissiveness toward aggression and subsequent TAT aggression. *Journal of Abnormal and Social Psychology,* 1962, **65,** 1–5.

Weinberg, W. L. The relationship of the extrapunitive category of the Picture-Frustration Study to an independent criterion of aggression in prisoners. Unpublished Master's thesis, University of Oregon, 1953.

Weissman, S. L. Some indicators of acting out behavior from the TAT. *Journal of Projective Techniques and Personality Assessment,* 1964, **28,** 366–375.

Welsh, G. S., & Sullivan, P. L. MMPI configurations in passive-aggressive personality problems. Unpublished materials, 1952. Cited in W. G. Dahlstrom & G. S. Welsh (Eds.), *An MMPI handbook: A guide to use in clinical research and practice.* Minneapolis: University of Minnesota Press, 1960. P. 308.

Wetsel, H., Shapiro, R. J., & Wagner, E. E. Prediction of recidivism among juvenile delinquents with the Hand Test. *Journal of Projective Techniques and Personality Assessment,* 1967, 31 (4), 69–72.

White, W. Selective modeling in youthful offenders with high and low O-H personality types. Unpublished doctoral dissertation, The Florida State University, 1970.

Wirt, R. D. Ideational expression of hostile impulses. *Journal of Consulting Psychology,* 1956, **20,** 185–189.

Wirt, R. D., & Briggs, P. F. Personality and environmental factors in the development of delinquency. *Psychological Monographs,* 1959, **73** (Whole No. 485).

Wolf, I. Hostile acting out and Rorschach Test content. *Journal of Projective Techniques,* 1957, **21,** 414–419.

Wolfgang, M. E. Victim-precipitated criminal homicide. *Journal of Criminal Law, Criminology and Police Science,* 1957, **48** (1), 1–11.

Wolfgang, M. E. *Patterns in criminal homicide.* Philadelphia: University of Pennsylvania Press, 1958.

Wolfgang, M. E. Crimes of violence. Mimeographed paper prepared for the President's Commission on Law Enforcement and Administration of Justice, 1967.

Zaks, M. S., & Walters, R. H. First steps in the construction of a scale for the measurement of aggression. *Journal of Psychology,* 1959, **47**, 199–208.

Depression and Oral Contraception[1]

Eugene E. Levitt, John E. Kooiker, and James A. Norton
Department of Psychiatry
Indiana University School of Medicine
Indianapolis, Indiana

I. Introduction

The relationship between endocrine function and emotional reaction is firmly established, especially the connection between ephemeral mood changes and the menstrual ebb of female hormones (e.g., Benedek, 1952; Gottschalk, Kaplan, Winget, & Gleser, 1962). An oral contraceptive—the Pill—is essentially a dosage of female hormones which acts to prevent ovulation. Thus it would not be at all surprising if the Pill had emotional side effects, conceivably negative ones.

There is certainly no scarcity of reports of physiological side effects of the Pill, many of them negative. The findings of the 1965 National Fertility Study (Westoff & Ryder, 1968) indicate that 27% of married women who used the Pill for contraceptive purposes between the years 1960 and 1965 discontinued it because of physiological side effects, primarily pregnancylike reactions (weight change, fluid retention, breast tenderness, and nausea) and difficulties associated with the menstrual

[1] This report was supported by grants from the Indiana University Research Foundation and from the Association for the Advancement of Mental Health Research and Education. Statistical analyses were carried out by the Indiana University Medical Center Research Computation Center under United States Public Health Service Grant FR-00162. The authors are indebted to the following persons for their assistance in the study: Dr. Sprague H. Gardiner, Jane Young, and Barbara Mealey.

cycle (spotting, hemorrhaging, irregularity, and cramps). Other findings suggest; however, that the presence or absence of physiological complications is not the *sole* factor determining continuation or discontinuation of a Pill regimen. A study by Ziegler, Rogers, Kriegsman, and Marton (1968) indicated that the incidence of side effects does not differ between groups of women who voluntarily stopped using the Pill and those who continued to use it for years. A survey of women who had used the Pill for long periods of time (Klein & Levitt, 1967) found a generally favorable attitude and a high continuation rate despite a high incidence of negative side effects.

The relatively high rate of physiological complications in women who use the Pill is beyond question, but the incidence of psychological side effects has not yet been established. Several reviews of the literature have failed to clarify this relationship. Wallach and Garcia (1968) conclude only that "relatively little is known about various effects, especially those on personality and emotions." A recent, four-page summary by the AMA Council on Drugs (1967) devotes only three sentences to the subject of psychological side effects. Equivocality amounting almost to confusion is found in the review by Glick (1967):

Several studies indicate that these drugs do not cause depression . . . cases of depression in association with drug use are uniformly reported. Incidence has ranged from 2% to 30% depending upon the population reported . . . unfortunately, carefully controlled, conclusive evidence supporting the above generalizations does not exist at present . . . it seems clear that there is not enough evidence in the literature to make any definitive conclusions about the behavioral effects of the oral contraceptive agents . . . if depression does occur during drug use, it occurs rarely.

Glick rightfully points out that the bulk of the evidence concerning the relationships between emotional factors and oral contraceptives have either been anecdotal reports or investigations suffering from major methodological defects.

As Glick's review indicates, reports concerning depression, the most commonly reported psychological side effect of the Pill, are particularly conflicting. Most of the positive reports are anecdotal or based on clinical impressions (Behrman, 1964; Bryans, 1965; Drill, 1965; Goldzieher, 1965; Gray, 1966; McGregor, 1967; Rossi, 1966; Vennard, 1966). Other investigations show that psychological complications associated with the Pill tend to arise in women with an established history of psychological difficulties (Kaye, 1963; Kane, Daly, Ewing, & Keeler, 1967). Among the handful of actual experimental investigations employing objective measures of depression, only Nilsson, Jacobson, and Ingemanson (1967) had positive findings. They report that 20% of the Pill-taking subjects manifested an increase in depression. However, there was also a correlation between incidence of depression and history of previous psychiatric symptoms and previous use of psychoactive medication. Another 10% of the subjects experienced a *decrease* in depression, a finding also reported by Sluglett and Lawson (1967) and Kistner (1966). These findings of beneficial psychological effects of the Pill are similar in import to the occasional reports of psychotherapeutic use of the Pill (Kane & Keeler, 1965; Kane, Daly, Wallach, & Keeler, 1966; Simpson, Radinger, Rochlin, & Kline, 1962, Simpson, Rochlin, & Kline, 1964; Swanson, Barron, Floren, & Smith, 1964).

The results of the Nilsson study are counterbalanced by four other objective reports in which the findings were generally negative (Bakker & Dightman, 1966; Murawski, Sapir, Shulman, Ryan, & Sturgis, 1968; Sapir, Ryan, Shulman, & Murawski, 1965; Ziegler *et al.*, 1968). In addition, depression was not listed as a reason for discontinuance by Westoff and Ryder (1968) although nervousness, irritability, and tension were noted.

A temporal factor may be contributing to the confusion. A tacit implication of research concerned with the establishment of any side effect is that this effect must occur within some reasonable time after the initiation of therapy. If the interval is too great, the connection between drug and effect becomes questionable. An interval no longer than the time required for the drug to enter the bloodstream is the most convincing, but it is not possible to stipulate a general rule.

Some side effects can be an immediate consequence of the ingestion of a drug while the appearance of others may require prolonged drug usage. Drowsiness occurs within an hour after administration of the first dose of a phenothiazine, but side effects such as hepatitis and agranulocytosis only appear after weeks or months of the drug regimen. The onset of oral contraceptive side effects such as breast soreness or enlargement, spotting, and nausea usually occur during the first cycle after starting on an oral contraceptive, but facial freckling may not appear until a year or more later (Klein & Levitt, 1967).

Psychological side effects usually are classed in the long-range category. In 1964, the American Medical Association's Council on Drugs suggested that unlike most Pill side effects, depression tended to increase with continued usage. Nonpsychiatric clinical practitioners believe that the encroachment of depression is so insidiously slow that the sufferer is totally unaware of the connection between mood and drug. Vennard (1966), for example, states that some of his patients eventually visited psychiatrists for the treatment of Pill-induced depressions.

The impression of clinical practitioners is succinctly summarized by Neubardt (1967):

Anxiety and depression resulting from the pill are vague symptoms which are not easily recognized but seem to progress insidiously each month. Such symptoms may begin to appear about the third or fourth cycle and, because depression and anxiety are not exactly unheard of in our society, may well be attributed to causes other than the Pill. Husbands, children, parents, in-laws are always available to "hang the rap on." Sometimes the patient is not even aware of the change in her personality.

A side effect which begins to appear three or four months after initiation of therapy may or may not be measurably apparent by that time. Perhaps several more months must elapse. At any rate, it seems clear that depression should not be expected to be an *immediate* consequence of the Pill regimen, and it ought to be most pronounced in women who have been ingesting the Pill for long periods of time.

It is also conceivable that the psychological effect of the Pill may be intracyclic. The patient gradually becomes depressed as hormone levels rise during the month, reaching a peak of depression just prior to the monthly discontinuance of the Pill. Depression is relieved during menstruation, reaching a monthly low at the cessation of flow. This sequence is repeated in each cycle. It is possible that the two views of the Pill effect are interactive. The intensity of intracyclic depression may increase as a function of the duration of the Pill regimen. All of these possibilities are considered as implicit hypotheses in the present investigation.

II. Experimental Design

A report concerning side effects of a contraceptive procedure may be interpreted in at least three ways: (*a*) The reported effects are unique to the particular contraceptive procedure under investigation. (*b*) The findings are a function of contraception in general and are not unique to the particular procedure under investigation. (*c*) The side effects do not differ in any meaningful way from chronic conditions reported by many women who do not use any contraceptive procedure, and therefore are not side effects at all.

The first inference is not warranted unless the latter two are ruled out by the design of the study. A psychological side effect cannot be considered to be a consequence of the Pill unless the experimental design dismisses the possibilities that observed effects are a function of any kind of contraception or are found in sufficient frequency even among women who use no contraception. The basic design of our study thus required an Other Contraceptive control group, and a No Contraception control group in addition to the Experimental or Pill group.

All of the hypotheses which we are considering in this investigation imply that the connection between Pill and depression is direct—that hormones *per se* make the woman depressed. They do not merely render her more likely to experience depression as a consequence of environmental or interpersonal circumstances. At any moment in time, the Pill user should be depressed, not simply depression-prone. Hence, in measuring depression objectively, we will need an instrument which measures *state depression* in contrast to *trait depression,* as this distinction has been set forth by Spielberger (1966) and others.

Testing the various hypotheses necessitates measurements of depressed states, across a number of months and within each of those months. One measurement would be made at the end of each subject's menstrual period at which time, according to hypothesis, depression would be at a minimum. We decided to make weekly measurements thereafter for a total period of four months.

Thus the study involved four weeks and four months of measurements for four groups of subjects with four forms of an instrument designed to measure depression. These numerical identities fit precisely into a Latin Square experimental design with replicated subject data. The within-subject effects are Months, Weeks and instrument forms. The between-subjects variation may be partitioned into Groups and Subjects within Groups. The complete Latin Square design is shown in Table 1.

Obviously, the depression measurements are made at different times for different subjects and require a very large number of occasions for any substantial group of subjects. It was not administratively feasible, nor did it seem necessary, to bring subjects to a clinical laboratory or any other special place in order to make the necessary measurements. A

TABLE 1

THE EXPERIMENTAL DESIGN: A REPLICATED LATIN SQUARE

Factor
Between Groups
Between Subjects within Groups
Between Months
Interaction: Months × Groups
Interaction: Months × Subjects within Groups
Between Weeks
Interaction: Weeks × Groups
Interaction: Weeks × Subjects within Groups
Between DACL Forms
Interaction: Forms × Groups
Interaction: Forms × Subjects within Groups
Latin Square Residual
Interaction: Residual × Groups
Interaction: Residual × Subjects within Groups

self-administered instrument completed in the home at the subject's leisure appeared adequate.

A. THE DEPRESSION ADJECTIVE CHECKLIST

The design of the investigation required an instrument for the measurement of depression which had certain definite characteristics. (*a*) It must be capable of being self-administered. (*b*) Since it would have to be administered on sixteen different occasions to each subject, it was desirable that it have a number of parallel forms. (*c*) Again considering the number of administrations per subject, it was desirable that each administration should require as little of the subject's time as possible. (*d*) The instrument should measure state depression rather than trait depression.

Most of the available instruments for the measurement of depression, such as the MMPI D Scale or the Depression Inventory (Beck, 1961), are measures of either trait depression or combinations of trait and state depression. One of the few instruments which is clearly a measure of state depression is the Depression Adjective Checklist (Lubin, 1965, 1966). The DACL was found to fulfill all of the required characteristics for this study. It is self-administered and takes only a few minutes to complete. In addition, the DACL has seven parallel forms, A to G, each with 34 adjectives. The subject's score for depression consists of the number of depression plus adjectives which are checked added to the number of depression minus adjectives which are *not* checked.

Normative data on Forms A to D, those which are most valid for female samples, are presented in Table 2. The data are based on a sample of normal females with a mean age of 22.8 years and a mean

TABLE 2

STANDARDIZATION DATA FOR THE DEPRESSION ADJECTIVE CHECKLIST[a]

	Form			
	A	B	C	D
r_{11}	.92	.93	.92	.92
$\bar{X}$	7.8	7.3	7.9	7.9
r with				
MMPI D	.46	.31	.41	.36
Beck Inv.	.50	.39	.49	.38

[a] From Lubin (1965) based only on normal female sample with mean age of 22.8 years and mean educational level of 12.8 years. N is 469 for mean and reliability row, and 92 for correlations with MMPI D and the Depression Inventory. All coefficients are significant beyond the 1% level. Intercorrelations among the four DACL forms range from .86 to .91.

educational level of 12.8 years, reasonably comparable to the samples which we anticipated using. The data in Table 2 indicate that the DACL is a highly internally consistent instrument which has moderate positive correlation with measures of trait depression.

B. SUBJECTS

The design of the investigation created unusual sampling problems. The popularity of the Pill is so great, especially among young married women, that despite the alleged high drop-out rate, it is difficult to aggregate a substantial sample of women employing mechanical methods of contraception, without going beyond the population from which the Pill sample would be drawn. The Other Contraceptive control group inevitably would be small; its size might be further reduced by lack of motivation to participate since it is possible that women eligible for this group might be Pill drop-outs. On the other hand, some of those in this control group might be expected to switch to the Pill during the study and would have to be dropped, thereby causing further attenuation.[2]

Married women of child-bearing age who do not use contraceptives are either infertile or trying to become pregnant. Those who would succeed in becoming pregnant during the course of the investigation would have to be dropped from the No Contraception control.[3]

Again, it appears inevitable that the No Contraception control group would wind up composed largely, if not entirely, of infertile women. Whether or not such a group is a biased control for the purposes of our investigation was a moot question at the time that it was designed.

Thus, our control samples were expected to be relatively small and possibly biased. We found no way to circumvent these potential methodological shortcomings without introducing fresh defects in the experimental design or sampling procedures.

Subject losses might also be anticipated from the Experimental (Pill) sample as the investigation proceeded. These would result from switches from a Pill regimen to mechanical contraception (the Pill drop-outs) and decline in motivation to participate. The latter possibility is, of course, a liability common to projects involving repeated data collection from the same subject group. The question of sampling bias is again moot.

Our original sample consisted of 263 wives of Indiana University Medical Students and 109 clients of the Planned Parenthood Association Clinic in Bloomington, Indiana. All initially volunteered to participate and 249 actually began, but only 126 submitted a sufficient number of DACL protocols to be included in the statistical analyses of data. The

[2] The actual loss in the study was 15%.
[3] The actual loss was 63%.

TABLE 3
SAMPLE SIZES AT VARIOUS STAGES OF THE STUDY

Group[a]	Original sample	Beginning sample	Finished study	Used in statistical analysis
Pill (SW)	118	108	80	71
(PPA)	102	102	51	41
Other contraceptive (SW)	20	17	9	8
(PPA)	3	3	0	0
No contraception (SW)	25	15	7	6
(PPA)	4	4	0	0
Experimental total	220	210	131	112
Control total	52	39	16	14

[a] SW, student wives; PPA, Planned Parenthood Association.

breakdown by subgroups is shown in Table 3.

As anticipated, the losses in the control groups were the heaviest. The overall loss from the original response group to the group providing data for statistical analysis was 73%. Of those who began in the study, only 41% finished. All but one of the dropped control cases were due either to pregnancy or to a change in the contraceptive procedure, usually from Other Contraception to the Pill. In contrast, the overall loss in the Pill groups was 49%. Of those who began the study, 62% completed it. Reasons for dropping out are known for only a few cases. With such large subject losses, the probability of sampling bias, of course, is fairly high. However, the data in Tables 4 and 5 suggest that the samples are not biased. Table 4 lists descriptive data for 125 of the 131 Pill subjects who completed the study, 15 of the Control subjects who completed the study, 10 Control subjects who dropped out because of a change in contraceptive procedure, and 20 Pill subjects who dropped out for unknown reasons. The differences among the various groups are not only statistically nonsignificant, but are trivial in absolute size.

Table 5 shows a comparison of mean DACL scores for the 140 student wives who began the study and the 85 who provided the data for final statistical analysis. The scores were obtained from the first DACL administration of the study, the only one which was available for all 140 subjects of the beginning sample. None of the differences between beginning and final samples was statistically significant.

III. Results

The analysis of a Latin Square design requires that there be complete data, i.e., 16 scores for each subject. Thirty-seven of the Pill subjects

TABLE 4
SAMPLE DESCRIPTION

	Pill			Control			Drop-outs	
	Student wife	PPA	Total	No contraception	Other contraceptive	Total	Procedure change	Other reasons
N	79	46	125	6	9	15	10	20
$\bar{X}$ Age	23.7	24.2	23.9	24.8	24.7	24.7	24.0	24.9
Age range	20–33	20–34	20–34	22–28	22–33	22–23	22–26	23–27
$\bar{X}$ Educational level	15.8	16.1	15.9	14.5	15.6	15.2	15.6	15.8
Education range	12–19	8–20	8–20	13–16	12–18	12–18	12–18	12–20
$\bar{X}$ No. of children	0.3	0.8	0.34	0.0	0.9	0.5	0.3	0.4
No. of children range	0–3	0–5	0–5	—	0–2	0–2	0–1	0–1
Religion (%)								
Protestant	91	61	80	100	100	100	90	70
Catholic	1	2	2	—	—	—	10	15
Jewish	4	4	4	—	—	—	—	10
Other	1	2	2	—	—	—	—	—
None	3	30	13	—	—	—	—	5

TABLE 5

A COMPARISON OF THE BEGINNING AND FINAL STUDENT WIFE SAMPLES
ON THE FIRST DACL ADMINISTRATION[a]

	Beginning sample		Sample used in statistical analysis	
Group	DACL mean	N	DACL mean	N
Pill	9.4	108	9.4	71
No contraception	10.2	15	10.0	6
Other contraceptive	8.3	17	9.6	8
(Control total)	(9.2)	(32)	(9.8)	(14)

[a] No differences are statistically significant.

who completed the study and six control subjects had failed to complete
and return the DACL on one or more occasions. To avoid some of the
bias inherent in working with estimated missing data, it was decided
to omit from the analysis all subjects with two or more missing observations. This left 22 subjects—18 Pill subjects and 4 controls—each with
one missing observation. The data for these subjects were used in the
formula for least squares estimation of a single missing observation in a
Latin Square to fill in the hole in each case (Winer, 1962). All of the
data analyses presented in this section are based on 112 Pill subjects and
14 control subjects, as indicated in Table 3.

Group mean scores by Months and by Weeks for the various groups

TABLE 6

MEAN SCORES ON THE DEPRESSION ADJECTIVE CHECKLIST BY GROUPS

	Pill			Control		
	Student wife	PPA	Total	Other contracep-tive	No contracep-tion	Total
Week 1	8.8	8.9	8.8	7.6	9.3	8.3
Week 2	7.9	8.4	8.1	7.1	9.2	8.0
Week 3	7.7	8.1	7.8	8.2	8.3	8.2
Week 4	7.8	8.3	8.0	7.4	9.1	8.1
Month 1	8.2	8.3	8.2	7.9	8.9	8.3
Month 2	8.5	8.0	8.3	7.1	8.1	7.5
Month 3	7.9	8.9	8.3	8.1	9.9	8.9
Month 4	7.6	8.5	7.9	7.2	8.8	7.9
All	8.0	8.4	8.15	7.6	8.9	8.16

are shown in Table 6. The means range from 7.6 to 8.9 for the Pill groups, and from 7.1 to 9.9 for the control groups with almost identical overall means of 8.17 and 8.15. These are comparable to the mean of 7.7 obtained by Lubin (1965) in one of his standardization samples (see Table 2). The primary goal of the investigation was a comparison of subjects taking oral contraceptives with subjects using other forms of contraception, or no contraception. Because of the way in which the subjects were obtained, however, it was appropriate first to perform separate, replicated Latin Square analyses in each of the four groups of the total sample. These analyses are shown in Tables 7–10. Tables 9 and 10 show that in the two control groups there are no significant effects attributable to any of the three main factors (Months, Weeks, DACL Forms). In Tables 7 and 8, however, significant differences were found among DACL Forms in both Pill samples, and significant differences among Weeks in the student wife sample. The means representing these effects are shown

TABLE 7
SUMMARY OF ANALYSIS OF STUDENT WIFE SAMPLE DATA

Source of variation	df	Mean Square	F test
Subjects	70	76.449	—
Months	3	42.175	1.542
Months × Subjects	210	27.351	—
Weeks	3	67.559	2.804*
Weeks × Subjects	210	24.090	—
Forms	3	78.081	4.046**
Forms × Subjects	210	19.300	—
Latin Square Residual	6	21.401	1.070
Residual × Subjects	409	20.003	—

Week means

1	2	3	4	Total
8.75	7.85	7.71	7.79	8.02

Tukey 5% HSD between any two Week means = 1.066

Form means

A	B	C	D	Total
8.46	7.35	8.41	7.87	8.02

Tukey 5% HSD between any two Form means = 0.954

* Significant at the 5% level.
** Significant at the 1% level.

168   *Eugene E. Levitt, John E. Kooiker, and James A. Norton*

TABLE 8

SUMMARY OF ANALYSIS OF BLOOMINGTON PLANNED PARENTHOOD ASSOCIATION DATA

Source of variation	df	Mean Square	F test
Subjects	40	66.888	—
Months	3	22.884	1.274
Months × Subjects	120	17.961	—
Weeks	3	16.628	0.800
Weeks × Subjects	120	20.775	—
Forms	3	51.888	2.832*
Forms × Subjects	120	18.319	—
Latin Square Residual	6	20.392	0.984
Residual × Subjects	233	20.717	—

Form means

A	B	C	D	Total
9.21	7.90	8.35	8.22	8.42

Tukey 5% HSD between any two Form means = 1.232

* Significant at the 5% level.

at the bottoms of Tables 7 and 8. The mean difference required for significance at the 5% level according to the Tukey studentized Range Test (Winer, 1962) is also given in each case.

Differences among Forms in the two Pill samples, though varying in magnitude for the two groups, arise from means which are in the same rank order for both groups; from high to low: Forms A,C,D,B. The Weeks effect in the student wife sample appears to be primarily due to Week 1, during which subjects tended to have higher DACL scores than in subsequent weeks. Note that the same pattern holds in the

TABLE 9

SUMMARY OF ANALYSIS OF OTHER CONTRACEPTIVE SAMPLE DATA

Source of variation	df	Mean Square	F test
Subjects	7	22.250	—
Months	3	8.333	0.293
Months × Subjects	21	28.464	—
Weeks	3	6.062	0.526
Weeks × Subjects	21	11.527	—
Forms	3	16.854	0.555
Forms × Subjects	21	30.390	—
Latin Square Residual	6	36.458	1.781
Residual × Subjects	41	20.470	—

Depression and Oral Contraception

TABLE 10
SUMMARY OF ANALYSIS OF NO CONTRACEPTION SAMPLE DATA

Source of variation	df	Mean Square	F test
Subjects	5	35.775	—
Months	3	13.069	1.543
Months × Subjects	15	8.469	—
Weeks	3	5.153	0.243
Weeks × Subjects	15	21.219	—
Forms	3	30.458	1.130
Forms × Subjects	15	26.958	—
Latin Square Residual	6	24.042	1.466
Residual × Subjects	27	16.398	—

Bloomington PPA Pill sample, though not to a degree sufficient to reach statistical significance.

The next step in the analysis was to compare the two Pill samples with one another, to determine whether they could be pooled into a single experimental group, and, similarly, to compare the two control samples, to determine whether they could be pooled into a single control group. These comparisons were accomplished by Between and Within Groups replicated Latin Square analyses using the method of unweighted means (Winer, 1962). The results are presented in Tables 11 and 12. In

TABLE 11
SUMMARY OF COMPARISON OF STUDENT WIFE SAMPLE AND PLANNED
PARENTHOOD ASSOCIATION DATA

Source of variation	df	Mean Square	F test
Groups	1	65.089	0.892
Subjects within Groups	110	72.972	—
Months	3	6.462	0.270
Months × Groups	3	53.510	2.236
Months × Subjects within Groups	330	23.936	—
Weeks	3	66.014	2.885*
Weeks × Groups	3	4.848	0.212
Weeks × Subjects within Groups	330	22.885	—
Forms	3	110.351	5.825**
Forms × Groups	3	12.542	0.662
Forms × Subjects within Groups	330	18.943	—
Latin Square Residual	6	37.309	1.841
Residual × Groups	6	4.346	0.214
Residual × Subjects within Groups	642	20.262	—

* Significant at the 5% level.
** Significant at the 1% level.

TABLE 12

SUMMARY OF COMPARISON OF OTHER CONTRACEPTIVE AND NO
CONTRACEPTION SAMPLES

Source of variation	df	Mean Square	F test
Groups	1	103.243	3.702
Subjects within Groups	12	27.885	—
Months	3	19.362	0.962
Months × Groups	3	2.731	0.136
Months × Subjects within Groups	36	20.133	—
Weeks	3	0.678	0.044
Weeks × Groups	3	10.450	0.671
Weeks × Subjects within Groups	36	15.565	—
Forms	3	32.529	1.123
Forms × Groups	3	16.725	0.578
Forms × Subjects within Groups	36	28.960	—
Latin Square Residual	6	23.105	1.226
Residual × Groups	6	35.646	1.891
Residual × Subjects within Groups	68	18.853	—

both tables the difference between Groups, and the interaction of each of the main effects with Groups, all fail to reach statistical significance at the 5% level. Accordingly, the samples were combined into a single Experimental Pill group of 112 cases, and a single Control, non-Pill group, of 14 cases.

In each of these combined groups, analyses were then carried out to test for main effects of Months, Weeks, and Forms. These analyses are presented in Tables 13 and 14, along with the corresponding means. In Table 13, there is a significant Week effect in the Pill group, with Week 1 high, Week 2 intermediate, and Weeks 3 and 4 low. There is a highly significant Forms effect in this group, with the same pattern as previously noted; from high to low: Forms A,C,D,B. In Table 14, we find none of the effects significant in the Control sample.

Finally, in Table 15, the combined Experimental group and the combined Control group are compared with one another. No significant differences between groups are detected. This may be attributable partly to the extreme disparity of the two group sizes, which results in some degree of insensitivity in the analysis of unweighted means for Months, Weeks, and Forms effects (Winer, 1962). However, the basic finding— that the Groups factor is not significant—was unaffected by the un- weighted means method. We may conclude that, overall, the Pill and Control subjects did not differ on DACL scores during the course of the study.

The duration of the Pill regimen in our Experimental samples ranged

TABLE 13

SUMMARY OF ANALYSIS OF COMBINED EXPERIMENTAL (PILL) SAMPLE DATA

Source of variation	df	Mean Square	F test
Subjects	111	72.901	—
Months	3	11.655	0.482
Months × Subjects	333	24.202	—
Weeks	3	79.381	3.494*
Weeks × Subjects	333	22.722	—
Forms	3	117.441	6.219**
Forms × Subjects	333	18.885	—
Latin Square Residual	6	37.448	1.862
Residual × Subjects	648	20.115	—

Week means

1	2	3	4	Total
8.79	8.06	7.85	7.98	8.17

5% HSD between any two Week means: 3.652 × .2252 = 0.822

Form means

A	B	C	D	Total
8.74	7.55	8.39	8.00	8.17

5% HSD between any two Form means: 3.652 × .2053 = 0.750

* Significant at the 5% level.
** Significant at the 1% level.

from a few months to more than two years with a median of 18 months. This provided an opportunity to determine whether there was a gradual encroachment of depression as a function of time on the Pill. Our subjects had classified themselves into four groups according to duration of the

TABLE 14

SUMMARY OF ANALYSIS OF COMBINED CONTROL SAMPLE DATA

Source of variation	df	Mean Square	F test
Subjects	13	33.718	—
Months	3	18.696	0.995
Months × Subjects	39	18.793	—
Weeks	3	0.815	0.054
Weeks × Subjects	39	15.168	—
Forms	3	30.589	1.092
Forms × Subjects	39	28.019	—
Latin Square Residual	6	24.851	1.229
Residual × Subjects	74	20.215	—

TABLE 15
SUMMARY OF COMPARISON OF COMBINED EXPERIMENTAL AND COMBINED
CONTROL SAMPLES

Source of variation	df	Mean Square	F test
Groups	1	0.061	0.001
Subjects within Groups	122	68.538	—
Months	3	19.024	0.807
Months × Groups	3	16.704	0.709
Months × Subjects within Groups	366	23.562	—
Weeks	3	12.469	0.563
Weeks × Groups	3	6.563	0.296
Weeks × Subjects within Groups	366	22.165	—
Forms	3	37.992	1.906
Forms × Groups	3	42.450	2.130
Forms × Subjects within Groups	366	19.928	—
Latin Square Residual	6	32.844	1.632
Residual × Groups	6	19.776	0.983
Residual × Subjects within Groups	710	20.127	—

Pill regimen.[4] DACL scores were averaged for each subject to provide a single score representing the degree of the subject's depression during the course of the study. Mean scores for subjects according to duration of the Pill regimen, and a summary of the subsequent analysis of variance, are shown in Table 16. The F ratio clearly shows that differences among groups were not statistically significant, supporting the conclusion that there was no relationship between DACL scores and longevity of the

TABLE 16
DEPRESSION AND PILL REGIMEN LONGEVITY

Duration of Pill (months)	N	Overall $\bar{X}$ DACL score	SD
1–6	5	8.9	1.82
6–12	19	8.2	2.14
12–24	44	7.7	2.20
More than 24	43	8.3	1.95

Summary of variance analysis

Source of variation	df	Mean Square	F test
Between Groups	3	4.067	0.939
Within Groups	107	4.331	—

[4] One subject whose Pill regimen was less than one month was discarded.

Pill regimen. Reference to the subgroup means in Table 16 shows that, if anything, there is a slight tendency for subjects who had been on the Pill for a year or more to have slightly lower DACL scores than those whose regimen was less than a year.

IV. On the Reliability of State Measures

The use of measures of personality states in behavioral science research is uncommon. It might be wise, therefore, to consider methods of computing reliability before attempting to estimate the reliability of the DACL in our study. Most of the objective verbal measuring instruments used in the behavioral sciences are operational definitions of hypothetical constructs which have reference to relatively stable conditions of the individual. These include such concepts as needs, personality characteristics, psychological adjustment, attributes, and aptitudes. They are assumed to derive from a host of antecedent factors—influences, events, heredity, and so forth—and are theoretically constant over time and across circumstances. Even during the developmental stages of life, they are considered to be relatively unchangeable over short periods of time like a week or a month, in the absence of a specific treatment designed to produce change. Such personal factors may be called *traits*, as a collective term, and the instruments which serve as their operational definitions are then called *trait measures*.

The conventional concept of reliability was developed for the trait measure. The idea of high test-retest correlation as a measure of reliability illustrates the point plainly. Reliability is the degree to which the individual's score is unaffected by influences other than the trait itself, especially by ephemeral factors in the testing situation such as motivation, fatigue, mood, and practice effects. These influences are ordinarily random in a particular group of individuals. At any testing moment, one person's score may be affected by his motivation, another's by his mood, another's by fatigue, and so forth. The net effect is to cause the distribution of scores to vary in a random, i.e., unpredictable, fashion. If any one factor is a constant influence over the group, for example, fatigue in the instance of a measurement made late at night, then the effect is no longer random and should not materially alter a test-retest correlation coefficient.

A reliability of .80 can be interpreted to mean that 80% of the observed score variation is a function of the trait being measured and 20% is due to the influence of random factors, the so-called *error variance*. If the correlation is .90—indicating greater stability of scores over time—then the error variance falls to only 10% of the total.

Feelings, moods, and emotional states are, in theory, inconstant over time in normal persons. A mood like anxiety, depression, joy, or anger is the immediate response to a situational stimulus and is expected to be dissipated when the stimulus is withdrawn or neutralized. (Moods which persist for any length of time are regarded as pathognomic of emotional abnormality.) We can call these ephemeral conditions *states*, and the instruments which serve as their operational definitions, *state measures*.

States are continually variable within individuals. A person may be angry on Monday, depressed on Tuesday, elated on Wednesday, and so forth. The influences which produce states are largely idiosyncratic and therefore largely random in any group of individuals. Any particular person might score high on a state measure of anger or depression at noon and low on that same measure at 5:00 P.M. on the same day.

Not all of the influences on a state measure are unpredictable. Most personality theories hold that individuals are more or less *predisposed* to experience various states. One person is more disposed to experience fear, another to experience anger, and so forth. These predispositions are conceptualized as traits. There is a trait known as anxiety (i.e., anxiety-proneness), a trait called aggressiveness (anger-proneness), and so on. These traits account for some part of the variance of the corresponding state measure. In theory, the influence is not great, on the average. We would ordinarily expect that a low trait-anxious individual under stress will obtain a higher anxiety state score than a high trait-anxious individual measured in a relaxed situation. Momentary influences are expected to have greater effect on state measure than does the corresponding trait.

The extent of the relationship between a state measure and its corresponding trait measure is unclear. Under normal circumstances, we might expect very little relationship, possibly a correlation no greater than .10. However, this may very well depend on the state which is being measured. Unfortunately, a measurement situation is itself stressful for individuals with certain traits. Thus, the relationship between trait and state anxiety measures in an unstressful situation found by Spielberger and Gorsuch (1966) was in the area of .40. A difference of almost 12 scale points on the state-anxiety measure was found between groups which were high and low on the trait-anxiety measure. Because anxiety is the state most affected by measurement situations, it is very probable that this coefficient represents a maximum state-trait correlation among various states.

The correlation indicates that no more than 16% of the variability of state measures is likely to be a function of variability in the corresponding trait, a characteristic which is stable in each individual across time. The remaining 84% of the variance is random, error variance in the conventional test-retest situation. If follows that the test-retest "reliability" of a state measure, even over a limited time period like 24 hours, would probably be quite low. This is due to the essential nature of the construct which is being measured, and cannot be attributed to shortcomings of the measuring instrument. It follows, also, that the test-retest method for estimating reliability is inappropriate to a state measure. In fact, this is simply an extreme case of a general criticism that can be levelled at the use of a test-retest coeffiicient as an estimate of reliability. A test-retest correlation is attenuated by any influence in the intervening time period which affects the testees differentially and which tends to alter their relative positions on the underlying variable. Such differential changes are all assigned to error variance by a test-retest estimate of reliability, but they are not true error variance in terms of the measure being evaluated. Methods of reliability estimation which do not permit the intervention of differential changes on the underlying variable being measured are preferable, in general, to test-retest.

There are several other ways in which the reliability of a measure may be estimated which involve the virtual simultaneity of supposedly parallel forms of the measure, or at least the lapse of only a very brief time interval. The conventional split-half technique for estimating reliability assumes that essentially half-length parallel forms of the measure have been administered simultaneously and intermixed. Another procedure is the actual use of parallel forms, administered sequentially without pause. Still another approach is the *internal consistency* estimate of reliability, sometimes called *coefficient alpha* (Cronbach, 1951). This has been shown to be the average of all possible split-half reliability estimates from the same set of items. Any of these methods, but especially the last, seems better suited to the job of estimating the proportion of non-error variance (i.e., reliability) in a measure with the ephemeral characteristics of a state measure.

To estimate reliability of a state measure in the conventional test-retest manner, it would be necessary to find some way to reduce sharply the apparent "error" variance due to state fluctuations in the individuals being used for reliability estimation. One possibility is the use of repeated stress situations. For example, a state measure of anxiety could be administered on two occasions widely differing in time but on both of which anxiety is induced in the subject group by the experimenter.

There are several problems with this approach. First, it is no simple matter to induce a specific emotional state in a group, even if we mean by this only that the state level would rise from an unstressed baseline in a majority of the group members. It is even less feasible to conceive of

TABLE 17

A COMPARISON OF TEST-RETEST AND SPLIT-HALF RELIABILITIES
OF THE DACL

DACL form	Mean test-retest	Split-half
A	.111	.914
B	.143	.921
C	.147	.900
D	.120	.901

carrying out this maneuver successfully with the same subjects on *two* occasions.

There is some evidence which suggests that the state-trait correlation rises when the state measure is administered under conditions of specific stimulation. For example, in the Spielberger-Gorsuch study, the state-trait correlation rose from .40 to between .50 and .60 under stress. The test constructor has therefore increased the variance of his "state" measure which is due to the trait. The improved test-retest correlation of the state measure is thus a function of the trait. Unless we can reasonably hypothesize that this apparent reliability is inherent in the state measure, the use of the stress situation to estimate state measure reliability is, at best, open to question.

Computations of DACL scores derived from our study provide an excellent illustration of the considerations of the reliability of a state measure. All possible intercorrelations among the 16 administrations of the DACL during the study yield a total of 120 coefficients. They range in magnitude from —.08 to .35 with an average intercorrelation of .133.

The four administrations of each DACL form furnish six intercorrelations among administrations of the same form. The average of the six coefficients for each form, and the split-half coefficients obtained for each form from all of its administrations, are compared in Table 17. Obviously, the test-retest coefficients are far below an acceptable, minimum level for a reliability measure by any standards, while the split-half coefficients are respectably large.

V. Comments by Pill Sample Subjects

Those subjects who completed the study were asked to fill out a personal data sheet which provided an opportunity for spontaneous comment. One hundred and twenty-five of the 131 Experimental sample subjects who completed the study also returned the personal data sheet.

Sixty, or 48%, volunteered comments on the study. This is a substantial proportion for an optional participation, no doubt reflecting the high educational level of the subject group. It also lends weight to those comments which were recurrent among the 60 respondents.

Examination of the content of the comments indicates that there are three types which occurred with a moderate frequency, and two others with a marked but somewhat lower frequency.

Thirty-three, or 55%, of the respondents indicated that stresses of everyday life and other causes of emotional variation appeared much more important than any pill effect. The following are some typical comments.

"There are so many variables when it comes to a study of emotions that it would seem difficult to me to figure which are the result of a person's contraceptive device."

"It seems to me that my emotional state was due to outside forces quite often rather than any cycle."

"I think many of my answers were influenced by the type of day I'd had."

"I don't understand what controls were used to eliminate the confounding variables of the influences of daily experiences on moods and feelings."

Twenty-six of the subjects, or 43%, commented that the time of day when the checklist was completed was a factor influencing responses. The consensus was that checklists filled out late in the day would have greater depressive content.

Twenty subjects, or 33%, voiced some criticism of the checklist itself. Some illustrations follow:

"There weren't enough word choices."

"I found that your choices of 'words to describe exactly how I feel' rarely described accurately any of my feelings. Needed more variety."

"The adjectives chosen to describe one's feelings were not complete. There were many times when I felt indifferent, average, etc., but few times when I felt the extremes of emotion indicated in the word list."

Seven subjects, or 12%, stated flatly that they had noticed no emotional change since beginning the pill regimen. A few others suggested that their mood had actually improved.

Six subjects, or 10%, indicated that the day of the week on which the checklist was filled out was a factor. The following comments suggest the effect of day of the week on mood:

"Another thing which might have bearing on my own contribution— Wednesday is my day off from work, and that may affect my emotional aspects."

"Saturday may mean a week's worth of cleaning, etc., whereas, Friday may mean 'thank goodness it's Friday' and let's celebrate!"

Overall, the many comments concerning the effect of everyday life stresses, time of the day and day of the week, strongly indicate that if the contraceptive regimen had any effect, it was submerged by other, more salient factors affecting the emotional state, and was thus of trivial consequence. This inference supports the conclusions deriving from statistical analyses of the data.

VI. Discussion

The inference that our Experimental subjects manifested no more depression than the Control subjects is based on four findings: (*a*) The means in Table 6 and the crucial analysis of variance comparing Pill and Control subjects, summarized in Table 15, show that there was no overall difference in DACL scores nor any significant interaction between samples and other main factors. The overall means for Experimental and Control samples are almost carbon copies: 8.15 and 8.16. (*b*) Within the Pill sample, there is no correlation between depression and duration of the drug regimen (Table 16). (*c*) The substantial internal consistency of the DACL as illustrated in Table 17 suggests that it is a highly reliable instrument. The very low test-retest correlations indicate that the state depression levels of our subjects fluctuated from week to week almost at random. This is precisely what one would expect to find if the state was influenced by a variety of factors occurring among the subjects with varying frequencies and intensities, and at different times. It is contrary to what would be expected if the state was influenced by a single strong factor. If a Pill regimen markedly affected the DACL scores of our Pill subjects, at least moderate test-retest coefficients would have been found. The very low coefficients therefore indicate an absence of any strong, constant influence on DACL scores. (*d*) The reasoning in the previous paragraph is supported by the spontaneous comments of our Pill sample subjects. More than half volunteered the opinion that, in essence, many factors influenced responses to the DACL. One subject concisely summarized the conclusion which derives from the test-retest correlations and the spontaneous comments of the Pill sample: "There are so many variables when it comes to a study of emotions that it would seem difficult to me to figure which are the result of a person's contraceptive device."

At the outset, we considered the possibility that the clinical notion of the insidious encroachment of depression might not be quite accurate.

Perhaps the depressive effect is intracyclic. Depression occurs as a function of the build-up of hormones during the month, is relieved by the menstrual period during which the contraceptive is not ingested and the hormone levels become low. It builds up again as the woman begins taking pills regularly during the next month. According to this hypothesis, depression as measured by the DACL should be lowest at the end of the menstrual period and highest just before the mentrual period.

The data in Table 6 show that exactly the opposite is true for the Pill samples. In both samples, mean DACL scores are highest for Week 1 and lower thereafter. The trend is statistically significant in the Student Wife sample (Table 7). Thus it appears that depression is *greatest* at the end of the menstrual period when the hormone level is *lowest*. After two weeks of taking the Pill, depression levels are lower. Inspection of Tables 6, 9, and 10 shows that this trend is not found in the Control samples. The difference between Week 1 and Week 4 means, which is 1.0 and 0.6 for the Pill samples, is only 0.2 for the Control samples. The Other Contraceptive sample reaches a clear peak at Week 3 while the No Contraception sample attains a definite low in the same week. Neither Control sample manifests a clear-cut trend over weeks.

The Experimental-Control Weeks comparison suggests that the Pill actually *reduces* depression during any one cycle, an inference which would be consonant with the few earlier reports of decreases in depressive symptomatology (Kistner, 1966; Sluglett and Lawson, 1967).

If we accept the Pill sample Weeks effect as genuine, it is necessary to explain why the overall mean DACL scores for the Pill samples are not lower than those of the Control groups. Possible corollary inference are: (*a*) the Pill regimen in some way causes a *rise* above normal in depression level at the end of menstruation; perhaps menstruation is more depressing for Pill users than for non-users; (*b*) Women who take the Pill are those who tend to be above average in depression-proneness; (*c*) Women who do not use the Pill tend to be below average in depression-proneness. Other corollary inferences are conceivable. Unfortunately, the data of the present study do not bear on the validity of corollary inferences.

It is possible to argue that those women who become markedly depressed due to the Pill are among the women who have discontinued the regimen and were thus not numbered among our experimental subjects. There are several arguments against this contention. First, depression was not offered as a reason by the discontinuers interviewed by Westoff and Ryder (1968). Second, the study by Ziegler *et al.* (1968) found that side effects were equally common among women who continued and discontinued a Pill regimen. Findings based on psychological test data suggested that personality factors rather than side effects themselves determined whether or not a woman would discontinue or continue the Pill.

Finally, the idea that Pill-depressed women discontinue the drug early clashes with the clinical hypothesis that the onset of Pill-induced depression is so gradual and insidious that the woman does not connect Pill and mood state. Obviously, a woman could not be expected to discontinue medication because of depression unless she believed that the former caused the latter.

VII. Conclusion

None of the hypotheses relating Pill and depression is supported by our data. There is no evidence that depression accumulates over a prolonged Pill regimen, nor that it rises intracyclicly. No doubt there are individual exceptions as a function of idiosyncrasies of personality or physical make-up. It is perfectly possible that our primary conclusion does not extend to populations of women whose mean age is considerably higher than 25 years. Perhaps the most important conclusion of our study is that it is unwise to draw significant inferences from clinical or other kinds of unobjective studies.

REFERENCES

AMA Council on Drugs. An oral contraceptive: norethindrone with mestranol (Ortho-Novum). *Journal of the American Medical Association,* 1964, **187**, 664–665.

AMA Council on Drugs. Evaluation of oral contraceptives. *Journal of the American Medical Association,* 1967, **199**, 650–653.

Bakker, C. B., & Dightman, C. R. Side effects of oral contraceptives. *Obstetrics and Gynecology,* 1966, **28**, 373–379.

Beck, A. T., Ward, C. H., Mendelson, M., Mock, J., & Erbaugh, J. An inventory for measuring depression. *Archives of General Psychiatry,* 1961, **4**, 561–571.

Behrman, S. F. Norethindrone, 2 mg., an evaluation. *Obstetrics and Gynecology,* 1964, **24**, 101–105.

Benedek, T. *Psychosexual functions in women.* New York: Ronald Press, 1952.

Bryans, F. E. Oral contraception. *Canadian Medical Association Journal,* 1965, **92**, 287–288.

Cronbach, L. J. Coefficient alpha and the internal structure of tests. *Psychometrika,* 1951, **16**, 297–334.

Drill, V. A. Endocrine properties and long-term safety of oral contraceptives. *Metabolism, Clinical and Experimental,* 1965, **14**, 295–310.

Glick, I. D. Mood and behavioral changes associated with the use of the oral contraceptive agents. *Psychopharmacologia,* 1967, **10**, 363–374.

Goldzieher, J. Oral contraceptives. *Medical Journal of Australia*, 1965, **1**, 991–992.

Gottschalk, L. A., Kaplan, S. M., Winget, C. M., & Gleser, G. C. Variations in magnitude of emotion: A method applied to anxiety and hostility during phases of the menstrual cycle. *Psychosomatic Medicine*, 1962, **24**, 300–311.

Gray, B. M. Oral contraceptives and depression. *American Journal of Psychiatry*, 1966, **123**, 373.

Kane, F. J., Daly, R. J., Wallach, M. H., & Keeler, M. H. Amelioration of pre-menstrual mood disturbance with a progestational agent (Enovid). *Diseases of the Nervous System*, 1966, **27**, 339–342.

Kane, F. J., Daly, R. J., Ewing, J. A., & Keeler, M. H. Mood and behavioral changes with progestational agents. *British Journal of Psychiatry*, 1967, **113**, 265–268.

Kane, F. J., & Keeler, M. H. The use of Enovid in postpartum mental disorders. *Southern Medical Journal*, 1965, **58**, 1089–1092.

Kaye, B. M. Oral contraceptives and depression. *Journal of the American Medical Association*, 1963, **186**, 522.

Kistner, R. W. Oral contraceptives: safety factors in prolonged use of progestin-estrogen combinations. Part 1. *Postgraduate Medicine*, 1966, **39**, 207–216.

Klein, E., & Levitt, E. E. Side effects of contraceptive medication in a university associated population. *Journal of the American College Health Association*, 1967, **16**, 182–184.

Lubin, B. Adjective checklists for the measurement of depression. *Archives of General Psychiatry*, 1965, **12**, 57–62.

Lubin, B. Fourteen brief depression adjective checklists. *Archives of General Psychiatry*, 1966, **15**, 205–208.

McGregor, C. M. Oral contraceptives and depression. *Lancet*, 1967, **104**, 1231.

Murawski, J. B., Sapir, P. E., Shulman, N., Ryan, G. M., & Sturgis, S. H. An investigation of mood states in women taking oral contraceptives. *Fertility and Sterility*, 1968, **19**, 50–63.

Neubardt, S. *A concept of contraception*. New York: Trident Press, 1967.

Nilsson, A., Jacobson, L., & Ingemanson, C. A. Side-effects of an oral contraceptive with particular attention to mental symptoms and sexual adaptation. *Acta Obstetricia et Gynecologia Scandinavica*, 1967, **46**, 537–566.

Rossi, G. V. Side-effects and possible complications of oral contraceptive drugs. *American Journal of Pharmacology*, 1966, **138**, 127–136.

Sapir, P. E., Ryan, G. M., Shulman, N., & Murawski, J. B. Emotional responses to the contraceptive agent, Enovid. Unpublished paper, American Society for the Study of Sterility, 1965.

Simpson, G. M., Radinger, N., Rochlin, D., & Kline, N. S. Enovid in the treatment of psychic disturbances associated with menstruation. *Diseases of the Nervous System*, 1962, **23**, 589–590.

Simpson, G. M., Rochlin, D., & Kline, N. S. Further studies of Enovid in the treatment of psychiatric patients. *Diseases of the Nervous System*, 1964, **25**, 484–486.

Sluglett, J., & Lawson, J. P. Side-effects of oral contraceptives. *Lancet*, 1967, **104**, 612.

Spielberger, C. D. Theory and research on anxiety. *In* Spielberger, C. D. (ed.), *Anxiety and behavior*. New York: Academic Press, 1966.

Spielberger, C. D., & Gorusch, R. L. Mediating process in verbal conditioning. Report of USPHS Grants MH 7229, MH 7446, and HD 947. September, 1966.

Swanson, D. W., Barron, A., Floren, A., & Smith, J. A. The use or norethynodrel in psychotic females. *American Journal of Psychiatry*, 1964, **120**, 1101–1103.

Vennard, W. O. Birth control pills. *American Journal of Psychiatry*, 1966, **123**, 1449.

Wallach, E. E., & Garcia, C. R. Psychodynamic aspects of oral contraception. *Journal of the American Medical Association*, 1968, **203**, 927–931.

Westoff, C. F., & Ryder, N. B. Duration of use of oral contraception in the United States, 1960–65. *United States, Public Health Reports*, 1968, **83**, 277–287.

Winer, B. J. *Statistical principles in experimental design.* New York: McGraw-Hill, 1962.

Ziegler, F. J., Rodgers, D. A., Kriegsman, S. A., & Marton, P. L. Ovulation suppressors, psychological functioning, and marital adjustment. *Journal of the American Medical Association*, 1968, **204**, 849–853.

The Quest for Valid Preventive Interventions[1]

James G. Kelly
Department of Psychology and Institute for Social Research
University of Michigan
Ann Arbor, Michigan

One should never wear one's
best trousers to go out and
battle for freedom and truth.
                Ibsen

I. Introduction

William James' legacy to psychology was remembered at the 75th anniversary meetings of the American Psychological Association in 1967 by a series of commemorative symposia focusing on humanism and the problem of will, the modern meaning of instincts, levels of awareness, and brain functions. In addition to James' substantive contributions to psychology and his eclectic and humanitarian concerns, he also began a quest for societal alternatives for social pathology that continues to speak directly to the emerging field of community psychology.

[1] An earlier version of this paper was presented in A Symposium on Community Psychology, Loyola University, Chicago, Illinois, May 6, 1968 and is one of the contributions of the Task Force on Community Mental Health, chaired by John C. Glidewell and Mortimer M. Brown. A summary of the final report "Priorities for Psychologists in Community Mental Health," is available from John C. Glidewell, University of Chicago. This chapter has benefited from the critical appraisal of Lenin A. Baler, Keith Smith, and Randolph Harper whose help is gratefully acknowledged.

There is still much unfinished business for this legacy of William James. He challenged psychologists to create new social institutions with varied means and open ends. His own eloquence was expressed as follows:

I spoke of the "moral equivalent" of war. So far, war has been the only force that can discipline a whole community, and until an equivalent discipline is organized, I believe that war must have its way. But I have no serious doubts that the ordinary prides and shames of social man, once developed to a certain intensity, are capable of organizing such a moral equivalent as I have sketched, or some other just as effective for preserving manliness of type. It is but a question of time, of skillful propagandism, and of opinion-making men seizing historic opportunities, . . . [James, 1911, p. 292].

There are numerous current and visible illustrations of the functions of crises and social disruptions that take on the properties of miniature warlike confrontations. The wisdom of Loaste's aphorism, "In every crisis there is opportunity as well as danger," has eluded citizens, government officials, and most change agents. We have failed, for the most part, to identify and moderate the social forces in our communities that are responsible for the personal and organizational casualties of change. What type of society can mobilize social change? Where in the life cycle of change programs are there opportunities to effectively influence social movements? How do interventions facilitate the evolution and development of social organizations? These searches, stimulated by William James, still are beyond the grasp of systematic knowledge.

The emergence of community psychology as a relevant area of professional engagement comes at a time when historic opportunity is seizing *us;* we certainly have not been effective in offering even miniscule suggestions for turning naturally occurring crises into social reform. While community psychologists have been active in proselytizing for change, we have not held positions of influence that would permit us to help identify opportunities for facilitating change, nor have we been able to pass on to others pragmatic and valid ideas that they might act upon. Eighty years after William James' words, we find that the community psychologist has joined the policy planner, the action researcher, the community developer, the urbanologist, and various groups of citizens working at making new communities. In the midst of this new and fast changing mix, we must ask: "What can we contribute that is unique?" and "How do we know that what we do counts?"

The operational issues which face community psychologists include such questions as: "When is an intervention by an outsider constructive?"; "When are interventions initiated?"; "How should interventions vary from place to place?"; "What criteria are employed to evaluate interventions?" Answers to these questions, generated out of involvement with real world affairs, suggest to the present writer that psychology must reorder its concepts for evaluating change and for conducting research, and must develop new methods to carry out its work.

What is effective, useful and sympathetic for the design of research in laboratory studies is inappropriate for the observation and evaluation of social change in natural settings and uncontrolled environments. Building toward a systematic account of the evaluation of change in social settings suggests an approach which involves multiple methods, an improvised style that emphasizes continuous participation with the local community, and a commitment to generate criteria for change. I am assuming that the community psychologist will increase his individual adaptation to social change by developing knowledge in different settings and by creating contrasting methodologies. The spirit of this personal response to the William James legacy is that adaptable knowledge will be best derived from work that emphasizes alternate methods stimulated by and appropriate to the requirements of natural settings.

In this chapter, I will present some personal views about these issues. Three approaches to preventive interventions are described in which methods are contrasted and aims are compared. In addition, examples are offered of the type of questions that these new methods generate for verifying knowledge about personal, organizational and community change. The main thesis is that the uniqueness of community psychology is in the verification of interventions that work in a variety of social settings. If we are ingenious enough to create ways to validate these ideas, we may eventually contribute to a redefinition of scientific activity in psychology.

II. Three Methods for Preventive Interventions

The following comments pertain to preventive interventions that are closely identified with three types of therapeutic programs. The clinical approach, which focuses upon changes in individuals or small groups, provides a setting for interventions that radiate effects resulting from services offered to relevant individuals. Programs designed to initiate systematic change in an organization can also provide the setting for interventions that assist an organization to deal with future crises. Community organization techniques that focus on ways to mobilize community resources for community action provide a heritage for preventive interventions that enable a community to plan for its future. For each of these prototypic approaches to personal, organizational, and community change, I have selected one example to illustrate the relevance of preventive programming.

For the clinical method, I have selected mental health consultation as an example of how the behavior of a consultee can be altered to affect the immediate larger environment. While most organizational change methods focus on redesigning role assignments and communication networks, altering the form of an organization also has the advantage of providing a context for developing capacities within the organization to handle future crises. The assumption is that the life style and ways of doing business of a social organization can be shifted to reduce the paralyzing features of an emergency which may face the organization. Community development is based on a dominant premise that the survival of a community depends upon its capacity to reach a new level of adaptation. With its tradition of multiple approaches and improvised formats, community development offers a setting for defining community change efforts that provide important guidelines for preventive intervention. In this case, the preventive intervention is developing criteria for the community to employ when setting goals for its own future.

When consultation services enable the immediate social environment to benefit from such help, this work contributes to an intervention that is preventive. If an organizational change program can rearrange the social fabric so that a new organization can deal effectively with internal and external crises, then the change program is, by definition, a preventive intervention. Community development programs function as a preventive intervention when they enable a community to plan more effectively for its future.

It is the present writer's view that these approaches to community change: (*a*) represent contrasting premises about the change process; (*b*) have quite different aims; (*c*) employ new types of data for evaluation; and, most importantly, (*d*) demand different principles for inferring verification of knowledge. While programs of personal and organizational change serve to generate goals that are valid as discrete accomplishments, new goals are required in order for such services to reduce expressions of maladaptive behavior. Viewing prototypic change programs as preventive interventions suggests different criteria for each evaluation. These criteria provide new options for linking change programs to social processes which may help them to become more directly related to the host community.

A. Intervention I: Mental Health Consultation
   as a Radiating Process

Descriptions of mental health consultation methods are legion, including an increasing number of efforts at evaluation that are now appearing in print (see Cowen, Gardner, & Zax, 1967; Iscoe, Pierce-Jones, Friedman,

& McGehearty, 1967). The work of Caplan (1964), Berlin (1962), Bind-man (1959), Morse (1967), Spielberger (1967), White (1966), and others has been effective in contrasting the professional activities of a psychotherapist and a mental health consultant. All of these writings emphasize an implicit premise: the aim of the consultant is to improve the functional competence of the consultee, for example, to improve the teaching effectiveness of the classroom teacher, to assist the principal in administering his school. The primary focus is the consultee's performance of occupational roles, and not necessarily the consultee's own personality structure or his overt expression of mental strain. The consultant's diag-nostic task is to assess the consultee's competence and his ability to carry out his job in a natural setting. The assessment process differs from the diagnostic process that takes place with clients in mental health treat-ment facilities by including data from the immediate social environment.

The historic focus for clinical work has been the patients' or clients' feelings, perceptions, and attitudes about their environments. Community mental health practice has emphasized the extension of clinical practice so that effort is expended to discuss feelings, attitudes, and perceptions that relate directly to concerns about occupational role. This type of intervention gives great emphasis to clarification of how the individual copes with his environment. It also involves an active, detailed exposition of the interrelationship between an individual's present behavior and his future interactions with key persons.

If we take preventive intervention seriously, we need to derive new types of criteria for assessing its effectiveness. The payoff from a consulta-tion program is not limited to an alteration in the feeling states, belief systems, and aspirations of the consultee; it should also reflect a change in a person's relationships with those significant others who directly participate in his life setting. Therefore, evaluation studies should not measure changes in attitudes of consultees, nor analyze samples of the interactions between a consultant and consultee, nor note changes in a consultee's self-concept, for such attempts at evaluation are not congruent with a conception of consultation as a preventive intervention.

One of the early rationales for developing consultation techniques was that they allowed the professional to work with key resources in the community who in turn would have direct access to large segments of the population (Klein & Lindemann, 1961). If this rationale is taken seriously, we are faced with establishing new standards for verification. If, for example, consultation is effective in initiating a change process, then indices of effectiveness should be defined not only by changes in consultee performance, such as that of the classroom teacher, but by cumulative and successive changes in the behavior of significant others, for example, students in the classroom as well as other teachers in the same school environment. The evaluation of such activities has not progressed, however, and new criteria for designing studies are needed. When considering research designs to document the effectiveness of consultation methods as a preventive intervention, it is essential to provide for the assessment of the radiating effects of the intervention. Since the creation of pre- and post-group comparisons and control groups to verify radiation effects would be prohibitive, it will be necessary to take into account what Campbell and Stanley (1963, p. 37) have termed "as quasi-experimental design" in which attention is given to time and spatial effects. This type of design permits periodic measurements of selected individuals, in this case students and classroom teachers, over a period of time and before and after the introduction of an intervention such as consultation. A schema for consultation as a radiating process is illustrated in Figures 1, 2, and 3.

In Figure 1, an example is presented for two classroom teachers where one teacher is the consultee (Teacher A). This design is relevant for assessing the radiating effects of the consultation process when the consultee has frequent interactions with other persons. The elements of

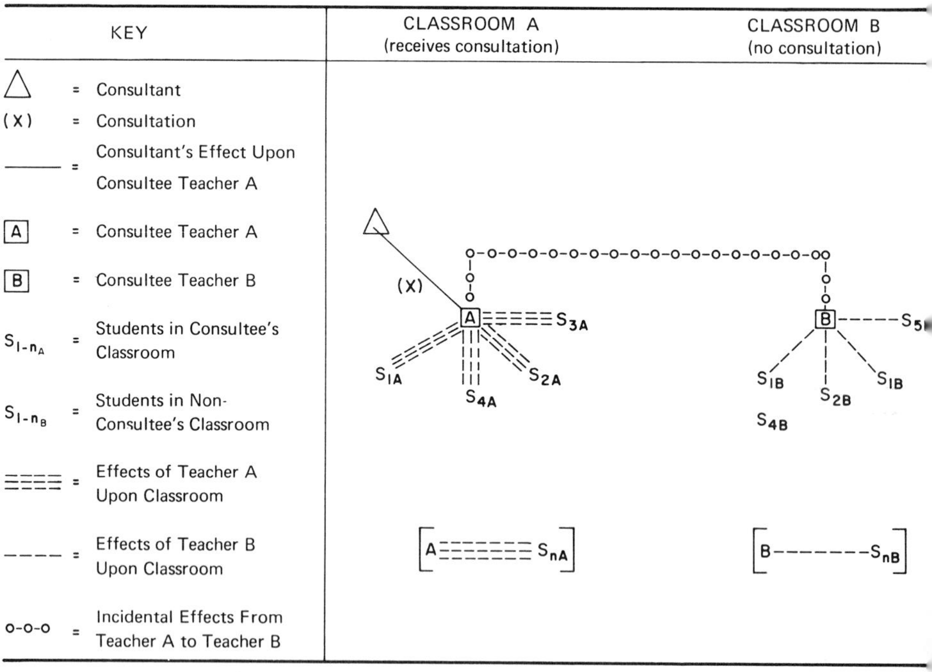

Fig. 1. Consultation: as a radiating process.

KEY	TIME-SERIES DESIGN
S_{1-n_A} = Observations of Students in Classroom A	
S_{1-n_B} = Observations of Students in Classroom B	Classroom A : $\left(S_{1-n_A}\right)_{T_1}$ $\left(S_{1-n_A}\right)_{T_2}$ × $\left(S_{1-n_A}\right)_{T_3}$ $\left(S_{1-n_A}\right)_{T_4}$
$T_{1\ldots n}$ = Times for Observations	
X = Intervention of Consultation	Classroom B : $\left(S_{1-n_B}\right)_{T_1}$ $\left(S_{1-n_B}\right)_{T_2}$ × $\left(S_{1-n_B}\right)_{T_3}$ $\left(S_{1-n_B}\right)_{T_4}$

Fig. 2. Consultation: as a radiating process.

this design which have been diagrammed provide for measuring changes in the behavior of the students in each teacher's classroom. It is expected that changes in students' behavior in Teacher A's classroom (S_{1_A} . . . S_{n_A}) will be more salutary than those observed in students in Teacher B's classroom (S_{1_B} . . . S_{n_B}). Thus, the thesis is that an intervention, such as consultation, can be preventive if the consultee produces change in significant others.

Figure 1 illustrates that Teacher A, who receives consultation, is the medium for producing change in the students in her classroom. Figure 2 diagrams a time-series design which involves repeated measurements of the students in both classrooms before and after the introduction of the intervention. Through the use of change scores and trend analysis, it should be possible to note any shifts in the behavior of students in the two classrooms, one in which the teacher receives consultation, a second

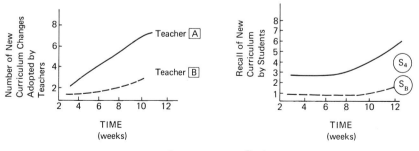

Fig. 3. Consultation: as a radiating process.

in which the teacher does not receive consultation. An additional feature of this design is that it permits documentation of the exact stages in the time sequence of the consultation process where its effects are seen in the behavior of students. Such research could help to clarify the meter of the consultation process and provide direct feedback for the practice of consultation.

Figure 3 presents examples of dependent variables which reflect the effects of the consultation intervention. In the rationale for consultation previously stated, an effort is made to influence the occupational role of the consultee. Criteria for evaluating consultation as a preventive intervention can be specifically related to occupational activity such as a teacher's ability to revise her teaching methods or the quality of teacher-student interactions. In the present example, the choice was to identify the number of changes in the teaching content of the teacher. The rationale for this example is that changes in the content of the curriculum reflect a central behavior of the teacher and define a major segment of teaching competence. In the example, Teacher A, who received consultation, increased the number of changes in her lesson plan more than did Teacher B who did not receive this service.

The same type of predictions can also be applied to students in the classroom. If consultation has been effective as a prevention intervention then students will be able to discriminate such effects as curriculum changes. Verification of the effectiveness of the intervention is derived from assessing changes in outcome patterns. Such quasi-experimental designs have been regarded as valid in the more successful sciences even though, as Campbell and Stanley (1963) have pointed out, they have rarely been accepted in the social sciences.

A source of uncontrolled variance that is intrinsic in this design is any unanticipated historical event unrelated to the intervention that brings about a discontinuity in performance. One approach to controlling this effect is to select and stratify teachers and students on the basis of the amount of contact with the consultee. As with most designs for interventions, concurrent field assessments of the local setting are required in order to provide contextual evidence for changes in the performance of students and teachers that are inferred to be a consequence of the intervention. This type of research design reduces so-called progression effects and selection biases that often plague studies of behavior in natural settings.

With such designs, we can test directly the effectiveness of consultation as a preventive intervention. We are no longer restricted solely to the behavior of the consultee as the criterion for outcome since we can assess "fallout" effects of the consultative relationship via the performance of others in the consultee's immediate environment. This design can also provide for the assessment of intermediate effects, such as comparisons of consultant-consultee interactions and changes in the attitudes of a consultee regarding performance of work roles. Such observations help to establish an empirical basis for defining the process of carrying out interventions, and link outcome criteria to intermediate effects. This phase of the evaluation of intervention effects requires the identification of precise points in time where the intervention is affecting change. Suchman (1967) has an additional review of this topic in discussing outcome and process research designs.

B. INTERVENTION II: ORGANIZATIONAL CHANGE AS ENVIRONMENTAL RESTRUCTURING

Recent work by Katz and Kahn (1966) and by Bennis (1966) presents a view of organizations, such as neighborhoods or communities, as open systems. These conceptions are based upon a premise that an organization is a series of interdependent units, and analogies have been drawn from cybernetics and general systems theory. The view of the organization as a biological process is conspicuously missing in psychological treatises on organizational development. Most approaches have concentrated upon analyses in which individuals and the total organization are seen as aggregates of disconnected parts bearing little relationship to one another. The axiom of interdependent units provides a basis for a view of an organization that comes closer to the ways in which people, roles, and organizational tasks are tied together under natural conditions. The behavior of people *in* organizations should be the focus of analysis in contrast to more abstract formulations of a model social structure. This point of view comes closest to an organic formulation of organizations which allows for simultaneous assessment of both organizational and personal behavior as they are portrayed through the performance of organizational roles *and* roles by individuals.

Interventions designed to affect the life of an organization can be validated via changes in the adaptive behavior of interdependent units, usually through a redefinition or realignment of various parts of the organization. If the creation of new organizational groupings, or the revision of existing social groupings, brings about overt changes in an organization's performance in coping with crises, then the intervention can be assessed by observing how the organization responds to crises. This thinking assumes that the restructuring of an organization is reflected in the total organization's ability to deal with emergencies without a significant loss in personal or operational effectiveness, and without a reduction in communication with other related organizations.

In the same way that consultation is used as a treatment rather than as a preventive intervention, organizational change programs often deal with momentary personnel conflicts, such as, for example, issues of productivity and management-labor issues that do not involve plans for assisting the organization with long-term development. Kahn (1968) in discussing the implications of organizational research for community mental health, commented that there have been a variety of methods to initiate change in organizations through: "various mixtures of cognitive input and peer group interaction . . . These include T-group or sensitivity training (Bradford, Gibb, & Benne, 1964; Schein & Bennis, 1965); the managerial grid (Blake & Mouton, 1964); the earlier work of the Tavistock group (Jacques, 1951); and the feedback discussions in overlapping groups as developed by Mann (1957, 1964) [pp. 68–69]." In commenting on these change programs, Kahn noted at least two generalizations that apply to all of these approaches; they all have been shown "to produce changes in interpersonal behavior in preceptions of self, and in attitudes toward others. Secondly, these changes are harder to produce, but more likely to endure, when they are generated in live, organizationally-embedded, ongoing groups [Kahn, 1968, p. 69]."

It is one thing to observe that an organizational change program affects the behavior of individuals in organizations, but quite a different problem to determine whether current change approaches influence the performance of individuals and organizations under conditions of stress. Still another new question is to relate change programs to role relationships in an organization which bear directly upon the performance of the total organization in dealing with planned and unplanned change. The present writer believes that change programs which help the organization deal effectively with its future must include criteria for judging effectiveness, and must focus on additional elements of the change process. More attention must be given to changes in social influence for the help-giving behavior of persons, independent of their roles, as well as help-giving behavior that can be added to the performance of key roles within the organization. Following Katz and Kahn's (1966) formulations, such changes should substantiate precisely how the organization is interdependent. If a change effort can increase the expression of spontaneous help-giving behavior in members of the organization, and create social norms so that the performance of executive functions can include help-giving behaviors, there is a possibility that there will be increased interaction and support for a wide variety of help-giving acts. The assumption is that an appropriate "organizational climate" will provide a social structure which can generate adaptive solutions for dealing with internal and external events.

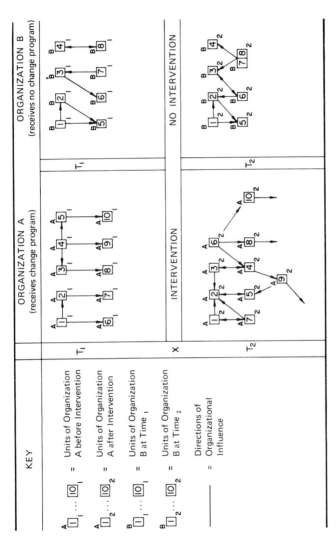

Fig. 4. Organizational change: as a process of restructuring the environment.

The creation of an experimental design to evaluate change programs is complex and difficult to formulate. The use of pre- and post-test designs and controlled measures in the study of organizations is not generally feasible since the natural life of an organization does not coincide with the aperiodic and unanticipated social events indigenous to organizations. There is one type of design, however, that may be relevant for identifying changes in the adaptive behavior of an organization. This design involves the use of similar, yet nonmatched organizations, and is called, in the terminology of Campbell and Stanley (1963), "the Nonequivalent Control Group Design [p. 47]" In this design, pre- and post-measures can be obtained on two organizations, with one of the organizations participating in the intervention. For the design to be optimally effective the two organizations should be selected with attention to equivalence of their general function. This is desirable in order to provide measures to control for possible source of "error," such as historical events affecting the organization, and maturation of the organization as well as the effects of the evaluation process. Such controls may be obtained by systematic or naturalistic observations prior to the onset of the intervention and further enhanced by continuous documentation of critical events in *both* organizations during the intervention. This operating procedure makes it possible to infer that any detected differences between the pre- and the post-tests in the adaptive behavior of the organization receiving the change program are not readily explained by the effects of extraneous variables. The possibility that differences in post-intervention scores may vary directly with differences between the populations from which the selection was made can be managed by covariance analyses and other statistical techniques (Campbell & Stanley, 1963, p. 49).

The design for this type of intervention is illustrated in Figures 4, 5, and 6. Figure 4 presents an illustration of a prototypic statement of directional influence in two organizations. At T_1 the form of the influence varies for the two organizations, but it is assumed to be equivalent in direction and magnitude. Following the preventive intervention, which has as its purpose the linking of directional influence, help-giving behavior and coping skills, Organization A is expected to develop not only a quantum increase in level of influence but also an increase in the level of reciprocal influences in the organization. In sum, the aim of the intervention as a change program is to increase the interdependence of the members with each other. Figures 4 and 5 illustrate the structure of the design and the types of predictions that can be made in differentiating responses of the members of the two organizations before and after the intervention.

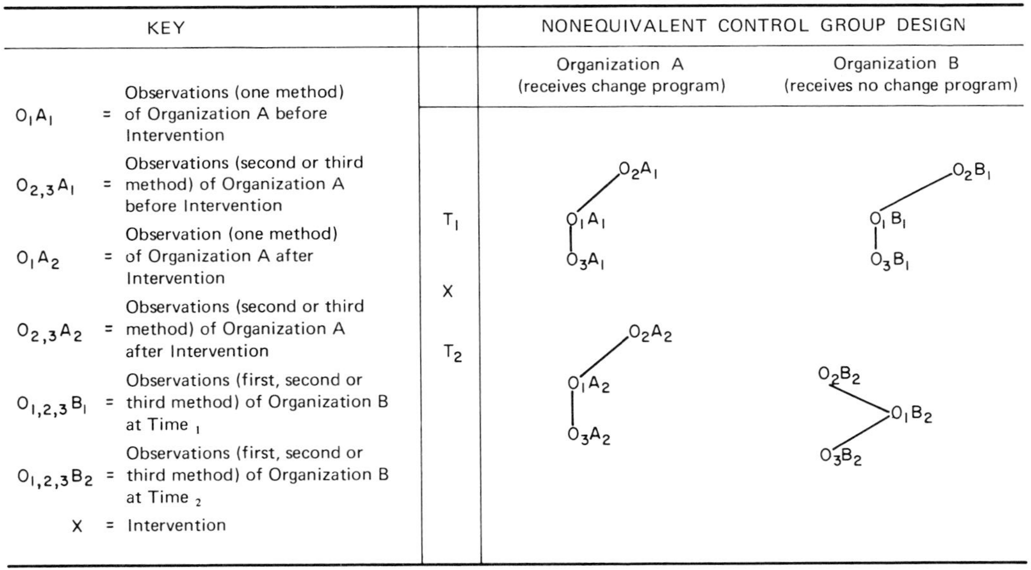

Fig. 5. Organizational change: as a process of restructuring the environment.

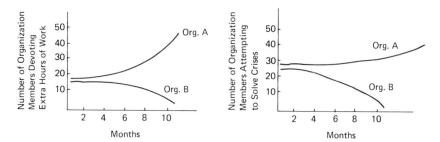

FIG. 6. Organizational change: as a process of restructuring the environment.

As an example of dependent variables that reflect an influence of the intervention, the members of Organization A are expected to voluntarily devote more effort (e.g., man hours of work) to solve problems than the members of Organization B, who have not experienced such a change program. If such predictions can be made and verified then the specific program has met the criteria of producing long term effects for the organization as well as changes in perception, attitudes and role behaviors. The primary criterion for evaluating the change program is dependent upon identifying how *both* organizations deal with future crises. It is assumed that the organization hosting the change program will expend fewer resources, suffer fewer casualties, and revise more functions after coping with crises such as budgetary cuts, shifts in public support, or loss of decision makers than will the "control" organization.

This type of design is relevant for the evaluation of community mental health programs. Many community mental health services have increased their liaison and visibility in their local communities, with the result that the public has increased its demands for accountability for services, and this often poses a genuine threat to the mental health program. As a result of attempts to develop preventive programs, increasing efforts have been expended by the mental health program and citizens to create additional community resources. If organizational change programs are viewed as a lever for initiating change and rearrangements or redefinitions of community services that result in a decrease in specific *direct* mental health services, then an organizational change program for the community mental health center staff can be classified as preventive. Efforts at program evaluation will require coordinated and integrated studies which simultaneously assess intraorganizational activities along with morbidity rates for relevant population groupings outside the immediate organization which are directly influenced by it. For such community studies, the Non-Equivalent Control Group Design provides an important approach for specifying the fallout effects of interventions.

Organizational change programs with staffs of mental health programs have characteristically employed laboratory training methods (T-groups). Such programs designed as inservice training for the staff of community mental health programs often serve to realign staff resources and redistribute decision making functions regarding patient care. One potential effect of such change programs is to make it possible for the professional staff of community mental health centers working inside the center to accommodate to criteria for relevant community services developed by citizens. As roles for community mental health practice respond to change methods such as the ones described above, criteria for community mental health programs will be expected to shift, and new types of data will be required for verification.

A synthesis of intervention methods can eventually bring about a greater affiliation between the clinician and the action researcher in the development of methods for assessing personal effectiveness and organizational effectiveness as reciprocal processes (Kelly, 1968). Through a combined program of interventions, such as consultation and organizational change methods, interventions in a variety of settings can be more closely assessed for positive and negative functions for the organization and for the broader community.

C. Intervention III: The Development of a Community
   as an Evolutionary Process

The previous interventions described in this chapter have been derived from contrasting premises about the change process. Consultation as a preventive intervention was viewed as a process of "radiating" change from the consultant to the consultee and to the consultee's clients. Organizational change programs were presented as examples of preventive interventions for restructuring the environment, with the goal of facilitating the organization to be more effective in dealing with crises. The third example of an intervention strategy which will now be presented is community development. This approach rests on the premise that social change is *not* a consequence of discrete man-made interventions, but rather that change occurs as a result of the evolution of functions in a society (Biddle & Biddle, 1968). The goal for community development is to create opportunities for a community to plan for its own change. In this class of interventions, the change agent is neither

a passive observer nor the final architect for plans, but a creative participant working with communities in the design and reorganization of their
activities.

The term community development, like consultation and organizational change, can refer to a euphemism for Utopia or Pollyanna, or it
can be used to denote an ethnocentric enterprise. There are few examples
to cite in which a professional change agent has been a "participant
conceptualizer" in the collaborative work of a community.[2,3] More
often we have been protagonists for change and have been invested in
interventions without regard for the goals of the community. Our statements regarding community goals have been largely limited to our own
entrepreneurial interests. In the present writer's opinion, until community
psychology can formulate new definitions of professional practice for
community development, we will not achieve the unfinished business
which was so eloquently prescribed by William James (1911).

Community development is a radical departure from most professional practice in community mental health because it commits the
designer of an intervention to be quite clear about goals and values he
elects for himself and espouses for "his" community. It is one thing to
mobilize citizens to fight for a cause, it is another to mobilize citizens to
develop plans and actions to guide their own future. This distinction is
very easy to articulate but very difficult to translate into reality, which
is the heart of the matter. Biddle and Biddle (1968) have written at length
on this theme and make the following observation:

Most believers in democracy have advanced to the point of admiring controversy
and stopped there. They are fighters for what they deem to be righteous. Some have
advanced further to an admiration of compromise but the compromise they have in
mind usually means a yielding of some demands when opponents will also yield a few,
a type of horse-trading. Only a few have advanced to an appreciation of creative
reconciliation, in which new and undreamed of solutions to problems arise out of
cooperative thinking and working together. Here is the great need and opportunity
in an age of increasingly complex problems and interdependent solutions. An
encourager belongs in the company of the creative reconcilers.

By accepting developmental goals, he does not reject political controversy. He
merely leaves this necessary activity to someone else. His job is not to encourage
attack upon rivals but to strengthen people's abilities to find creative solutions to

[2] The phrase "participant conceptualizer" has become an apt identification for
the unique role of the community psychologist. For future archival value, this phrase
was first coined by Forrest Tyler, then of the National Institute of Mental Health,
now at the University of Maryland, in group discussions at the Boston University
Conference on Community Psychology, Swampscott, Massachusetts, May 5, 1965.

[3] One exception where there has been a report of a long-term collaborative work
with a community is The Cornell-Peru Project (Holmberg & Dobyns, 1962; Dobyns,
Carlow, & Vazquez, 1962; Lasswell, 1962).

conflict. He is not a political controversialist. He is a reconciler of conflict, to the end that people may become more competent to create their own solutions to problems [p. 48].

This quotation could be interpreted as espousing special kinds of persons who can encourage community development. The intent of the statement can also mean, however, a value to expand and diversify resources from all segments of the population. As the above comments indicate, designs for documenting this type of change program are non-existent. What little evaluation that has been accomplished is preserved in the accumulated wisdom of the change agent or in the archives of anthropological field notes.

The community psychologist has an obligation and a rare opportunity to contribute to the definition of criteria for community development. Designs for community change require momentum and the resources to sustain evaluations of the process over a long period of time. Asking any professional to think in terms of decades is unique and presents a series of taxing requirements for the research process. The dependent variables considered useful in the evaluation of consultation as a preventive intervention were the performance levels of students and teachers in the classroom setting. The criteria suggested to assess organizational change were measures of coping with crises. In contrast to coping with change events, the type of dependent variables that will be required to evaluate community development are measures of *planning* for change. It is assumed that planning for change represents a higher level of organizational adaptation then either coping with crises or radiating change.

Campbell and Stanley (1963) provide a provocative initial suggestion for a design for community development known by the folksy title, "the patched-up design," or, if you prefer a more technical term, "the recurrent institutional cycle design." They describe this design as:

a strategy for field research in which one starts with an inadequate design and then adds specific features to control one or another of the recurrent sources of invalidity. The result is often an inelegant accumulation of precautionary checks which lacks the intrinsic symmetry of the 'true' experimental designs but nonetheless approaches experimentation [p. 57].

In this case the research design is selected to accommodate to the unpredictable and tentative events that are generic in mobilizing citizen groups to work toward goals for achieving change at the community level. Rather than an integrated attempt to reduce sources of error, this design defines a variety of procedures to maximize opportunities for specifying the conditions under which change takes place. In this

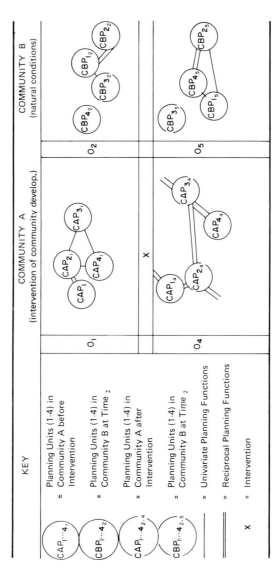

FIG. 7. Community development: as an evolutionary process.

sense it is an approximation to laboratory conditions, but only an approximation. The design requires that both longitudinal and cross-sectional studies be continuous. It also assumes that (*a*) a variety of methods will be employed; (*b*) the research process will be flexible in spirit; and (*c*) the project will be bountiful in resources so that unanticipated, spontaneous community events can be assessed.

In the same sense that consultation and organizational change programs have intrinsic validity in their own right, community development in its aims to mobilize citizens for change also has intrinsic merit. The thesis here is that community development becomes a preventive intervention when aroused and motivated community groups work together to effectively plan for unknown future events. This assumes that the aroused citizenry is able to utilize current resources, create new resources, and link to a maximum number of constituencies. The elements of the design are presented in Figures 7, 8, and 9.

The design combines the longitudinal and cross-sectional approaches commonly employed in developmental research. It assumes that scheduling is such that, at one and the same time, a community *in* development and a community prior to development can be assessed, e.g., comparisons of observations can be made at O_1 and O_2. As Figure 7 indicates, Community A, which is in the process of development, has similar planning functions to Community B early in the development cycle. The planning that is ongoing in each community is relatively autonomous, largely *ad hoc*, and likely to be tied to a few individuals in formal governmental positions. Measurements in this case might be surveys, naturalistic observations, in-depth interviews, participant observations, and other types of field work including attendance at formal and informal community functions. The measurements should include all that is possible and feasible in conducting a community study.

Following the community development program, observations are repeated so that a detailed evaluation of the planning process can be charted. If the program has succeeded, it would be expected that Community A will have developed more viable reciprocal planning functions, created more and better new resources, and included more new citizens in its planning. As Figure 8 indicates, this type of design allows for taking advantage of unexpected events to document critical unplanned occurrences in the life cycle of the program, such as at time O_3, as well as comparative data collection in both communities at other times such as O_4 and O_5. Observation points can be as close as several weeks, or only every six weeks, depending upon when the real life events take place. The total time period needed to evaluate and document the planning process per se may take several years.

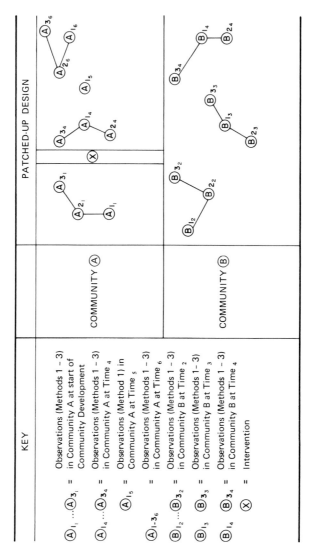

Fig. 8. Community development: as an evolutionary process.

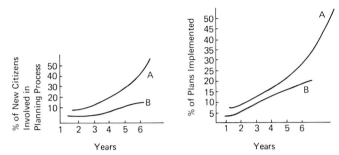

Fig. 9. Community development: as an evolutionary process.

Reassessing the functions of the two communities in their ability to plan for change provides a basis for many comparisons in the life of the change program. While the design does not directly control for maturation effects over time, it can be extended to assess such effects since maturation effects can be made a basic part of the study. Figure 9 presents an example of two types of predictions that can be made in assessing community development. One example is a prediction of the different number of citizens involved in working directly on the formulation and implementation of community change. The basis for this prediction is that the community development process is effective when it can continuously involve over time different citizens. Of specific interest is the proportion of new citizens who were not previously a part of the community planning effort. The criteria refer to the number of new citizens involved, who have not been involved previously in such work, and may also refer to the increasing proportion of persons from minority groups, who are otherwise not active in the development of their local community. The goal of the community development process as a preventive intervention is to increase the diversity of citizens who are influencing change in their community.

It is expected, for example, that an effective intervention with its accompanying social processes would produce a community participation curve which is S shaped. In contrast, the predicted curve for the number of persons involved and number of actions and plans implemented in control communities would not be expected to vary over time, or would be only slightly positively accelerating. Such positive acceleration is expected to reflect the effects of changes outside the community upon the local population.

Much of the emphasis in community work has been placed on the prevention of pathological conditions in individuals. The prospect of obtaining knowledge about the positive development of persons in natural settings could be increased if psychologists worked to create empirical data about the ways in which communities evolve and how they establish criteria and norms. One of the important by-products of the evaluation of community development programs is the creation of a psychology of social change. How groups of persons are mobilized, how impediments to action are reduced, how old investments of citizens are redefined and replaced by indigenous efforts are examples of discrete activities which combine to affect community goals. The evaluation of community development can also provide hypotheses about the success and failure of broader societal changes, in that they provide a more restricted setting to observe the diffusion of change processes into local communities.

There is a critical need for research centers and universities to focus on the aspirations and interests of their local host communities. The contributions of the social sciences have limited relevance to under-standing contemporary social problems in communities, and most public issues raise questions which go beyond the social scientist's traditional data source. We cannot expect to understand the problems of community conflict without attempting to understand the delights and the hazards of positive community change. Our present knowledge of community development comes largely from cultures beyond our own,. which illustrates our ideological and motivational constraints. It should be less difficult to work towards community change in the U. S. than in a Peruvian village, and thereby to help our citizens to affect their own destiny. Community development is thus offered as a critical area for psychologists to offer new commitments that are expressed daily and that are lasting.

III. Conclusion

The three contrasting approaches for preventive interventions that have been described suggest new critiera for change programs. Con-sultation methods as a preventive intervention do not focus on the symptomatic or expressive behavior of the consultee, but rather upon the radiating effects of the consultee's clients. Organizational change methods are not concerned with the productive behavior of the members of an organization, but with the members' ability to handle crises. The verification of community development does not depend solely upon economic development, but also considers the community's competence to plan for its future (Meier, 1956, 1965).

These new criteria are required if community psychology is to contribute verifiable knowledge about the effectiveness of individuals in organizations and communities. The main thesis in these comments is that the community psychologist should view the development of knowledge as an ecological enterprise, an enterprise in which the conditions for verification are defined in terms of the specific host environment and its requirements for intervention (Barker, 1965; Kelly, 1966). A science of intervention encompasses a series of diverse and interdependent sciences, each with its unique requirements and principles for verification, and its own methods for the control of error. Psychologists can participate in this redefinition of the scientific process if we obtain for ourselves a liberal education. We can then contribute to social betterment without the hidden costs of social engineering!

Each of the three types of interventions which have been described involves unique experimental designs and methods of quality control that generate their own built-in ethics. These designs provide for the observation of naturally occurring events to help confirm or disconfirm the effects of interventions. This kind of research obviously requires a strong commitment to longitudinal studies as well as the development of research facilities that are organized to take account of unanticipated and spontaneous community events.

The proper goals of the scientific enterprise as presented in this paper have been simply stated by the philosopher of science, Herbert Feigl (1951): "scientific explanation is where most specific or more descriptive statements are derived from general or more hypothetical assumptions [p. 182]." The linkage between our general statements and our assumptions of the rate and direction of social change can permit the design of intervention in social settings to create a science of community psychology. For this adventure man is best viewed in his natural setting, rather than as an atom in a smasher.

REFERENCES

Barker, R. G. Explorations in ecological psychology. *American Psychologist*, 1965, 20, 1–14.
Bennis, W. G. *Changing organizations*. New York: McGraw-Hill, 1966.
Berlin, I. N. Mental health consultation in schools as a means of communicating health principles. *Journal of the American Academy of Child Psychiatry*, 1962, 1, 671–679.
Biddle, W. W., & Biddle, L. J. *Encouraging community development*. New York: Holt, Rinehart, and Winston, 1968.
Bindman, A. J. Mental Health Consultation: Theory and practice. *Journal of Consulting Psychology*, 1959, 23, 473–482.
Blake, R. R., & Mouton, J. W. *The managerial grid*. Houston: Gulf, 1964.

Bradford, L., Gibb, J., & Benne, K. (Eds.). *T-group theory and laboratory method: Innovation in re-education.* New York: Wiley, 1964.

Campbell, D. T., & Stanley, J. C. *Experimental and quasi-experimental designs for research.* Chicago: Rand McNally, 1963.

Caplan, G. *Principles of preventive psychiatry.* New York: Basic Books, 1964.

Cowen, E. L., Gardner, E. A., & Zax, M. (Eds.). *Emergent approaches to mental health problems.* New York: Appleton-Century-Crofts, 1967.

Dobyns, H. F., Carlos, M. M., & Vazquez, M. C. Summary of technical-organizational progress and reactions to it. *Human Organizations,* 1962, **21,** 109–115.

Feigl, H. Principles and problems of theory construction in psychology. In *Current trends in psychological theory.* Pittsburgh: University of Pittsburgh Press, 1951. Pp. 179–209.

Holmberg, A. R., & Dobyns, H. F. The process of accelerating community change. *Human Organizations,* 1962, **21,** 107–109.

Iscoe, I., Pierce-Jones, J., Friedman, S. T., & McGehearty, L. Some strategies in mental health consultation: A brief description of a project and some preliminary results. In E. L. Cowen, E. A. Gardner, and M. Zax (Eds.), *Emergent approaches to mental health problems.* New York: Appleton-Century-Crofts, 1967. Pp. 307–330.

Jacques, E. *The changing culture of a factory.* London: Tavistock, 1951.

James, W. From The moral equivalent for war. In *Memories and studies.* London: Longmans, Green and Co., 1911. Also appears in *The philosophy of William James.* New York: The Modern Library. P. 264.

Kahn, R. L. Implications of organizational research for community mental health. In J. W. Carter, Jr. (Ed.), *Research contributions from psychology to community mental health.* New York: Behavioral Publications, Inc., 1968.

Katz, D., & Kahn, R. L. *The social psychology of organizations.* New York: Wiley, 1966.

Kelly, J. G. Ecological constraints on mental health services. *American Psychologist,* 1966, **21,** 535–539.

Kelly, J. G. Toward an ecological conception of preventive interventions. In J. W. Carter, Jr. (Ed), *Research contributions from psychology to community mental health.* New York: Behavioral Publications, Inc., 1968.

Klein, D. C., & Lindemann, E. Preventive intervention in family crisis situations. In G. Caplan (Ed.), *Prevention of mental disorders in children.* New York: Basic Books, 1961. Pp. 283–306.

Lasswell, H. D. Integrating communities into more inclusive systems. *Human Organizations,* 1962, **21,** 116–124.

Mann, F. C. Studying and creating change: a means to understanding social organization. In *Research in industrial human relations.* Industrial Relations Research Association, 1957, No. 17, 146–167.

Mann, F. C. Toward an understanding of the leadership role in formal organizations. In R. Dubin, G. Homans, & D. Miller (Eds.), *Leadership and productivity.* San Francisco: Chandler, 1964.

Meier, R. L. *Science and economic development.* Cambridge, Mass.: M. I. T. Press, 1956.

Meier, R. L. *Developmental planning.* New York: McGraw-Hill, 1965.

Morse, W. C. Enhancing the classroom teacher's mental health function. In E. L. Cowen, E. A. Gardner, and M. Zax (Eds.), *Emergent approaches to mental health problems.* New York: Appleton-Century-Crofts, 1967. Pp. 271–289.

Schein, E. H., & Bennis, W. G. *Personal and organizational change through group methods.* New York: Wiley, 1965.

Spielberger, C. D. A mental health consultation program in a small community with limited professional mental health resources. In E. I. Cowen, E. A. Gardner, and M. Zax (Eds.), *Emergent approaches to mental health problems.* New York: Appleton-Century-Crofts, 1967. Pp. 214–238.

Suchman, E. A. *Evaluative research.* New York: Russell Sage Foundation, 1967.

White, M. A. The mental health movement and the schools: Theory evidence, and dilemma. In R. H. Ojemann (Ed.), *The school and the community treatment facility in preventive psychiatry.* Iowa City, Iowa: The University of Iowa Department of Publications, 1966. Pp. 49–68.

Author Index

Numbers in italics refer to the pages on which the complete references are listed.

210

Author Index

Daly, R. J., 158, 159, *181*
Daniels, A., 10, 59
Darley, F. L., 10, 21, 29, 57
Darley, J. G., 94, 95
Datel, W. E., 120, *148*
David, C., 126, *152*
Davidoff, R. A., 39, 55
Delgado, J. M. R., 51, 55
Deming, R. W., 124, *148*
Dennerll, R. D., 10, 17, 18, 55
De Renzi, E., 23, 25, 26, 28, 29, 31, 32, 34, *54, 56*
De Vos, G. A., 120, 136, *148*
Dightman, C. R., 159, *180*
Dinitz, S., 120, *153*
Dinwiddie, F. W., 112, *148*
Dobyns, H. F., 198, *206*
Doehring, D. G., 24, 56
Drill, V. A., 158, *180*
Drummond, F., 145, *148*
Durkee, A., 112, 118, *148*

E

Edwards, A. L., 76, 95
Efron, R., 21, 25, 56
Eichenwald, H., 3, 56
Elizur, A., 133, *148*
Epstein, S., 127, 128, *153*
Erbaugh, J., 162, *180*
Erikson, R. B., 111, *148*
Ervin, M. D., 51, 55
Ewing, J. A., 158, *181*

F

Faglioni, P., 23, 25, 31, 32, 34, 56
Fedio, P., 20, 51, 55
Feigl, H., 205, *206*
Feldman, M. J., 115, *149, 154*
Feldman, S. E., 120, *149*
Fennell, E., 6, 8, 59
Ferracuti, F., 139, *153*
Fine, H. J., 134, *149*
Finney, B. C., 134, 136, 141, *149, 154*
Fisher, D., 126, *152*
Fisher, G., 117, *149*
Fisher, H., 119, *148*
Fisher, S., 137, *149*
Fiske, D. W., 61, 63, 65, *94*

Fitzhugh, K. B., 18, 56
Fitzhugh, L. C., 18, 56
Floren, A., 159, *181*
Frank, C. H., 10, 17, 56
Freedman, D. X., 35, 58
Freedman, L. Z., 124, *150*
Freeman, R. A., *150*
Friedman, S. T., 187, *206*
Fry, P. C., 3, 56
Fumagalli, R., 7, 58
Furth, H. G., 22, 56, 126, *152*

G

Garcia, C. R., 158, *182*
Gardner, E. A., 186, *206*
Garmezy, N., 7, 56
Gazzaniga, M. S., 19, 20, 56
Geschwind, N., 20, 21, 41, 51, 56
Ghent, L., 15, 29, 30, 59
Giannitrapani, D., 20, 56
Gibb, J., 192, *206*
Gleser, G. C., 65, 66, 72, *94*, 157, *181*
Glick, I. D., 158, *180*
Goldberg, L. R., 62, 95
Goldman, R., 123, *147*
Goldstein, K., 5, 21, 32, 33, 35, 41, 42, 45, 47, 49, 56
Goldzieher, J., 158, *181*
Goodglass, H., 21, 56
Gorlow, L., 134, *149*
Gorusch, R. L., 174, *181*
Gottlieb, A. L., 43, 56
Gottschalk, L. A., 157, *181*
Gough, H. G., 116, 119, 120, 121, *149*
Gray, B. M., 158, *181*
Green, B. F., 65, 95
Guertin, W. H., 10, 17, 56
Gulliksen, H., 66, 77, 82, 84, 95
Guthrie, G. M., 89, 95

H

Hafner, A. J., 133, *149*
Haganah, T., 94, 95
Hagiwara, R., 51, 55
Hahn, S., 123, *150*
Hall, G. C., 43, 56
Hall, M. M., 43, 56
Halstead, W. C., 6, 13, 24, 34, 36, 56, 59

Subject Index

215